W9-AOT-841

Fodor's

EXPLORING

SOUTH AFRICA

FODOR'S TRAVEL PUBLICATIONS, INC.

NEW YORK • TORONTO • LONDON • SYDNEY • AUCKLAND

HTTP://WWW.FODORS.COM/

Published in the United States by Fodor's Travel Publications, Inc.
Published in the United Kingdom by AA Publishing.

ISBN 0-679-03215-0
First Edition

Fodor's Exploring South Africa

Author: **Melissa Shales**
Joint Series Editor: **Josephine Perry**
Copy Editor: **Audrey Horne**
Original Photography: **Clive Sawyer**
Cartography: **The Automobile Association**
Cover Design: **Louise Fili, Fabrizio La Rocca**
Cover photograph: **Nik Wheeler**

Special Sales

Printed in Italy by Printer Trento srl
10 9 8 7 6 5 4 3 2 1

How to use this book

This book is divided into five main sections:

❑ Section 1: **South Africa Is**
discusses aspects of life and living today, from economic power to the Rainbow Nation

❑ Section 2: **South Africa Was**
places the country in its historical context and explores past events whose influences are still felt

❑ Section 3: **A to Z Section**
covers places to visit, arranged by region, with suggested walks and drives. Within this section fall the Focus-on articles, which consider a variety of topics in greater detail

❑ Section 4: **Travel Facts**
contains the strictly practical information that is vital for a successful trip

❑ Section 5: **Hotels and Restaurants**
lists recommended establishments in South Africa, giving a brief resume of what they offer

How to use the star rating
Most places described in this book have been given a separate rating:

▶▶▶ **Do not miss**

▶▶ **Highly recommended**

▶ **Worth seeing**

Not essential viewing

Map references
To make the location of a particular place easier to find, every main entry in this book is given a map reference, such as 54A2. The first number (54) indicates the page on which the map can be found; the letter (A) and the second number (2) pinpoint the square in which the main entry is located. The maps on the inside front cover and inside back cover are referred to as IFC and IBC

Contents

Quick reference

This quick-reference guide highlights the elements of the book
you will use most often: the
maps; the introductory features;
the Focus-on articles; the walks
and the drives.

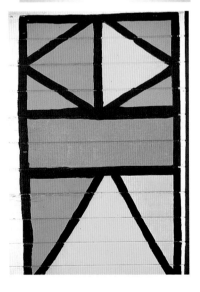

My South Africa by Melissa Shales

As a child, living in sanctioned, war-torn Zimbabwe (then Rhodesia), I saw South Africa as our land of plenty and sophistication. Once a year, the family would pile into the car, hitch up a caravan and head south on a holiday and shopping bonanza, stoking up with a year's supply of everything from dried fruit to Marmite, theatre, ballet and beaches. I was vaguely aware that there were problems, but never saw beyond the gates of Eden. In 1977, when I returned to the UK, my eyes were opened abruptly by the horror of the nightly news broadcasts from Sharpeville and Soweto. They seemed to come from a different universe.

I didn't return to South Africa until 1995, when Mandela was in power and I started researching this book.

Over three months and 10,000 miles, I traveled by boat, plane, car, bus and helicopter. I stayed in guesthouses, game lodges and historic homes, business hotels and tents. I watched whales tumbling in Hermanus Bay, sat breathlessly still as an overly playful elephant tickled the back of my neck, and ate crocodile and ostrich, washed down with ambrosial wines. I played tourist under indigo skies and a blazing sun, in sandstorms and heaven-splitting thunderstorms, gossiped to a positive army of kindly Afrikaner landladies, saw Cape Dutch mansions, Zulu huts and elegant Victorian town houses. Everywhere I went, I was overwhelmed by kindness and generous hospitality; it seemed an almost perfect holiday destination.

Yet, try as I might, I found myself still in a segregated, almost schizophrenic society. The mere handful of black people I talked to were welcoming, but even they agreed that it was unsafe to wander the townships or villages. There is the inevitable, inexorable rise of reverse discrimination. I grew tired of hearing how much better things were in the old days, angry at the unnecessary violence and anarchy rampaging through the cities, and despairing at the vastness of the task facing the Government. In the end, my emotions and impressions were still scrambled. I'd seen the beautiful but fragile mask and caught glimpses of a tortured soul. The real face of the new South Africa is yet to be revealed.

Melissa Shales

SOUTH AFRICA IS

■ Dismayed by horrific film of squatter camps and township violence, of police brutality and children lying dead in the dust, many tourists stayed away from South Africa until the 1994 elections. Now they are arriving in droves in search of the New South Africa; the number of overseas tourists doubled in 1995 alone. What most of them have found is a politically acceptable version of the old regime. ■

The European image At first glance, South Africa looks like an affluent suburb superimposed on the African bush—exactly the impression its former rulers, middle-class urban whites to a man, tried so hard to create. If it seems a little old-fashioned in some ways, it is also superficially comfortable, familiar, well tended and nonthreatening.

South Africans used to pride themselves on clinging to the old virtues by which everyone went to church on Sunday, women stayed at home to look after their families and the niceties of afternoon tea were strictly observed. It was a squeaky clean image based on the biggest conjuring trick in history—nearly 40 million people were made to vanish. The

Above: sprawling shanties in Soweto. Below: the Dutch Reformed church is the social center of most small Afrikaans communities

harsh laws of apartheid kept Africa and poverty out of sight in huge settlements of corrugated iron and cardboard that appeared on no map or signpost. Black people were only allowed into view if they were smiling and subservient. Most towns were—and are—as European as possible, filled with chintz and antiques, bijou boutiques and coffee shops.

Tourism, designed largely for the South African home market, has always concentrated on the coast, whites-only game parks and cool, green uplands where golf courses stretch amid the pine plantations.

The New South Africa Of course, this image of rich white/poor black, good black/bad white is as simplistic and unrealistic as any other cultural stereotype. The truth is far more complicated. South Africa has a population of about 45 million, with 11 official languages and cultural

traditions from across Europe, Asia and Africa. There has been violence and oppression, the nonwhites have been shamefully used and the townships are a sin against humanity, but today luxury dwellings and run-down shanties stand side by side on the same street. Tribal chiefs and traditional healers live and work alongside pinstriped politicians and orthodox medical professionals. There are black millionaires and professors, white taxi drivers, waiters and beggars, and even, astonishingly, black people who mourn the passing of apartheid.

The New South Africa is a mind-bending paradox: a sunny land of apparent peace and harmony with a boiling undercurrent of violent crime in its centers. Voices of doom mutter about chaos and corruption or talk of

Below: fruit stalls are affordable and accessible. Right: middle-class suburbia lives behind tight security

betrayal. A surprisingly large number of people embraced the Government of National Unity's call for "Masakhane" ("Working together for a better future"). Most people, of whatever color, are still waiting to see what will happen.

It may seem as if little has changed so far, but these are still early days

for the New South Africa. It will take time for people to be rehoused, for economic as well as political power to shift, for the richness of African culture to emerge from the townships and villages, for the history books and museums to be revised and for a people used to being invisible to take possession of their true heritage. Meanwhile, tourists still live largely in a luxurious and almost totally white world, with only a quick tour of black South Africa. The difference is that they can now wander the lush gardens, swim in limpid pools and quaff fine wines without the slightest twinge of conscience.

■ **Most world maps, with their Eurocentric projection, give little idea of how large South Africa actually is. With an area of 474,276 square miles, it is five times the size of the U.K. and one-eighth the area of the U.S.A. The Kruger National Park alone is as big as Wales, and the distance between Johannesburg and Cape Town is the same as from London to Rome. The country has 1,835 miles of coastline bordering the Atlantic and Indian Oceans, which meet at Cape Agulhas, the southernmost tip of Africa.** ■

Boundaries South Africa has land borders with Mozambique, Swaziland, Zimbabwe, Botswana, and Namibia, and totally surrounds the enclave of Lesotho. Since the 1994 elections, the country has been redivided into nine provinces, along roughly tribal lines—Western Cape, Eastern Cape, Northern Cape, Northwest Province, Gauteng, Northern Province, Mpumalanga, the Free State and KwaZulu-Natal. At the time of writing, it still has three capitals, a legacy from the Anglo-Boer War. The legislature is in Cape Town (former British capital); the administration is in Pretoria (capital of the old Transvaal); and the judiciary is in Bloemfontein (capital of the Orange Free State). Pretoria is currently leading the betting to become sole capital should they decide to consolidate them into one.

❏ Cape Town is at about the same latitude as Sydney in Australia and Rio de Janeiro in Brazil. If folded into the northern hemisphere, it would be level with Cyprus or Los Angeles, while the Kalahari Desert would fit neatly into the Sahara. ❏

Geography The terrain ranges in altitude from sealevel to South Africa's highest peak, Injasuti (11,178 feet) in the Drakensberg, near the border with Lesotho, and covers ecosystems from tropical forest to desert dunes. Almost every crop known to humanity can find a natural home somewhere in the country.

The Western Cape, cut off from the hinterland by the mountains of the Cederberg, Hex River and Swartberg, has a distinct, Mediterranean climate with cool, gray, wet and windy winters and warmer, sunny summers. It is ideal for wine and deciduous fruits. The more northerly KwaZulu-Natal coast, also cut off by the vast wall of the Drakensberg, is subtropical, hot and humid, clipped by the southwest monsoon. Here, the main crops are tropical fruits, such as bananas (the country's most profitable product), pineapples, and sugarcane.

Beyond the mountains is the Karoo, a dramatic semidesert capable of supporting only sheep, ostriches and, increasingly, antelope, while in the west blow the barren red sands of the Kalahari. In the center, the land climbs on to the high, flat central plateau, to the cattle and corn prairies of the Free State and, most importantly, the gold and diamond deposits of Kimberley and the Witwatersrand (see pages 137 and 160–1).

Finally, in the northeast, the highveld drops off a dramatic escarpment in a flurry of mountains where tea and avocados, cherries and bananas, eucalyptus and pine all flourish cheek by jowl. Below, the lowveld provides a hot, dry habitat for baobabs and acacias, elephant and lion.

Water South Africa is a land of plenty, rich in agriculture, industry and minerals, but there are only two

From roads across the Free State to the Kalahari and the fruit farms of the Cape, distances are vast and the horizons endless

major rivers, the Vaal and the Orange. The whole subcontinent has been gripped by drought for many of the last 15 years, the population is rising steadily, and with the new government have come schemes for creating proper water supplies, plumbing and drains in all the black towns and villages. The demands on the water supply are increasing sharply and, in spite of careful water management, and the occasional season of magnificent rains, the water table is dropping below the level of the boreholes, and the desert is expanding. In some areas people have already been forced off the land, while the government is hurriedly trying to implement massive projects to bring water down from the mountains of Lesotho and even from as far north as the Zambezi (despite the fact that Zimbabwe has its own serious problems to contend with).

■ **South Africa is wealthy, one of the world's top 25 trading nations and among its largest producers of many minerals, notably gold and diamonds. It accounts on its own for 25 percent of the GNP of the African continent, but it also has Third World slums, horrendous unemployment, homelessness and increasing crime levels. Vast problems must be overcome if the country's two societies are ever to come together without the entire economic structure collapsing.** ■

Sanctions During the last years of apartheid, sanctions were enforced officially by the United Nations. However, South Africa was situated strategically across the Cape sea route and was a major supplier of vital minerals such as uranium and chrome. Most First World countries continued to trade under the counter, while neighboring black countries were totally reliant on South Africa's ports for survival. The economy was battered but it survived and, turning inwards, became broad-based and self-sufficient.

The new world Since the 1994 elections the country has been welcomed back into the global fold. Exports are rising rapidly and multinational companies are lining up for information, with the government doing all it can to reassure anyone prepared to invest. Everything should be rosy. However, massive new imports are

> ❏ South Africa is the world's leading supplier of alumino-silicates, chromium (72 per cent), gold (40 per cent), platinum (88 per cent) and vanadium (44 per cent). It ranks second for vermiculite and zirconium; third for antimony, fluorspar, phosphate rock, and uranium; fourth for diamonds, titanium and zinc; and fifth for coal and nickel. It also has significant deposits of iron, lead, manganese, silver and copper. ❏

damaging the balance of trade, and increasingly powerful trades unions are making vociferous demands for black wages to meet those of the white workers, a shorter working week, better conditions and improved housing. Meanwhile, the Government of National Unity instituted a policy of affirmative action, providing much-needed fast-track promotion for black managerial candidates.

All these are laudable aims, but there has been a heavy price to pay. Nervous white workers are creating a brain drain before there are enough well-qualified and experienced black workers to take their place. Constant strikes, lockouts and other industrial action are crippling some industries, while wage demands are pushing prices up so sharply that some South African products are in danger of becoming too expensive to survive in the world market.

Unemployment is running at over 40 percent; the drift from the land to the cities has become a deluge; the black market or "informal sector" runs most small businesses in the townships; and, as a final complication, an estimated 4 million illegal immigrants from elsewhere in Africa have flooded the job market.

Redevelopment The main economic focus of the government is the implementation of the Reconstruction and Development Programme (RDP), a nationwide scheme to provide a suitable infrastructure, including housing, water,

drainage, electricity, schools and clinics, for all black townships and villages. Enormous amounts of money are needed, with global development aid being poured into the gaping void alongside every available scrap of tax revenue. The fledgling welfare system is already stretched way beyond its limits; inessentials and luxuries are being stripped away. Disgruntled whites, who still form the vast majority of taxpayers, seem unable to understand why they are paying more and receiving less and, the honeymoon over, the black community is waiting impatiently for its slice of the cake.

So far, the government has steered a skillful route along this narrow, potentially treacherous divide, preaching a gospel of self-help, patience and understanding, sustainable and environment-friendly development, the expansion of legal business and equal opportunities, and capital investment for the common good. If they can convince their electorate and the international business community to back them with hard cash, South Africa has the potential to become an economic Utopia.

Above: downtown Johannesburg. Below: the Rand Club, still a focus for Gauteng's financiers

■ "Let us be channels of love, of peace, of reconciliation. Let us declare that we have been made for togetherness, we have been made for family, that, yes, now we are free, all of us, black and white together, we, the Rainbow People of God!" Archbishop Desmond Tutu. ■

The New South Africa has adopted Archbishop Desmond Tutu's catchy phrase as the slogan of its quest for racial harmony. It is singularly apt, given the country's complicated population mix. Of its estimated 45 million people, 4 million are white, 3 million of mixed race, 1 million Indian and 37 million black.

The black population is subdivided into nine main tribal groupings based on language. Zulu (22 per cent of the population) and Xhosa (17 per cent) are the largest groups. Ndebele, Northern Sotho, Southern Sotho, Swati, Tsonga, Tswana and Venda are all first languages for more than 1 million people, and each is further divided into local tribal groups. Minorities include the all-but-extinct San (Bushmen) and Khoikhoi (Hottentots), the aboriginal inhabitants of the country, and the Cape Malays, whose ancestors came as slaves from the Dutch East Indies in the 18th century.

The "coloreds" are mixed-race people, the result of early black-white or Khoi-San-Malay contact, although in recent years they have largely married among their own ranks, creating a distinct cultural group. The Indians, brought in to work the Natal cane

Desmond Tutu, archbishop of Cape Town during the years of struggle

fields and lumped together ethnically under apartheid, came mainly from the south, but most of India's 65 main "tribes" are represented, all with a different heritage and customs.

Most whites are Afrikaner (of Dutch extraction) or English. However, the 17th century saw significant immigration of German, and French Huguenots fleeing religious persecution. Later additions include Greeks, Italians, Portuguese, as well as immigrants from every other nation in Africa and Europe. Finally, there is a substantial Jewish community.

Language Afrikaans is the first language of around 15 per cent of the population, including many of the

South Africa's "colored" community has evolved its own distinctive and vibrant culture

❑ The Zulu, Xhosa and Ndebele all belong to a related racial group, the Nguni. Though similar in language and culture, they have been responsible for some of South Africa's most persistent conflicts: 19th-century frontier wars between the Zulus and Xhosa; traditional conflicts between the Xhosa and their offshoot tribe, the Mfengu; the Zulus' attempted slaughter of the renegade Ndebele in the early 19th century; and the current township wars between the largely Xhosa-run ANC and the mainly Zulu Inkatha Freedom Party (IFP). ❑

that allowed freedom of religion—a liberal policy that survived even the darkest years of apartheid. The nearest thing to a State Church has been the sternly Protestant Dutch Reformed Church, the most influential of the myriad Christian churches. Other important Christian denominations include the Church of England, the Roman Catholics, the Methodists and the thriving Church of Zion. There are significant numbers of Hindus, Muslims and Jews, while many people still follow traditional African religions—often in tandem with Christianity.

Whatever their faith, South Africans are a fairly religious people, many of them deeply shocked by so-called Western liberalism and the upsurge in pornography since censorship was abolished. Most are also conservative (with a small "c") when it comes to women's rights in the home or workplace. Though more women work today, few so far have risen higher than junior management.

coloreds, and English of 9 per cent. These and the nine main black languages are now all official languages of the country. English is used as the main language of government and business, and each province uses English, Afrikaans and whichever African language predominates. Most people speak fluent English and Afrikaans as well as their home tongue. The television news is presented in different languages on different evenings, and many programs are multilingual.

The conservative majority South Africa has always been a secular state

Right: Ndebele woman. Top: traditional bead work

■ From the time in 1652 when Jan van Riebeeck laid out his kitchen garden in the settlement that was to become Cape Town, to Johannesburg's dramatic skyline emerging from the squalor of a mining camp, South Africa's towns and cities were carefully planned. ■

Gracious living Most towns were built on a grid layout, with Dutch-style squares and English-style parks to give a feeling of space, and broad streets lined with ornamental trees. Official buildings became ever larger and grander, culminating in Herbert Baker's superb Union Buildings in Pretoria. Until the early 20th century, the towns were relatively multiracial, with areas like Cape Town's District Six and Johannesburg's Sophiatown as vibrant cultural melting pots that produced innovative art, music and dance and created pockets of bohemian life beneath the stern noses of the Dutch Reformed pastors.

From the turn of the 20th century onwards, South Africa experienced an explosion of immigration from Europe. While suburbs of mock-Tudor houses cocooned in cool green gardens sprouted across the

Above: Jacarandas shade many of Pretoria's streets. Below: some of Soweto's better housing

hills, the urban centers became crowded. The whites were increasingly anxious to enjoy their idyll untroubled by signs of poverty or race. A series of forced "slum clearances" began as distraught nonwhites were dumped far out of town to restart their lives as best they could. As soon as they were gone, their properties were bulldozed and the land redeveloped.

Townships Satellite townships grew up rapidly around every city. Few were marked on the maps or street signs, even though many were soon larger than their white neighbors. Some had family dwellings, serried rows of tiny tin-roofed houses. Others consisted of squalid barrack-style hostel accommodations for male workers living three to a room and sharing a basic kitchen and bathroom among 12. Wives and families remained in the villages, seeing their men only once or twice a year. A very few of the larger townships

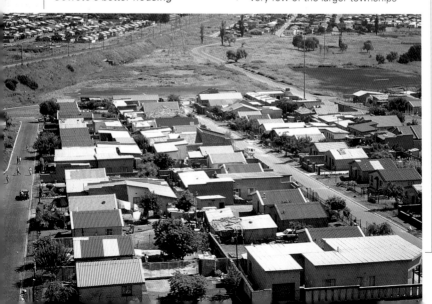

like Soweto—already the size of a major city—developed small middle-class areas with good houses and suitable facilities. On the whole, however, there were few real stores, the only food available sold from tiny market stalls. Clinics and schools were scarce and many of the latter were boycotted by children refusing to learn in Afrikaans. A boycott of the white alcohol trade led to the growth of shebeens, illegal drinking haunts. By the 1980s, shanty towns began to grow up around the official town-ships, vast, desperate seas of plastic, corrugated iron and cardboard. With the repeal of the Pass Laws in 1986, the situation became even worse, as families flocked to the city to join their men, where they lived three families to a room or built shanties on any available patch of ground.

Development The government now has to sort out the mess. Most of the townships have been incorporated within the municipal bound-aries of the white towns and money is being poured into development. The first phase alone of the Reconstruction and Development Programme aims to build 10,000 new houses. In some areas, the authorities are simply building streets, drains and lavatories. Families are allocated a plot with a lavatory and it is up to them to build their house around it. Black stall-

Souvenir sellers liven up Adderley Street, Cape Town

holders are beginning to take their wares to the streets of the white cities, but outside Johannesburg, few black families have moved into the white suburbs.

Levels of violent crime are on the increase everywhere and tourists should be cautious in all the cities, especially Johannesburg. The black townships are no-go areas for white people, unless they have a black friend or guide to vouch for them.

❏ In 1991, official figures showed that 60 per cent of the population lived in towns. Today, the figure is probably closer to 80 per cent and the rush to the cities continues unabated. ❏

■ **Most of South Africa's large population is clustered in a few key cities. Much of the rest of the country seems almost empty. Large tracts of the Kalahari are virtually uninhabitable with settlements spread sparsely along the few remaining watercourses, while farms in the Free State and Karoo stretch over vast areas.** ■

The remote life The farmers are almost all white, many the descendants of trekboers who set out into the unknown in order to shake off the constraints of civilization. Today they pride themselves on being rugged individualists, living self-contained lives, mixing only with their families and a small handful of neighbors within driving distance. Water comes from boreholes run by windmills; many have their own electricity generators, although the national electricity grid is spreading. The arrival of TV satellite dishes, video recorders and fax machines has given them their first access to daily news and entertainment. All shopping is done by mail or on infrequent sorties into the nearest market town. Even these can be remote. Upington in the Northern Cape is 500 miles from its nearest city, Kimberley. Those who can afford it run small planes and plan their rare shopping trips to the city like a military campaign.

From sheep to antelope The huge farms of the Free State and Karoo run half-wild cattle across virgin bush, or grow vast prairies of wheat and corn. In the Karoo, ostrich farming is making a triumphant return and many farmers are restocking the land with game shot out by their ancestors. Some are breeding antelope for the table, but more deal in live animals to sell to other farmers; others hope to set up private game reserves. Many are creating hunting concessions for the foreign market.

The good life Near the coast, the landscape changes. In KwaZulu-Natal, there are still huge plantations of pineapple, sugar-

Top: picking onions in Ceres. Left above: Venda village; below: farming in the Transkei

cane and bananas, but most are within a few hours' drive of Durban and the resort towns on the coast. People here have far more contact with the outside world, while in the Western Cape, farmers are wealthy and lead the good life. The area specializes in intensive farming of high-yield fruit crops and, above all, wine. The valleys are patterned by small, neatly combed vineyards, and life is far more sociable, with everyone within easy reach. Because of the international nature of the wine trade, the strong French Huguenot influence and the proximity of Cape Town, the winelands are a remarkably sophisticated area with some of the finest hotels and restaurants in the country—and some of the finest architecture in the white Cape-Dutch houses built by the early settlers.

Black life Outside those areas once designated as tribal homelands, there is virtually no independent black rural life. All nonwhites were removed from any usable land. Some remained on the white farms, each of which has a thriving village housing the farm workers and their

Grapes are one of South Africa's most important crops

families. The work is hard and the pay poor, but in other ways life is not all bad. Apartheid was always prepared to be paternal to those who toed the line and asked for little. Workers' houses are very basic, too small but hygienic; rudimentary medical care and schooling are provided; the pay often includes a ration of basic foodstuffs; and the farmer's wife usually runs a general store selling everything from canned foods to patent medicines, pens to beer. Some even provide staff and retirees with small plots to grow things for themselves.

The traditional villages have all but disintegrated. The men have long worked away while the women brought up the children and took what work they could find locally. Some of the villages have grown into towns in all but name; others have been left to the old while the youngsters flock to the city. Hardly anywhere do you see the tiny patches and tethered goats of traditional rural life in Africa.

SOUTH AFRICA IS *Liberal*

■ **South Africa's constitution is one of the most liberal ever written, with a bill of rights guaranteeing equality for men and women of all races, creeds and color, with freedom of speech and expression. It takes into account tribal as well as Roman–Dutch law.** ■

South Africa is now a republic within the Commonwealth, with two houses of parliament, the National Assembly and a National Council of Provinces. Until 1996, Vice Presidents Thabo Mbeki from the ANC (African National Congress) and former President F. W. de Klerk acted as deputies to Nelson Mandela as President. In 1996, shortly before the new permanent constitution came into effect, de Klerk resigned and the National Party withdrew from the Government of National Unity.

The nine provinces all have a high degree of regional autonomy. Eight seem happy with this arrangement. The exception is KwaZulu-Natal where the IFP (Inkatha Freedom Party), led by Chief Mangosuthu Buthelezi, is still embroiled in a violent struggle for further autonomy as a Zulu kingdom or even outright independence. There is also a demand for an all-white Afrikaaner Volkstaat, led by the Vryheidsfront (Freedom Front), the largely discredited AWB and several small ultraright wing parties.

❏   Born July 18, 1918 at Qunu, near Umtata, Nelson Rolihlahla Mandela graduated in law from the University of the Witwatersrand and started South Africa's first black law practice, in partnership with Oliver Tambo. In the 1950s, he became active in the emerging ANC, holding various offices including Commander-in-Chief of the militant wing, *Umkhonto we Sizwe* (Spear of the Nation). In 1963, he was sentenced to life imprisonment on Robben Island. Released unconditionally on February 11, 1990, he headed the ANC delegation in talks leading to South Africa's first truly democratic elections. Later he and F. W. de Klerk were awarded the Nobel Peace Prize for their success in dismantling apartheid. On May 10, 1994 Mandela became President of the Government of National Unity. ❏

22

SOUTH AFRICA WAS

■ **One of the great debates of all time hovers over a single question: what are the origins of humankind? Charles Darwin was convinced that Africa held the clue, though his contemporaries ridiculed that idea. Man, they thought, was too grand for the dark continent.** ■

It seems that Darwin may have been right after all. With each new find, it becomes more certain that Africa was the cradle of mankind. Research this century seems to have established that the emergence of the forerunner of modern man from ape-like prehuman forms took place in East Africa about 6 million years ago. Recent attention has been focused on the Leakey family's discoveries in the Rift Valley, at such sites as Olduvai Gorge and Koobi Fora, but some of the earliest discoveries that helped create the timetable of evolution were made in South Africa.

The birth of humanity The earliest of the protohumans were the australopithecines (literally "southern apes"). The first discovery came in 1924 when a fossilized skull of an infant *Australopithecus africanus* (the "Taung baby") was found at Taung in the Northern Cape, by a workman digging in a limestone quarry. Its canine teeth, like those of man, were small, and from the shape of the skull its brain showed humanoid features. The discovery was of immense importance and led to the hunt for an adult specimen. In 1936 Dr. Robert Broom found the first adult cranium in the Sterkfontein Caves, near Johannesburg. Exposed after a 2.5-million-year interment, the species was triumphantly hailed as the "missing link" between ape and man. In 1945 came definitive proof that the species had walked on two legs.

Australopithecus africanus lived between 1 and 3 million years ago; further discoveries have since identified several other species (or possibly subspecies) in Africa: *Australopithecus robustus*, and the even earlier *Australopithecus boisei* and *Australopithecus afarensis*, thought to date back 5.5 million years.

From about 2 million years ago, a new species emerges. *Homo habilis* ("handy man") walked upright with an awkward gait and dramatically outsplayed feet, and probably lived partially in trees. He had a brain with less than half the capacity of that of a modern human, but his hands were flexible and capable of fashioning crude stone tools for hunting.

Top: reconstruction of Australopithecus africanus. *Right: fossil bones offer clues to early man*

An artist's impression of
Australopithecus africanus

Upright man *Homo erectus*, the
first of the protohumans to be fully
adapted to standing and walking
upright, with leg bones barely distin-
guishable from those of modern
man, lived 1.6 million to 250,000
years ago. His brain was smaller than
ours, but it is thought that he could
speak, and his hands were free to
develop the most crucial of human
skills: the ability to make and to use
tools. He was also the first to kindle
a fire, and the first to have wandered
beyond the African continent—*Homo
erectus* bones have been found in
China and Java. Some of the earliest
remains were excavated in 1948 at
Swartkrans, near Krugersdorp.

Homo sapiens Modern man is still a
babe in arms in this time frame. The
earliest *Homo sapiens* and Nean-
derthal subspecies are believed to
have emerged about 100,000 years
ago. By about 40,000BC, *Homo sapiens sapiens* (modern man) was dominant and spreading fast, with a varied
array of cultures. Southern Africa
was inhabited by the Bushmen
whose life as nomadic hunters
continued with few variations until
the arrival of black tribes from the
north and white tribes from the sea.
  The story has not ended, however.
Each new find adds another piece to
this most difficult of puzzles. In 1995,
some foot bones from Sterkfontein,
lying forgotten in a museum, were re-
examined. They belong to an australo-
pithecine nicknamed "Littlefoot," have
a slightly divergent big toe and weight-
bearing arch, are extraordinarily early,
at about 3.3 million years ago, and
have overturned all existing theories
on how man came to walk upright.

■ **The history of the Cape of Good Hope is inextricably linked with the search for and defense of a sea route to India. It is a history of rivalry in trade and war between the Portuguese, the Dutch, the English and, to a lesser degree, the French.** ■

26

Portuguese explorers The earliest recorded voyage round the Cape was made in 1488 by the Portuguese navigator, Bartolomeu Dias. He never discovered the long-searched-for route to India, but in 1498 another Portuguese, Vasco da Gama, triumphantly rounded the Cape, reached India and returned to Europe in 1499. The route to the Indies had been found. The trade potential was enormous. The Portuguese moved quickly to consolidate and protect the route, claiming the right to overlordship of the Indian Ocean and domination of its trade.

Early expeditions all called into southern Africa as they passed, to collect water or barter with the Khoikhoi for fresh meat, but no efforts were made to set up a permanent outpost. Table Bay itself was not explored until 1503 when Admiral Antonio de Saldanha climbed Table Mountain and visited Robben Island. Later that century the Portuguese lost their dominant trad-

ing position, and the Netherlands and England both set about finding routes to the East.

Dutch settlement In 1580 Sir Francis Drake rounded the Cape, and by 1591 the first English expedition bound for the Indies had left Plymouth. By 1594 the Dutch too were on their way. Early in the 17th century, national efforts were controlled respectively by the British East India Company and the Dutch East India Company. It was the Netherlands, with their larger merchant fleet, who dominated trade. The Dutch East India Company established a victualing station at the Cape, and in 1652 Jan van Riebeeck was dispatched to command it. His task was to provide fresh water, vegetables and meat for passing Company mariners, who suffered all kinds of deprivation on the long voyage from Europe, as well as repair for their vessels.

A strategic base Dutch rule came to an end with the first British invasion in 1795 as part of the military strategy of the Napoleonic Wars. The colony was handed back in 1803, only to be invaded again in 1806

Top: Table Mountain. Left: a 16th-century view of Africa

when Napoleon once more became a danger. This time, the Congress of Vienna (1815) confirmed the British occupation and the Cape colony was ceded formally to the British Crown. The aim was strategic: by then, the Cape had become a naval base on the sea route to India and the Far East.

The Cape became an important focus of imperial communication—a vital link between the motherland and far-flung territories. Mail ships came and went, the Royal Navy set up its local headquarters in Simon's Town, and many thousands of eager white immigrants landed here, ready for the long trek north to try their fortunes in the diamond and gold fields. The 1890s was a decade of almost unparalleled growth as South Africa's economy boomed. During World War I the route became strategically important, as merchant shipping which might otherwise have used the Suez Canal was diverted south. After the war, the route was no longer profitable and trade dwindled until the fresh outbreak of war in 1939, when history repeated itself.

Decline and recovery The Egypt-Israeli war of 1967, which closed the Suez Canal, once again focused attention on the Cape. With the end of that crisis, trade sanctions were imposed on South Africa in the 1980s and traffic tailed off until the Cape's most frequent visitors were bulky supertankers simply too big to pass through the Suez Canal. Regular passenger transportation declined massively; the last mail-ship voyage took place in October 1977. Today, sanctions over, ships are lining up to get into South Africa's ports, the cruise ships are heading south, and the future looks hopeful.

Left: Jan van Riebeeck. Below: Cape Town in the 17th century

27

■ **The arrival of the first Dutch settlers in the Cape in the 1650s was to have far-reaching consequences not only for the locals, but for the very survival of stable African societies throughout the entire sub-continent.** ■

Early links The Khoikhoi (called Hottentots by the early Dutch colonists) were mainly gentle pastoralists who were happy to barter sheep and cattle for iron and other metals. It was a trade that became vitally important to the survival of European mariners on their months-long voyage to the East.

For centuries, the sailors came, looked, traded and went away again. A few stayed a while on dry land. The Portuguese who pioneered the route to India were sometimes ship-wrecked, having to stay on the shores of Table Bay until rescued by the next passing fleet. In 1615 the British left a small party of convicts, but they retreated to Robben Island until rescued. Then in 1647 the crew of a wrecked Dutch East Indiaman, the *Haerlem*, built a fort during their yearlong stay.

Founding of the Cape colony It was only in 1682 when the Dutch East

India Company established the Cape refreshment station for the scurvy-ridden crews of passing ships (see page 26) that a settled white community came into existence, with a set policy and continuity of command.

The local Khoikhoi welcomed the Dutch settlers at first, conducting trade as usual. Jan van Riebeeck, the first commander of the new Cape colony, successfully gained their trust, all the while claiming the Cape Peninsula and adjacent land for the VOC (Verenigde Oost-Indische Compagnie—Dutch East India Company, see box below). Contact with the Khoikhoi was at first restricted by the Company. As a result, a small number of Company employees—particularly those free burghers the Company had released from its service, and to whom it had granted land—were unable to find local labor, and imported slaves from the East Indies.

By the 1680s, the settlers were moving out from the embryo Cape Town, and were successfully raising their own cattle. The Khoikhoi not only lost their barter livelihood, but gradually also their grazing land and water rights as the Europeans moved farther out from the town. The Khoikhoi society began to disintegrate. In 1713 smallpox decimated the people of the southwestern Cape and by the 1740s the remaining few were working as laborers for the colonists, many of them in conditions of dreadful servitude.

Expansion In the early years settler numbers increased slowly. The majority were Dutch, members of the Dutch Reformed Church, but their numbers were augmented by Germans and French Huguenots fleeing religious persecution. Many of

❑ In 1602, the Dutch East India Company received a charter to conduct all Dutch trade between the Cape of Good Hope and the Strait of Magellan. With its headquarters in Batavia (Jakarta), it acted more like a nation than a trading company, conquering and ruling huge territories and fighting off all competition. The profits were enormous in the 17th century, but tailed off over the next hundred years until, by 1799, with corrupt officials, it was nearly bankrupt. The company was dissolved and its possessions and debts taken over by the Dutch state. ❑

28

Ox wagon, a major form of transport, approaching a Boer farm

these settlers brought to Africa a tradition of dissent and a legacy of resentment against Europe. As the settlement expanded, borders were extended: when the burghers sought to beat the Company's often draconian rules by quitting areas under their control, the authorities simply extended their influence into the newly formed districts.

By the 1770s many settlers had drifted well beyond the confines of van Riebeeck's original territory, heading northwards as far as the Orange River and eastwards toward the Great Fish River. The more determined were farmers driven by a ruthless quest for land, larger herds and, above all, total independence. They drew European control far into the hinterland, eventually coming into conflict with more warlike indigenous people—such as the Xhosa on the Eastern Frontier—who found themselves having to defend their territory against the gun.

Governor Willem van der Stel at his farm, Vergelegen

■ ***Mfecane*** **is a Zulu word (literally "crushing") used to describe the ripple effect of the early 19th-century process of Zulu expansion and empire-building in what is now KwaZulu-Natal. The key to these bloody events was an ever more pressing need for land.** ■

Among the often warlike Nguni societies of the 18th century (see page 17), chiefdoms expanded, spilling over into ever more virgin territory so that by the beginning of the 19th century there was a land shortage, aggravated by a devastating drought, overgrazing, serious soil erosion and the ever closer presence of the white Voortrekkers (see pages 32–33). A scramble for power and influence ensued, forcing many smaller chiefdoms into defensive alliances against land-hungry foes. This led to larger groupings, like the southern Mthethwa whose ruler (from about 1809) was Dingiswayo, normally considered to be the first of

the great Zulu kings. Another such group included the northern Ngwane who, under Sobhuza, were to flee inland, defeating smaller Sotho and Nguni clans they met on the way and eventually amalgamating them into what became the Swazi nation.

Shaka In 1815 Dingiswayo was murdered by a rival clan, the Ndwandwe. Shaka emerged as the new king. Born in 1787, the son of a minor Zulu chief, he grew up in Dingiswayo's court and became a military commander. One of his first acts was to change the name of the ruling tribe and all the conquered clans to that of his clan, the Zulus. Shaka was a military genius and totally ruthless. From the moment he took power, he set about expanding his army, turning it into one of the deadliest fighting forces in Africa. He invented the hugely effective short stabbing assegai to replace the traditional javelin-style throwing spear, allowing the army to reuse their weapons. He also developed brutally efficient new tactics such as the terrifying *impi* with the warriors attacking in a curved "bull-and-horns" formation. In this, the main army advanced on the enemy from the front, while units of the fastest runners created diversions down the opposition's flanks, and troops from the rear circled round outside the horns to close the circle. By the end of his reign, Shaka had subjugated most of the smaller, weaker clans and controlled a vast area of land, left vacant by the flight of those who refused to submit to his authority. Murdered in 1828 by

British Lieutenant Farewell negotiates with Shaka

his half brothers Dingane and Mhlangane, he remains one of the greatest heroes of the Zulu nation.

❏ A second word, *Difaqane*, also describes this period of black South African history. A Sotho word, it is used for the intertribal wars west of the Drakensberg that followed invasions of peoples fleeing the Mfecane wars farther east. Of all the conquered and dispossessed tribes the Sotho were the most affected, and their word has connotations of defeat and loss. ❏

The battle for land It was the ripple effect caused by the refugees from Zulu might that created such widespread upheaval. As terrified peoples moved north, they collided and clashed with other settled inhabitants spread in a wide arc from what is now Swaziland to the highveld and Lesotho, displacing them in turn as they secured land on which to graze their cattle and grow their crops.

The events of this period gave rise to an enduring myth: that the land into which the Voortrekkers and other early pioneers stepped in the 19th century was empty country, depopulated by the Mfecane. The reality was quite different. In fact, this was a land where people had gathered in places of safety and were desperately endeavoring to re-establish order in their shattered societies. The presence of the settlers—with their guns, wagons and horses—only exacerbated an already unpleasant situation, eventually leading to appalling violence and some of the most tragic episodes in South Africa's history, among them the horrifying Battle of Blood River (see page 204).

Boers charge Dingane's army

■ **The Great Trek signaled the determination of Dutch-speaking farmers (Boers) to find a "Promised Land" where they would be "free and independent," beyond the limits of British control. This bold venture led briefly to the establishment of several independent Boer republics. The Great Trek is a landmark in the history of South Africa, heralding an era of expansionism, bloodshed and land seizure.** ■

Into the interior The Trek began in 1835, when the first of many groups of bitter Voortrekkers left Grahamstown, Uitenhage and Graaff-Reinet and headed for the largely unknown interior. The Eastern Cape was a particularly tense region, being the frontier between Xhosa territory and the Cape Colony and a focus for refugees who had fled the rise of the Zulu state. The Boers were unhappy about having to fight the Xhosa for land or submit to British rule. They felt that the colonial government had failed to provide them with sufficient protection against the Xhosa, while the abolition of slavery (1834) had robbed them of valued possessions. In 1834 reconnaissance expeditions claimed that Natal was fertile and largely uninhabited. In fact, the Africans had only moved away temporarily in the wake of the Mfecane and were soon to return, only to find themselves ousted by Boer intruders (see page 31).

During the following decade, thousands more Boers migrated, many of them the so-called "trekboers," semi-nomadic pastoral farmers; others were cattle ranchers or sheep farmers. Each group of Voortrekkers had its own leader but they all followed much the same route through "Transorangia" (the highveld), only splitting when some went into Natal while others continued north.

Voortrekker life A family might have more than one wagon, carrying all its worldly goods. Drawn by oxen, the wagons could carry a surprising amount—household effects, furniture, bedding, clothes, food, agricultural implements, weapons and shot, even fruit trees. They were narrow and designed to put as little weight as possible on to the oxen. In the evenings the wagons were drawn into a protective circle (laager), the gaps and space under the wheels filled with thorn branches. The laager became an instant fort for the Voortrekkers who would hide behind the wagons and shoot at any attackers. The cattle and other livestock were herded into a kraal (corral) in the center. People would gather around a fire to sing, pray, chat—and even dance.

Top: tapestry homage to the Voortrekkers, Pretoria. Left: statue of Piet Retief, Pietermaritzburg

The Boer republics The varied terrain the Voortrekkers covered, at a rate of about 6 miles a day, was treacherous. Not only was the topography often difficult, but they ran the risk of encounters with wild animals, the tsetse fly and the malarial mosquito. The courage they displayed is still a key feature of Afrikaner folklore. They also ran into strong local resistance. Small parties of trekboers, missionaries and adventurers had preceded them, so the Africans were not completely unused to the white man. But this was the largest group they had ever seen. In 1838 a party led by Piet Retief was massacred by Dingane. Desire for revenge led to the Battle of Blood River (see page 204) and eventually to Dingane's death and the creation of the Boer Republic of Natalia (1838), which was promptly annexed by Britain. The Boers then trekked north, and in 1860 formed the South African Republic (ZAR) in Transvaal. Another party proclaimed the Orange Free State (1854) beyond the Vaal and Orange Rivers. Others headed for Delagoa Bay and were annihilated by the Tsonga, while a party led by Louis Trichardt ended up in Lourenço Marques where most died of tropical diseases.

33

Voortrekkers crossing the Transvaal

■ **The British ruled this corner of Africa for most of the 19th century. Their initial occupation of the Cape in 1795 had little impact. Only from 1814 onwards, eight years after they had wrested the Cape colony from the Dutch for the second time, did they start to develop the Cape's potential for settlement and trade. This African subcontinent, Britain finally realized, would be a great source of labor and raw materials and a market for manufactured goods. ■**

British rule in the 19th century was characterized by certain key events now regarded as milestones in South Africa's history. It started with the mass immigration in 1820 of settlers from Britain, which resulted in exhausting conflict with the Xhosa on the eastern frontier, and the gradual settling by whites of what is now called KwaZulu-Natal following the Great Trek. In 1843 Natal was annexed by Britain as a second colony. Subsequent bloody clashes between Zulu, Boer and Briton punctuated the following decades.

Boers versus Britain In 1852 and 1854 Britain recognized the independence of two new Boer republics, the fledgling South African Republic (ZAR) in the Transvaal and the Orange Free State. Then in 1877 it annexed the Transvaal in the first attempt to create a federation in southern Africa. In 1880, the Boers under Paul Kruger revolted against their new government. Within a few weeks they had won the first Anglo-Boer War, enjoying a crushing victory at the Battle of Majuba (1881). Kruger became President of the ZAR while Gladstone's government agreed to withdraw the large British force and restore internal self-government to the Boers. Kruger grudgingly accepted this arrangement, which

Above: Model soldiers in Talana Museum, Dundee. Left: the Battle of Majuba— a crushing defeat for the British

Jameson Raid (see page 37). The raid was a disaster, but it indicated to Kruger British intentions. The Second Anglo-Boer War was not long in coming (see pages 38–9). The victorious British granted limited self-government to former Boer Republics, but from then on, they effectively controlled the whole of modern South Africa and all its mineral wealth.

Above: Cape Prime Minister Cecil Rhodes. Right: ZAR President Paul Kruger

was formalized by the Convention of Pretoria in 1881.

The Empire-builders were far from content. They had visions of controlling territories in Africa from the Cape in the south to Cairo in the north, and although Britain still claimed status as paramount power in South Africa and reserved to itself ultimate control over the Transvaal's foreign affairs, it could not now claim the republic as a colony. Many resented this, among them the multi-millionaire diamond magnate, Cecil John Rhodes (prime minister of the Cape in the 1890s).

The discovery of gold (1886) made the Transvaal the richest and most powerful nation in southern Africa— and that made Britain nervous. It also made Randlords Cecil Rhodes and Alfred Beit a second fortune, and brought Boer and *uitlander* (foreigner) into conflict. The wealth of the Witwatersrand proved too alluring a prize. In 1895, Rhodes and others conspired to take over the Transvaal and install a British administration by means of the ill-fated

Union After the war, the colonial government began the process of reconstruction. The mines were put back into operation and, by 1907, the former republics were given representative government. In 1910 the Cape, Natal, the Orange Free State and the ZAR were bound into a single national entity, the Union of South Africa. The local black Africans were not consulted. Voter franchise —or the lack of it—was the single most negative outcome. Only whites could be elected to Parliament, and English and Dutch became the official languages. By excluding blacks, the Act of Union sowed the seeds of discontent resolved only with the freeing of Nelson Mandela in 1990.

■ **In the last quarter of the 19th century, the discovery of diamonds in Kimberley, followed by the first gold diggings on the Witwatersrand, transformed the landscape, population and history of South Africa. Almost overnight, what had been a poor and little-known country became rich, famous and powerful thanks to the mines—and the mining magnates.** ■

Fortune hunters rushed to the arid zones of discovery from every corner of the globe. They included some two dozen men, most of them immigrants from England, Holland and Germany, who staked claims, but also started auxiliary services. They opened hotels, set up dealerships and even ran the lifts which gave the men access to their diggings. They also built alliances, fed feuds and appetites and, in the 1870s and 1880s, went on to take control of the diamond fields. From 1886 onwards they moved north to finance and run the gold mines. Nicknamed the Randlords by the British press, they acquired immense wealth, power and influence.

Wealth and power Supreme among the Randlords was Cecil John Rhodes—diamond magnate, gold mine owner, politician and empire-builder extraordinary. His chief rival for control of the diamond fields was showman Barney Barnato, who combined financial wizardry and cabaret. Other highfliers in this mixed bunch were Lionel Phillips, Alfred Beit, Joseph Robinson, Julius Wernher, Solly Joel, and Samuel Marks. Later Ernest Oppenheimer founded the dynasty which still controls the world's diamond market.

The Randlords' lives were colorful and controversial. Their ostentatious wealth contrasted dramatically with the increasing poverty of the rural poor, both white and black. Only the feather barons in Oudtshoorn (see page 80) came anywhere near matching their flamboyant lifestyle. They built large, showy mansions in and around fledgling Johannesburg as well as in fashionable parts of London. They collected art, much of which forms the core of major national galleries in Cape Town and

Top: the diamond diggings at Kimberley. Above left: the Oppenheimer family in 1933. Left: showman millionaire Barney Barnato

Prospectors used simple methods to find gold in 1900

Johannesburg, sponsored foundations, and set up scholarships. But this wealth brought with it a lust for power—those who controlled the gold controlled the country.

Photo: *Mr. G. T. Ferneyhough*
PROSPECTING FOR GOLD ON THE RAND.

The shaping of modern South Africa

The Randlords' most enduring legacy is to the economy of South Africa. The discovery of gold and of diamonds contributed hugely to South Africa's regional power base and gave it a crucial standing in the world economy. Mining has affected the lives of every one of the social and ethnic groups in the country. One of the first pieces of discriminatory legislation to be passed on the way to apartheid was designed to oust black miners from their diamond claims, make sure that claim ownership was white and reduce the blacks on the diamond fields to a cheap, compliant labor pool. Gold was vital to the subcontinent and cheap labor was vital to gold if profit margins were to be kept high on international sales. The Randlords were easily persuaded to ally themselves with many of the worst racial excesses of the republican and, later, the South African government.

The Jameson Raid

The struggle for control finally toppled into intrigue and war. Rhodes, as prime minister of the Cape Colony, wanted to oust Paul Kruger, leader of the Transvaal Boers, and set up a British-ruled Federation of South Africa. With his sights on yet another personal fortune, he was convinced that only Britain possessed the know-how to exploit the region's immeasurable riches. The deeply religious Kruger not only regarded the discovery of gold as a mixed blessing, but was hostile to the presence of the British and other *uitlanders*. In 1895, Dr. Leander Jameson, a close associate of Rhodes, led a raiding party into the Transvaal aiming to cause an insurrection and remove Kruger. The Jameson Raid not only ended in ignominious defeat and finished Rhodes' political career in South Africa, it also sowed the seeds for the Second Anglo-Boer War.

■ **The first of the two Anglo-Boer Wars was won by the Boers. In 1870 the British annexed a small hill on the Orange Free State border, which turned out to be the Kimberley diamond pipe; then gold was discovered and in 1877, they annexed the South African Republic (ZAR). The furious Boers fought for their independence and won, at the Battle of Majuba in 1881.** ■

The path to war The ZAR was officially given its independence again in 1884, but by then its gold was attracting huge interest from scores of foreign prospectors. British imperialists, goaded on by the enormous wealth being engendered, instigated the Jameson Raid (1895), hoping to ignite an uprising which would lead to the installation of a British administration in the ZAR. It was a disaster, and subsequent events led President Kruger to demand that Britain withdraw the troops massed on his border. Ignored, he invaded Natal in 1899, and so began the Second Anglo-Boer War.

Kruger's commandos were in essence a "people's army," wearing civilian clothes. But they had a distinct advantage over the regular British troops because they knew the countryside and climate and were excellent horsemen. Before the war was over, Britain had committed 448,715 troops—outnumbering the Boers by nearly five to one.

The Siege of Ladysmith The Boers started well: they beat the British at Talana Hill and routed them at Nicholson's Nek. But their four-month siege of Ladysmith in northwest Natal was ill-timed and ended in disaster. The Boers' original aim was to advance into Natal and the Cape to stem the influx of British troops, but the siege lasted too long. Even though it tied up four-fifths of the British army, the road to Durban was left virtually open, and the Boers—aside from attacks at Weenen, Estcourt, and Mooi River—remained far too cautious. The British had time to bring up fresh troops via Durban, the Boers lost their advantage—and ultimately lost the war. Various, unsuccessful attempts were made to relieve Ladysmith, such as the disastrous Battle of Colenso, but it was not until after such famous battles as Spienkop and Paardeberg that the siege was lifted.

Above: the Battle of Majuba, 1881. Left: Jameson captured by the Boers in 1895

Le Petit Journal

SUPPLÉMENT ILLUSTRÉ

Huit pages : CINQ centimes

DIMANCHE 19 JANVIER 1896

AU TRANSVAAL
Le docteur Jameson prisonnier des Boers

Concentration camps In 1900 Pretoria surrendered, and then Johannesburg, but the war was not yet over. A rural guerilla war began as Boer commandos split up, continuing the fight in smaller, more mobile bands in an effort to deny the British control of the countryside. Retribution was swift—and terrible: for every belligerent act, every sabotage of railroad lines, the British reacted with twice the force. They burned farmhouses, instituting a devastating scorched-earth policy. Anything that might sustain the guerillas was flushed out of the countryside, and that included horses, cattle, sheep, women and children. Boer women and children—so-called refugees—were dumped into huge camps, located near the railways and run along military lines—the world's first concentration camps. Neglect of elementary precautions led to epidemics of typhoid and dysentery. By the end of the war, 136,000 Afrikaners were imprisoned in 50 camps; over 26,000 women and children had died of disease and neglect. The horror of the camps was brought to light by an English philanthropist, Emily Hobhouse, and these revelations helped bring about the Peace of Vereeniging (1902). There is a memorial to the Afrikaner dead in Bloemfontein (see page 127).

❏ Whites were not the only inmates of the concentration camps. Entire populations of black locations or mission stations were uprooted and transferred to sites adjoining the Boer camps. By the end of the war, it is believed that there were some 115,700 Africans in 66 camps. Unlike the whites, they were used as a labor force for the British army, and were not fed, as they were expected to be self-sufficient. More than 14,000 deaths are recorded; there were undoubtedly many others. There is no memorial to the African dead. ❏

Boers hold their position against the Grenadier Guards, 1900

■ **"Apartheid" means the segregation and separate development of the races. Though its roots go back to the slave-owning colonists and to economic and political developments in the 19th century, much of the legislation which made up the core of apartheid policy was in fact born of British policies of the early 20th century.** ■

First steps Basing their thinking on the teachings of John Ruskin, the British colonial administrators came up with an ideal of separate development, by which the superior (i.e., white) race assisted the other races towards an eventual goal of equality and reintegration. Meanwhile, they would be given tasks suitable to their abilities and progress (i.e., menial). It was, of course, in the interests of the dominant whites to insure that progress was not too swift. The ultra-right-wing Afrikaner Broederbond (Brotherhood), founded in 1918, took the notion much further.

It was Jan Smuts's Native Affairs Act (1920) that took the first step toward real political segregation, establishing the principle that African political activity should be divorced from "white" South Africa. It ushered in a period of intense debate on "native policy," during which state ideology was refined and clarified.

Apartheid legislation Nearly 30 years on, in 1948, the Afrikaner National Party under Hendrik Verwoerd and D. F. Malan coined the word "apartheid," and fought and won the election on a ticket of oppression. It immediately adopted apartheid as a national political program, bringing in many new laws. What is called "petty" apartheid was instituted: separate beaches, public benches, building entrances and public lavatories. These regulations were united under the Separate Amenities Act. Sex outside marriage between races was already banned, but the 1949 Mixed Marriages Act and the Immorality Act of the following year banned any sex between the races. The Population Registration Act of 1950 legislated for a national register according to racial classification, with every citizen to be issued with documents stating their racial group. Race was identified by physical attributes, "measurable" in ways which beggar belief: for example, if an official stuck a pencil in your hair and it stayed fast, you were Black, not Colored.

Laws allowing Africans into urban areas were redefined; Africans had to carry a pass at all times and wherever they went. Failure to do so was a criminal offence. This effectively made Africans aliens in their own land. "Group Areas" defined as White, Black, Indian or Colored (mixed race) made physical separation absolute. You lived where the state told you to. If you tried to resist, you were forcibly removed. On the crucial issue of land, the Prevention of Illegal Squatting Act (1951) gave the government power to move African tenants from privately or publicly owned land.

Top: apartheid even led to separate beaches.
Left: Hendrik Verwoerd, architect of apartheid

More and more demonstrators braved the police

All this was only the completion of legislation begun under Cecil John Rhodes as prime minister of the Cape Colony from 1890 to 1895. The exclusively Afrikaner Nationalist politicians justified the ruthless apartheid system as the only alternative to segregation and the end of white South Africa.

The death of apartheid For 30 years the National Party government wrestled with the implementation of apartheid, an unwieldy, contradictory and deeply unsavory policy. There was heavy media censorship, a total lack of freedom of speech and increasing violence, with torture, poorly explained deaths, disappearances and attendant horrors. But the level of protest, at home and abroad, grew steadily and bravely until white South Africa was an international pariah.

Under the force and effect of economic sanctions and diplomatic pressure, President F. W. de Klerk announced that he would repeal discriminatory laws. Seizing the political initiative, he surprised his supporters by unbanning the African National Congress (ANC), the Pan African Congress (PAC) and the Communist Party—and releasing from jail the popular hero Nelson Mandela. The government, bowing to the inevitable, finally abandoned the indefensible apartheid policy, explaining it away as an experiment that foundered and did not work.

■ **The roots of the Struggle are nearly as deep as those of the oppression itself. By the end of the 19th century, a feeling of African nationality was emerging among Christian-educated blacks. At first this was centered on religion, with the foundation of many independent African churches, but political movements were not far behind.** ■

First stirrings In 1912 a handful of mission-educated black men in the Eastern Cape and Natal founded the South African Native National Congress (SANNC), the forerunner of the ANC. Four years later the University of Fort Hare opened, giving blacks a first chance at higher education. Around the same time, a young Indian lawyer, Mohindas Karamchand Gandhi, began the first of his many campaigns of nonviolent protest on behalf of the Natal Indians. In the 1920s, the mainly Zulu Inkatha Movement was founded, also in Natal. Any small political successes were met with a massive right-wing backlash.

In 1923, the SANNC became the African National Congress (ANC),

which in 1928 began to work with the Communist Party. The war years saw the creation of the African Miners' Union and the ANC Youth League, the first mass protests in the townships, bus boycotts, squatter camps, and black-run strikes in the mines. All were crushed violently by the police. The outcome was the Nationalist victory in the 1948 elections, and the official implementation of apartheid.

Below and opposite: violence and death dogged the fight for freedom. Right: Steve Biko

Protest and suppression In 1959 the more militant Pan African Congress (PAC), was formed by breakaway members of the ANC, led by Robert Sobukwe. In 1960 Sobukwe persuaded thousands to burn their pass books. In Sharpeville, south of Johannesburg, the police panicked and fired on a crowd, killing over 200 people. The government declared a state of emergency, arrested Sobukwe and banned the PAC and ANC. Both organizations went underground and formed military wings, the PAC's *Poqo* and the ANC's *Umkhonto we Sizwe.*

Oliver Tambo and several other key leaders fled into exile. In 1962, many remaining ANC leaders, including Nelson Mandela and Walter Sisulu, were charged with treason and sabotage in the Rivonia Treason Trial, and sentenced to life imprisonment—most on Robben Island. Effective protest was over for nearly a decade.

Township violence By the early 1970s, a new generation of young, bright and committed activists was ready to take up the struggle. The most charismatic and famous was Steve Biko, leader of the Black Consciousness movement. Speaking to black and white students, he aimed to raise black awareness and pride. Biko was to die under dubious circumstances in a police cell in 1977.

Meanwhile the schoolchildren of Soweto took to the streets. The police responded brutally and many hundreds were killed, injured or arrested while others fled to ANC camps outside the country. By 1980, violence on the township streets was commonplace. The media was heavily censored, but pictures of singing children facing armed police and attack dogs were being daily flashed on to TV sets across the globe. There was a permanent state of emergency with tens of thousands detained without trial to face torture, police brutality and poorly explained deaths in custody. Zulu Chief Mangostho Buthelezi, who revitalized Inkatha, was not prepared to play second fiddle to the ANC. Horrific factional violence broke out in the townships and workers' hostels between supporters of the various political parties and tribal groups, with so-

called traitors burned alive, a car tire filled with gas around their necks.

In 1986 international sanctions were imposed and the first cracks were seen in the apartheid armor. The pass laws were repealed, the Indians and Coloreds were given a limited franchise, and many of the petty rules of apartheid were abolished. The real drama was still to come.

■ **The road to freedom was finally opened in 1990, when President F. W. de Klerk made a momentous and unexpected speech in Parliament, repudiating the concept of apartheid, repealing the laws that held discrimination in place and unbanning organizations such as the ANC. He withdrew the South African army from Angola, gave Namibia its independence and pledged to work toward a truly democratic society.** ■

But the greatest indication that freedom was here to stay came with the release of Nelson Mandela from his 27-year imprisonment on Robben Island. He would accept his own freedom only when all South Africans had theirs. Over 100,000 people waited for hours on the old Parade Ground in the heart of Cape Town before Mandela stepped out on to the balcony of City Hall to give his first public address.

❏ "We have, at last, achieved our political emancipation. We pledge ourselves to liberate all our people from the continuing bondage of poverty, deprivation, suffering, gender and other discrimination.
Never, never and never again shall it be that this beautiful land will again experience the oppression of one by another...The sun shall never set on so glorious a human achievement.
Let freedom reign. God bless Africa!"
Nelson Mandela, Presidential Inaugural Address, quoted in *The Long Walk to Freedom* (1994) ❏

Talks now began in earnest between the government and the various opposition parties. In 1992, to the astonishment of the world, a referendum held among white South Africans resulted in an overwhelming vote to end apartheid. The violence continued unabated until the last moment, with massacres at Boipatong south of

Johannesburg and Bisho in former Ciskei, and has still not died away completely, with ongoing trouble in KwaZulu-Natal to this day. In 1994, however, the country held its first truly democratic elections, and Nelson Mandela and F. W. de Klerk jointly accepted the Nobel Peace Prize. On May 10, with the eyes of the world watching, Nelson Mandela took office as President of the New South Africa.

Above: Nelson Mandela and F. W. de Klerk. Below: ANC election poster

A to Z

WESTERN CAPE

WESTERN CAPE

What's in a name
Bartolomeu Dias rounded Cape Point on a bad day and called it "Cabo Tormentoso," "Cape of Storms." The name that actually stuck was the Cape of Good Hope, donated by Sir Francis Drake who sailed it in benign sunshine in 1577 and was moved to describe it as "the fairest Cape we saw in the circumference of the world."

First intentions
"It is apt to be forgotten that the Cape was not occupied with the view to the establishment of a European colony in our present sense of the word. The Dutch took it that they might plant a cabbage garden: the English took it that they might have a naval station and half-way house to India."
James Bryce, *Impressions of South Africa*, 1897.

Western Cape The Western Cape's plump, roughly L-shaped body lies along the edge of the Indian Ocean, stretching a long, languid arm up the Atlantic coast to the Kalahari desert. At its heart, where the two oceans meet, is Cape Town, a lifeline to sailors and a magnet to tourists. The city is the single biggest tourist attraction in South Africa. The authorities are aiming for 4–5 million tourists a year by 2004—when they hope to host the Olympic Games. It is hard to imagine how these extra people will all fit in when there are already three-hour lines for the Table Mountain Cableway.

The founding fathers chose well when they colonized the coastal strip. The climate is moderate and pleasant, the land fertile and well watered, and the scenery superb. As might be expected when a colony is founded by a gardener, the first farms were up and running within a very few years. With the planting of the first vines only three years after Jan van Riebeeck's arrival in 1652, the Cape had found its true vocation. The area surrounding Cape Town is as steeped in wine as Bordeaux—and has its roots in the same place. It was the arrival of the French Huguenots from 1685 that spurred the industry into something more than the occasional flagon of cheap wine, while the German contingent provided the fruity tones, redolent of the Mosel, that characterize so much of the best South African white wine. Today, the industry is up there with the best, and for the connoisseur or the

tippler, a dozen local wine routes offer an extraordinary range of tasting opportunities.

Beyond these tidy, whitewashed valleys lies a jagged line of craggy mountains, the Cederberg, the Hex River Mountains, and the Swartberg. The south faces, slapped by ocean clouds, are thick with forest or powerfully scented by the Cape's unique herbal *fynbos* (see page 74). On the dry far side, the picture is very different. People either love or hate the Karoo. It is rocky, dry and dusty, twisted at times into fantastic rock formations. From a distance its scrubby vegetation looks unimpressive, but if you look closely and carefully it is magnificent, and when the spring flowers are in bloom it is an artwork worthy of Jackson Pollock. The inhabitants of this tough land are as rugged as their surroundings. Their ancestors headed into the unknown with nothing more than a flimsy wagon and a few cooking pots to escape the ordered urban life with all its rules and regulations. These communities are hospitable but introverted. Most are more concerned with physical survival than metaphysics, but the desert has sometimes borne extraordinary blooms in the occasional powerful writer or artist.

Then there is the coast itself, a delightful playground of rocky headlands and golden beaches, where whales and surfers alike frolic in the crashing waves. A major road, the N2, runs straight along the coast, linking the numerous small towns of the Garden Route, so called because

Above: the lush Breë Valley is perfect for growing fruit

Below: weird rock formations, like the "Sewing Machine," crown the Cederbergs

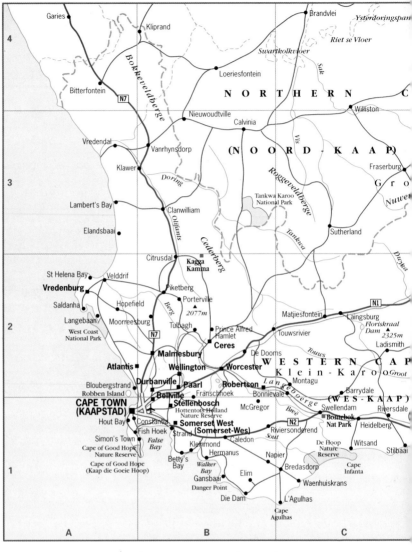

of its rampantly green forests. This has long been one of the white South Africans' favorite vacation destinations and inevitably has become more crowded, with bungalows and vacation homes stretching along the dunes to link many of the towns in continuous ribbon development. At the same time, the forest has been pushed a little farther away and the coast has lost a little of its beauty, but at least there are now facilities and entertainment for the many thousands who flock here each year. And there are still plenty of isolated coves and deserted dunes for those who care to seek them out.

This is a patchwork land, the ideal vacation destination with something for everyone, and all within a reasonable distance. It may not be "real" Africa, but the Western Cape has a magic all its own.

Tourist information
Western Cape Tourism
Board, PO Box 1403, Cape
Town 8000 (tel: 021-418
3716, fax: 021-214 875).

*Brightly colored
beach huts stand
sentinel at
Muizenberg*

Cape Town

Even before Vasco da Gama first rounded the Cape in 1498, sailors kept a lookout for Table Mountain, visible from 90 miles out to sea. The Phoenicians and Arabs thought it was filled with magnetism that could draw a ship in to its doom, while the massive mythical bird, the roc, nested on the slopes, and a race of dwarves called the Wac-wac lived in the bay area. When later sailors actually stepped ashore, they discovered good fresh water and the cattle-farming Khoikhoi, who were willing to trade fresh meat and milk. Table Bay became a regular revictualing stop, but it was 150 years before any Europeans came to stay, although several nationalities made abortive and short-lived attempts.

Foundations Then the Dutch got serious. In 1652, a small fleet of three ships, commanded by Jan van Riebeeck, was sent to the bay by the Dutch East India Company. Their mission was to provide fresh produce for passing ships. Van Riebeeck laid out the 45-acre Company's Garden as a market garden, built a fort in which to live, founded a small hospital and made a safe area for ship repairs. The foundations of modern Cape Town had been laid and the city has since grown from strength to strength, much loved and with numerous nicknames, from the "Mother City" to the "Tavern of the Seas."

Today, this is one of the world's prettiest cities, famously cocooned into a shallow bay by the looming bulk of Table Mountain, its tiny center neat and elegant. If it can be compared to anywhere else, Cape Town is most akin to San Francisco. Like that city, it owes its existence

*Windsurfers enjoy
spectacular views in
Table Bay*

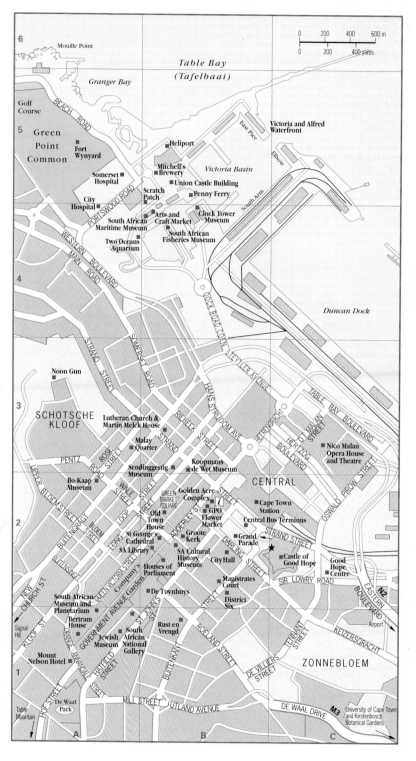

CAPE TOWN

Mouille Point

Table Bay
(Tafelbaai)

Granger Bay

Golf
Course

**Green
Point
Common**

Fort
Wynyard

Somerset
Hospital

City
Hospital

Victoria and Alfred
Waterfront

East Pier

Heliport

Mitchell's
Brewery

Victoria Basin

Union Castle Building

Penny Ferry

Scratch
Patch

Elbow

Arts and
Craft Market

Clock Tower
Museum

South Arm

South African
Maritime Museum

South African
Fisheries Museum

Two Oceans
Aquarium

Duncan Dock

Noon Gun

**SCHOTSCHE
KLOOF**

Lutheran Church &
Martin Melck House

RIEBEEK STREET

HANS STRIJDOM AVE

TABLE BAY BOULEVARD

Malay
Quarter

Koopmans
de Wet Museum

HERTZOG BOULEVARD

Nico Malan
Opera House
and Theatre

Sendinggestig
Museum

Bo-Kaap
Museum

GREEN
MARKET
SQUARE

Golden Acre
Complex

CENTRAL

OSWALD PIROW STREET

Old
Town
House

GPO
Flower
Market

Cape Town
Station

Central Bus Terminus

St George's
Cathedral

Groote
Kerk

Grand
Parade

STRAND STREET

SA Library

SA Cultural
History
Museum

City Hall

Castle of
Good Hope

Good
Hope
Centre

Houses of
Parliament

Magistrates
Court

SIR LOWRY ROAD

N2

South African
Museum and
Planetarium

De Tuynhuys

District
Six

EASTERN BOULEVARD

Airport

Bertram
House

Jewish
Museum

South
African
National
Gallery

Rust en
Vreugd

Signal
Hill

KEIZERSGRACHT

Mount
Nelson Hotel

ZONNEBLOEM

Table
Mountain

De Waal
Park

MILL STREET   JUTLAND AVENUE

DE WAAL DRIVE

M3

University of Cape Town
and Kirstenbosch
Botanical Gardens

A   B   C

CAPE TOWN

The perfect garden
When Jan van Riebeeck laid out his market garden in 1652, the first things he planted were Turkish and broad beans, peanuts, aniseed, fennel, medlar, quince, Spanish oranges, cucumber, pumpkin, onions, watermelon, endives and beet. The following year, the gardens were enlarged, adding parsnips, chives, artichokes, pimpernel, rosemary, gooseberries, blackberries, apricots and plums. The garden was tended by 300 slaves. The first oranges were picked by Mr. and Mrs. van Riebeeck in 1661.

to a sweeping bay and natural harbor. It lives on the edge of winelands, has the same mix of old, pretty buildings, a lively waterfront and serious business, in this case as the legislative capital of South Africa and one of the country's most important business centers. Publishing, the arts and the gay community all flourish, and the city prides itself on being liberal and bohemian, although until very recently this cosmopolitan approach only extended as far as the boundaries of the white community.

Kirstenbosch National Botanical Gardens

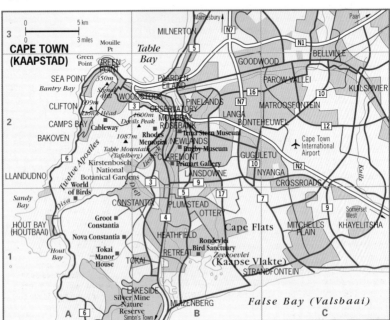

Suburban Cape Town under the Lion's Head

European style Cape Town does not seem like part of Africa. The climate is Mediterranean, the buildings European and most of the faces you see around you light skinned. Nevertheless, it has real magic and charm, providing plenty of mellow history, fascinating museums, good shopping and enchanting gardens such as the superb Kirstenbosch National Botanical Gardens. There is pleasant walking, both in gentle strolls around town or serious hikes on the mountain, where you also find some of the world's most dramatic views and spectacular sunsets. There are great beaches and countryside, wineries and wine cellars, where wine tasting is all part of the experience and even, in season, whale watching within easy day-trip distance. At night, there is superb food and drink from haute cuisine to sumptuous seafood, live music (particularly jazz), theater and dancing. For the moment, it is even relatively safe, although you should be careful after dark. The only blot on the landscape is the city's sometimes changeable and bad-tempered weather. When good, it is superb, but it can blanket the city in gray cloud on a whim, send bitter winds whistling through the winter streets, and drop dank English-style rain for days on end.

Around the gentle urban center, Greater Cape Town is vast. Leafy white suburbs stretch up the slopes, around the mountain and along the coast to merge almost imperceptibly into the commuter towns of the peninsula. To the east, on the Cape Flats, the black townships and squatter camps spread as far as the eye can see, an ocean of corrugated iron and cardboard, plastic bags and wooden boxes. Local population estimates range at anything from 1.5 to 3.5 million. Even the census takers have no idea. For tours see page 238.

Not so liberal
Cape Town has always prided itself on being sophisticated, liberal and cosmopolitan—the one place in South Africa where the races could mingle freely. Yet it is the site of the very first forced clearance, in 1901, long before the official start of apartheid and while the colony was still under British rule. Whole communities have been forced from their homes no fewer than 46 times in the city's history.

Anton Anreith
The sculptor Anton Anreith (1754–1821) was, together with Louis Thibault, responsible for revitalizing Cape architecture. Born in southwest Germany, he served his apprenticeship under a rococo sculptor—which led to what has been called his "high baroque" style—then came to the Cape where, first a carpenter, he went on to become a master sculptor. His best work can be seen in the Groote Kerk, the Lutheran Church (see page 57), the Castle's Kat Balcony, and on the pediment of Groot Constantia's Wine Cellar (see page 68).

▶　　**Bertram House**　　51A1

Company's Gardens, top of Government Avenue (tel: 021-24 9381)
Open: Tue–Sat, 9:30–4:30. Admission charge: inexpensive
This beautifully proportioned redbrick house was built in 1830 for an English lawyer, John Barker. A rare example of early 19th-century Cape British domestic architecture, its Regency-style rooms are rich with furniture, ceramics and silver illustrating the lifestyle of a well-to-do English family in the Cape.

▶▶　　**Bo-Kaap**　　51A2

Bounded by Rose, Wale, Chiappini and Shortmarket Streets
For walking tours of the area, contact Tana-Baru Tours, tel: 021-240 719; Community Guided Tours, tel: 021-240 014; Tasneem Tours, tel: 021-261 977
Built in the late 18th and early 19th centuries for European artisans, the little cube houses of Bo-Kaap were taken over by the Muslim Cape Malays (see pages 64–5), whose community survived as the only nonwhites in central Cape Town. These days the steep streets are once more bright with color and life.

The **Bo-Kaap Museum** (71 Wale Street, tel: 021-24 3846. *Open* Tue–Sat 9:30–4:30. *Admission charge* free on Fri), in one of the finest surviving houses, offers a fascinating glimpse into late 19th-century Muslim life and the contribution of Islam to South African history, culture, food and the Afrikaans language.

▶▶　　**Castle of Good Hope**　　51C2

Castle Street (tel: 021-469 1111)
Open: daily. Conducted tours hourly, 10–3; no unaccompanied sightseeing. Admission charge: moderate
Founded by Simon van der Stel as the headquarters of the VOC (Dutch East India Company), this solid pentagonal fort is the oldest European building in South Africa (1666–79). Five bastions surround utilitarian structures from dingy, graffiti-covered cells to armories. From 1691, several officers' houses were built on to a massive defensive wall, the Kat. The Secunde's House, home of the deputy-governor (1695), has rooms furnished in 17th-, 18th- and early 19th-century style. The Governor's Residence,

Anton Anreith's Kat Balcony in the Castle of Good Hope

best known for Anton Anreith's magnificent baroque Kat Balcony (*c.* 1785), is furnished in grand style with military and maritime artefacts and part of the William Fehr Collection of furniture, paintings, china and glass with an African theme. Look for the many paintings of Cape Town through the ages, and paintings by Thomas Baines.

► **City Hall and the Grand Parade** see page 66.

►►► **Company's Garden and Government Avenue** see page 67.

► **District Six** *51B2*
District Six began life as a cosmopolitan port area where some 60,000 people of a dozen races and every color mingled to create a vibrant community. In 1966, it was declared whites-only and all other races were shipped off to townships; in 1979, the area was bulldozed and the rubble used to build the new harbor. Since then, protests have been so vociferous that the land has remained empty. Today, a fascinating **Museum** (Buitenkant Methodist Church, 25a Buitenkant Street, tel: 021-461 8745. *Open* Mon–Sat, 10–4; Sun by appointment. *Admission charge* moderate) displays photos and recollections of the district and its street signs, saved from the bulldozers. Past inhabitants all sign a cloth (now over 225 feet long) and write down memories on a huge floor map.

Former residents re-create their bulldozed home in the District Six Museum

► **Greenmarket Square** *51B2*
The second oldest square in Cape Town, built in 1710 as a market, is still home to one of the city's liveliest and most popular flea markets, and also contains the city's first civic building—the Old Town House (see page 58).

► **Groote Kerk** *51B2*
Adderley Street, entrance in Church Square, off Parliament Street (tel: 021-461 7044)
Open: Mon–Fri 10–2. Admission free
Until a wood and thatch church was commissioned by Governor Willem Adriaan van der Stel in 1678 and consecrated in 1704, services were held on van Riebeeck's ship, the *Dromedaris*. The original church was replaced by this rather drab, but much larger building in 1841. Only the pretty clock tower belongs to the first edifice.

Inside, the huge room has sturdy box pews and a magnificent wooden pulpit, carved by Anton Anreith in 1788. The organ is the largest in the southern hemisphere, with 6,000 pipes and 32 foot pedals. This is the Mother Church of the Dutch Reformed Faith.

A venerable pear
The oldest tree in Company's Garden is a saffron pear, near the café, believed to have been imported from Holland in the time of Jan van Riebeeck and to have provided fruit for 17th-century sailors. It needs careful treatment but still produces edible fruit each year, most of which is pickled.

Commercial art galleries
Cape Town is not as well blessed with commercial art galleries as Johannesburg. However, there are several which run constantly changing exhibitions of the best of contemporary South African art: Primart Gallery (Warwick Square, Claremont, tel: 021-644 440); SA Association of Arts (35 Church Street, Cape Town, tel: 021-24 7436); and The Alfred Mall Gallery (Shop 9A, Alfred Mall, Pier Head, Waterfront, tel: 021-419 9507). Galleries, hotels and tourist information centers stock arts and crafts maps illustrating a useful "arts and crafts route" around the Cape Peninsula.

Houses of Parliament 51B2

Parliament Street and Government Avenue (tel: 021-403 2911).
Enter via Parliament Street gate. Tickets available for parliamentary sessions (Jan–Jun) on presentation of passport. During recess (Jul–Jan) guided tours Mon–Fri 11AM and 2PM. Jacket and tie required during parliamentary sessions. Admission free

Cape Town's imposing brick and stucco Houses of Parliament (1884) are the seat of the country's legislative government. Inside, a breath of fresh air is sweeping through the corridors of the gloomy old building, generated by the enthusiasm and the jazzy African dress of the new multiracial parliamentarians.

Next door, De Tuynhuys (1700) is the office of the State President (see page 67).

▶ Irma Stern Museum 52B2

The Firs, Cecil Road, Rosebank (tel: 021-685 5686)
Open: Tue–Sat 10–5; weekends 10–1 and 2–5.
Admission charge

Once the home of South Africa's best-known painter, Irma Stern (1894–1966), this little museum houses an excellent collection of the artist's own work and the souvenirs of her travels, from Zairi masks to oriental ceramics and old furniture. A follower of the German Expressionist movement, Irma Stern painted South African people and landscapes which were popular in Europe but unappreciated in her own country until after her death.

Powerful studies still crowd the walls of Irma Stern's studio

Jewish Museum 51A1

84 Hatfield Street, Company's Garden (tel: 021-45 1546)
Open: Tue and Thu 2–5; Sun 10–12:30. Admission charge: inexpensive

The first service in South Africa's oldest synagogue took place on Yom Kippur in 1841. The ornate Egyptian Revival building contains a museum of the Jewish communities in the Cape.

▶▶ Koopmans de Wet Museum 51B3

35 Strand Street (tel: 021-24 2473)
Open: Tue–Sat 9:30–4:30. Admission charge: inexpensive

This charming Georgian townhouse, on what was once the city's most fashionable street, was built in 1701, and much altered by later owners, particularly in 1771. The pink and white pilastered façade has been attributed (without proof) to Louis Thibault and Anton Anreith. Its name comes from its most famous inhabitant, Maria Koopmans de Wet (1834–1906) who, as well as being a noted hostess and art collector, was an enthusiastic advocate of the Afrikaans language.

The spacious rooms are decorated in European style

with *trompe l'oeil* pilasters, swags and friezes and are elaborately furnished in the late 18th-century manner. Behind the courtyard, in contrast, are the slave quarters.

▶ Long Street   51A2

Laid out in the 18th century, Long Street runs right through the center of town, from sea to mountain. Wander slowly, craning upwards at the delightful architectural details or peering under the shadowed balconies at the extraordinary shops. There are churches, mosques, banks, offices, apartment buildings, cafés, restaurants and clubs, art deco shop fronts, curly cast iron, double-tiered verandas on elaborate Victorian houses, and exuberant neoclassical buildings awash with brightly painted decorative plasterwork; the roofline is a profusion of turrets, gables and minarets.

The oldest inhabitants could pack a theater on tales of former residents: retired pirates, drag queens, exotic dancers... Tamer, but still lively, it now offers anything from Zulu beads to '70s nostalgia clothes, secondhand books, vintage wine, plumbers' fittings or 18th-century Cape Dutch furniture. Explore the back shelves of the **Junk Shop**, listen to live jazz at **Manenberg's Jazz Café** or have a sauna at the **Turkish Baths** (*Open* 8:30/9AM–8:30PM. Women—Mon, Thu, Sat; men—Tue, Wed, Fri, Sun).

Lone survivor
Although many 18th-century houses on Long Street are undoubtedly entombed within later shells, only one (no. 185, now the Palm Tree Mosque) survives intact. It was converted into a mosque in 1805 by a freed Malay slave, Jan van Boughies, who planted the two palms which gave the building its name.

Lutheran Church and Martin Melck House   51A2

96 Strand Street
Enquiries at Church House,
19 Buitengragt Street,
Mon–Fri 8:30–12:30.
Admission free

Until 1771 when the German immigrants were permitted freedom of worship, Lutherans and other denominations were forced to worship in the Dutch Reformed church. This, the country's first Lutheran church, was built in 1774 by a wealthy merchant, Martin Melck. Anton Anreith carved its magnificent wooden pulpit, and it so impressed the council of the Dutch Reformed church that they wanted one too (see page 55). Next door, the old parsonage, Martin Melck House, is a rare surviving building with a *dakkamer*—a room in the roof with windows looking toward the sea. It now houses an art gallery and restaurant.

A delicate relic, the Koopman de Wet House is dwarfed by office buildings

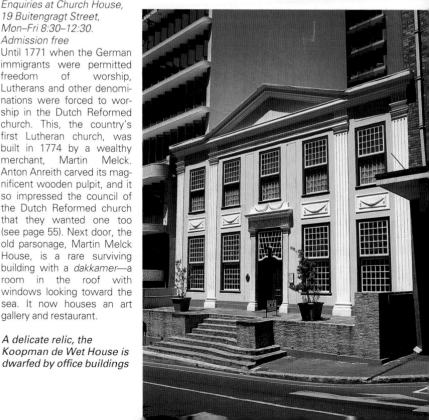

▶▶ **Old Town House** 51B2

Greenmarket Square (tel: 021-24 6367)
Open: daily 10–5. Admission charge: moderate
By the 18th century, the Burgher Watch, responsible both for law and order and fighting fires, was making nightly patrols of the city. Their base was in Old Town House (1755). Citizens were summoned by the bell in the tower to listen to proclamations read from the balcony. The building later became the town hall, superseded in 1905 by the present City Hall. Today it is an art gallery, containing the magnificent Michaelis Collection of 17th-century Dutch and Flemish paintings.

Rhodes Memorial 52B2

Off Rhodes Drive (tel: 021-689 9151)
Open access (tea garden closed Mon)
Cecil Rhodes (1853–1902) became a multimillionaire businessman, scholar, founder of several British colonies and builder of most of southern Africa's railroads. In between he found time to be prime minister of the Cape Colony. This memorial stands near the University of Cape Town campus and Rhodes' former home, Groot Schuur, a 17th-century barn sumptuously converted for him by Sir Herbert Baker in the 1890s. It is now the main residence of the President. There are fine views across the city from the memorial, and a pleasant tearoom near by.

Rugby Museum 52B2

Boundary Road, Newlands (tel: 021-686 4532)
Open: daily 9:30–4. Admission charge: moderate
Occupying the first floor of Josephine's Water Mill (1840), the world's largest rugby museum is also a shrine to South African greats of the game. Its collection of mementos dates back to 1891.

▶ **Rust en Vreugd** 51B1

78 Buitenkant Street (tel: 021-45 3628)
Open: Mon–Fri 9:30–4. Admission charge: moderate
(free with a Castle double ticket)
The name of this double-storied 18th-century house

A grandiose memorial to the arch empire-builder, the Rhodes Memorial offers superb views across Cape Town

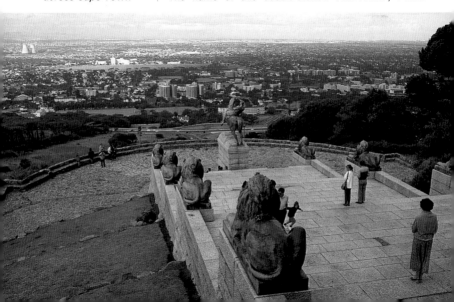

means "rest and joy." One of the finest domestic buildings in the Cape, it was once the home of the state prosecutor, and had a splendid view of the bay. Now it is tucked away inland behind the ugly foreshore. Inside is part of the William Fehr Collection of Africana (see also Castle of Good Hope, page 54), with fine watercolors by Thomas Baines, lithographs, engravings and paintings of the early Cape, and extraordinary cartoons by George Cruickshank.

Rust en Vreugd, built as the restful home of the Cape state prosecutor

▶ St. George's Cathedral 51B2

Wale Street
Open: daylight hours. Admission free
Consecrated in 1834, the first Anglican Cathedral of St. George the Martyr was felt to look like an average English parish church, not nearly grand enough for the Mother City. In 1901, architect Sir Herbert Baker was let loose, adding considerably to the length and grandeur of the building and replacing the neoclassical entrance with his favorite gray stone neo-Gothic design. The cathedral is much bigger now, but still looks like a large welcoming parish church. The vaulted interior is more imposing than the outside. The highlights are a series of modern stained-glass windows by Gabriel Loire. The eight along the nave depict the Creation; the Christ in Majesty above the transept is dedicated to Lord Louis Mountbatten. This was the seat of Cape Town's flamboyant archbishop, Desmond Tutu, also hosting events such as the memorial service for Joe Slovo, the communist, atheist, ex-Jewish Minister of Housing in the Government of National Unity, who died in December 1994.

Sendinggestig Museum 51B3

40 Long Street (tel: 021-236 755)
Open: Mon–Sat 9–4. Admission free
This charmingly decorative apricot and white mission church was built by the South African Missionary Society in 1804, and used both for worship and the education of slaves and non-Christians. It now houses a museum of mission work in South Africa.

Archbishop Desmond Tutu
Archbishop Desmond Mpilo Tutu was born on October 7, 1931. Ordained in 1961, he became Anglican Dean of Johannesburg (1975–6), Bishop of Lesotho (1976–8) and the first black Secretary-General of the South African Council of Churches (1979), representing around 12 million Christians. In 1984, he became the first black bishop of Johannesburg and was awarded the Nobel Peace Prize. In 1986, he was elected the first black Anglican archbishop of Cape Town. An outspoken advocate of nonviolent reform and black nationalism, he nevertheless avoided imprisonment and won the hearts of South Africans of all colors. He resigned as Archbishop in 1996, but continues to play an active role in the rebuilding of South Africa.

Big bang
Just below Signal Hill, the Noonday Gun shatters the air on the dot of 12 o'clock every day except Sunday. It was instituted to help ships in the bay correct their chronometers and, after 1918, to mark a two-minute pause in honor of South Africa's war dead.

▶ **Signal Hill** 52A2

Off Kloof's Nek, or reach on foot via Bo-Kaap and Longmarket Street

Forming one arm of Table Bay, Signal Hill is far smaller than Table Mountain but offers easy access, no lines and superb views across the bay and city, particularly dramatic at sunset and at night, when a vast field of lights spreads below. At the summit are picnic tables and short, pleasant (if windy) strolls. Nearby is the tomb of Saudi saint, Tuan Sayeed Alawie, incarcerated on Robben Island for 11 years.

▶▶ **South African Cultural History Museum** 51B2

49 Adderley Street (tel: 021-461 8280)
Open: Mon–Sat 9:30–6:30. Guided tours Sat 10:15, 12:15, 2:15. Admission charge: inexpensive

For 130 years, this long, low house (built in 1685) was used to house slaves working in Company's Garden. After the second British occupation in 1811, Louis Thibault converted it into government offices. Today it is one of the finest museums in the country, with beautifully displayed exhibits from Greek and Roman amphorae to ferocious throwing knives of the Sudan. The second half of the museum is dedicated to South Africa, with coins, weapons, ceramics, stamps, and textiles, excellent collections of furniture and *objets d'art* (particularly silver) from white South Africa, and tribal art and utensils from the black community. Notice the roughly engraved postal stones found in Table Bay near the Versse River (see panel opposite).

The National Gallery graces the end of Government Avenue

South African Library 51B2

Queen Victoria Street (tel: 021-24 6320)
Open: Mon–Fri 9–6, Sat 9–1. Admission free

Founded in 1818, this national copyright and preservation library is the oldest cultural institution in South Africa and one of the world's first free libraries. Regular exhibitions include the 5,000-volume private collection of former governor Sir George Grey, which holds the oldest book in South Africa, a gospel dating to AD900, several medieval illuminated manuscripts and a First Folio Shakespeare.

▶ **South African Maritime Museum** 51B4

Dock Road, V&A Waterfront (tel: 021-419 2506)
Open: daily 10–5. Admission charge: moderate

The Cape of Good Hope has produced some of the world's most fascinating maritime history, and here you can learn about it *in situ:* the all-too-frequent shipwrecks, Table Bay Harbour, shipping lines and maritime archaeology. There are models, a shipwright's workshop, the SAS *Somerset* (the world's only surviving boom defense vessel), and the *Alwyn Vincent*, built in 1959 and the only steam tug still in use in the southern hemisphere.

► South African Museum and Planetarium   51A1

25 Queen Victoria Street (tel: 021-243 330)
Open: daily 10–5. Admission charge: inexpensive; free on Wed

This stately building is South Africa's oldest museum (1825). The anthropology hall, specializing in southern African tribal culture, includes rock paintings, and several diaramas of San and Khoikhoi life. Some of the labels need changing but the exhibition itself is fascinating. Other sections include white South African furniture, silver and *objets d'art*, geology (with replica dinosaurs) and marine life in the Southern Ocean, with a 67-foot skeleton of a blue whale. The Planetarium offers a delightful explanation of the southern hemisphere's night sky.

►► South African National Gallery   51A1

Government Avenue, Company's Garden
(tel: 021-45 1628)
Open: Mon 1–5; Tue–Sun 10–5. Admission charge: inexpensive

Although it began life exhibiting mainstream European art with a number of fine oils and a collection of sporting pictures by such as Stubbs and Munnings, sanctions and the collapse of the rand forced the curators to buy locally. The gallery now has a good collection of contemporary South African art, an increasing amount of traditional tribal art, from decorated knobkerries to beadwork, and exciting work by modern black artists in both traditional and ultramodern styles. Traveling exhibitions include foreign work, photography, and experimental and ethnic art.

Postal stones
In the early days of the Cape Sea Route, sailors could be away for years on end. To send news home and make contact with other ships in their fleet, they would leave letters under a rock engraved clearly with the name of the ship from which it had come and for whom it was intended. The stones were also sometimes used to pass on personal letters, delivered by ships newly arrived from Europe, or on their last leg home.

61

View from Signal Hill, once used to watch for the arrival of ships to Table Bay

The tablecloth
Table Mountain is all too frequently covered by a swirling layer of white cloud which fits comfortably over the top like a cloth. Some say that each summer, the retired pirate, Van Hunks, has a pipe-smoking contest with the Devil (the rheumatic old man cannot climb in winter, so the mountain remains clear). In reality, the Cape's summer south-easterly prevailing wind (known as the Cape Doctor) sweeps into the bay, gets trapped and deposits its moisture neatly over the mountain.

The cable car up Table Mountain is South Africa's top tourist attraction

▶▶▶ **Table Mountain and Cableway**   *52A2*

Lower Cable Station, Tafelberg Road, off Kloof's Nek (tel: 021-245 148 or 248 409)
The cableway operates daily, weather permitting (not in cloud or high wind), Nov 8–9:30; Dec–end Jan 7AM–10:30PM; end Jan–end Apr 8AM–9:30PM; May–Oct, 8:30–5:30. Admission charge: expensive

Guarded by Lion's Head and Signal Hill (right) and Devil's Peak (left), Table Mountain towers dramatically 3,565 feet above Cape Town. Its gently sloping pedestal, covered with *fynbos* and forest, leads to a 1,640-foot-high sheer-sided slab of bare, layered sandstone marking the northern end of a craggy ridge stretching 30 miles to Cape Point.

The mountain started to form some 700 million years ago when mud and sand deposits were laid deep on the seabed; 600 million years ago, they were pushed upward and molten granite poured in around them. After 200 million years of erosion, a shallow sea returned, leaving mud, ripple marks and marine fossils, before the whole of southern Gondwanaland (a huge ancient continent) was covered in heavy sheet ice. Some 160–300 million years ago, shifting tectonic plates lifted the mountains clear of the water and Gondwanaland began to break up into the modern continents. About 70 million years ago, further upward movement re-exposed Table Mountain to the winds and rain.

A cable car offers easy access to the viewing platforms and restaurant. The weather can be treacherous, so get a guide if planning to go any distance.

During peak season, book in advance for the cable car and check ahead—lines can be as long as three hours. Tickets, bookable in advance, are available from Waterfront Information Centre (tel: 021-418 2369) and Lower Cable Station. For walking tours, contact Table Mountain Climb Company (tel: 021-419 2667); Walk Up Table Mountain (tel: 021-45 2503).

▶▶ Two Oceans Aquarium

51A4

Dock Road, V&A Waterfront (tel: 021-418 4644)
Open: daily 10–6:30 (last entry 5PM).
Admission charge: expensive

This beautiful aquarium concentrates entirely on the
wealth of species found in and around the Cape
Peninsula, from both Indian and Atlantic Oceans and from
the freshwater mountain lakes and streams inland. There
are 4,000 fish of 300 species in several large set pieces
including a kelp forest, an open ocean pool, a tropical tank
and seal and penguin pools, a tidal tank showing life
above and below the watermark, and an ecosystem
following the progress of river life from mountain stream
to estuary. Smaller tanks show sections of reef and water
management and there is a touch pool where children can
examine creatures like anemones and starfish.

▶▶▶ Victoria and Alfred Waterfront

51C5

Victoria and Alfred Basins, Table Bay Harbour
(tel: 021-418 2369)
Open: all hours. Admission free

In 1860, Queen Victoria's second son, Alfred, tipped the
first rock for the construction of the Victoria Basin. A
century later, Cape Town's old harbor was left virtually
derelict by the advent of the container port. Given a new
lease of life in one of the world's most successful urban
reclamation projects, it now hums as the heartland of the
city's nightlife. Working fishing boats, yachts and harbor
cruise boats skim the water, while wooden walkways
offer brightly lit shopping malls, the largest craft market in
South Africa, restaurants, and a fascinating maritime
museum (see page 60) and aquarium (see above). The
South African Fisheries Museum (West Quay Road, tel:
021-418 2312. *Open* Tue–Sun 10–4. *Admission charge*
inexpensive) has audiovisual presentations, model fishing
boats and fishing gear. There is an Imax Cinema (tel: 021-
419 7364) with a five-story screen, and regular boat trips
take you around the harbor from beside the Victoria and
Alfred Hotel. Boards throughout the development identify
old buildings and explain the area's history.

*The Victoria and
Alfred Waterfront is
a favorite evening
playground*

Hanging by a thread
The Table Mountain
Cableway was founded in
1926 by Sir Alfred
Hennessey. It runs 4,080
feet in a single span, lifting
the passengers 2,300 feet
up the mountain in around
five minutes, traveling at
about 10 mph. The latest
cabins carry 25
passengers; in all over 9
million have swung up the
mountain since the cable-
way first opened.

■ Under the old regime, there was a distinct hierarchy. First came the northern European whites, then the Latins, followed by the Japanese, Chinese, Cape Malays, Indians, Cape Coloreds and Blacks. Each had a different level of housing, education and social status. The different communities, particularly those imported from the east, retained their own cultural traditions, some stretching back for centuries. ■

The Sacred Circle
In 1693, Sheikh Yusuf, who claimed descent from Mohammed, was banished to the Cape where he and his followers continued to live and worship much as before. On his death in 1699 his tomb became a center of pilgrimage while the 25 holy men who followed him were buried in Constantia, Oudekraal, on Signal Hill, on the slopes of Table Mountain and on Robben Island. Their tombs (or *karamats*) form a "sacred circle" around Cape Town, and are said to give the city spiritual protection against natural disasters.

Safe journey
The most famous of Sheikh Yusuf's disciples was Paay Schaapie, a freed slave responsible for the establishment of Islam in South Africa. He was recognized as a saint while still living, and after his death it became the practice among his followers to take soil from his tomb when going on a journey. It is said he loved the Tana Baru, the burial ground at the top of the Bo-Kaap, so intensely that he would not let the soil remain away too long and thus a safe journey was ensured.

"Coloreds" There are about 1.4 million "coloreds" of mixed race. Some originate from the offspring of black servants and their white masters, some from the integration of the San and Khoikhoi (see page 132) to form the KhoiSan. Some of these then had children by white men, some intermarried with black tribes from farther north and east. In Europe and America today, anyone with any black ancestry is considered part of the black culture. This is not the case in South Africa; the coloreds were isolated, accepted socially by neither black nor white communities, while their only true heritage, the San culture, was destroyed by urban living.

By the late 19th century, there were sufficient numbers for them to form a distinct cultural group, mainly Christian, Afrikaans-speaking and working as skilled manual laborers, particularly on the railroads.

Cape Malays There is a large Islamic presence in the Cape region, drawn from Indian, Far Eastern, black and colored communities. The Cape Malays are a much smaller group of about 12,000 people, largely confined to the tiny Bo-Kaap district of Cape Town (see page 54). Virtually none has Malay ancestry, most having been imported as slaves from Singapore, Sri Lanka, Madagascar and, above all, Indonesia by early Dutch settlers. The name comes from the Malayal language used as a lingua franca among traders across the Dutch East Indies. The community calls itself either Cape Muslim or Indo-African.

Unlike most slave nations, these were highly educated and skilled people, prized as builders and carpenters as well as household servants. They brought with them Sufism (the mystical branch of the Islamic faith), holy men and teachers, and a strong cultural identity. Relatively few have intermarried with other ethnic groups and they are proud to have kept their nationhood and traditions, many of which have died out elsewhere.

Their language and history were officially banned during centuries of repression, but were kept alive by underground classes and texts written in Arabic script, known to all good Muslims but totally indecipherable to the Afrikaners. People do still speak Malayal today, but most commonly use Afrikaans. In fact, the first book in Afrikaans is said to have been written in Bo-Kaap and the language was taught formally for the first time at the Auwal Mosque in Dorp Street, one of the oldest mosques

in Cape Town (1804).

The holy men did their best to buy up the slaves and free them but it was not until slavery was banned throughout the British Empire in 1834 that the newly freed Muslims moved into Bo-Kaap. There are now 11 mosques scattered among the small, square, vividly painted houses which crawl up the side of Signal Hill. In 1966, the area was declared a slum and the Muslims were ordered out. Some went, but many more remained and eventually the authorities lost interest and left them alone, the only nonwhite community to survive in central Cape Town. Many of the houses were even rebuilt to the original design. Today, the area is a unique, fascinating testament to the old city, vibrant with noisy street life, as women in traditional *burkhas* and men in *kufias* gather on the corners to talk with relatives.

Yet the community is under threat once more, a victim of its success. Young trendy Capetonians have recognized the charm of the district and the fascination of the architecture and are snapping up houses, driving prices way out of the reach of locals.

The mainly Muslim Malay quarter of Bo-Kaap is rapidly becoming some of Cape Town's most sought-after real estate

Carnival Time

For two days a year (January 1 and 2) the colored community erupts on to the streets of Cape Town in a blaze of color and noise. Their exuberant Carnival began life as a thanksgiving for the abolition of slavery and, almost incidentally, welcomes in the new year. Preparations are intense and often competitive as district troops are formed, spending several months creating spectacular original costumes, music, and dance.

Walk Historic Cape Town

The old center of Cape Town is surprisingly small; much of it is built on reclaimed land and the harbor water used to lap the castle walls. This gentle stroll takes in most of the main attractions. Allow one–two hours, or a full day if you plan to visit the many sights *en route*. Start beside the **Castle of Good Hope** (see page 54).

Walk across into the **Grand Parade**, usually less than grand with a noisy mix of cars parking, taxis cruising for business and a colorful flea market full of buckets of flowers and bolts of cloth. Carefully positioned in front of Table Mountain, the positively imperial **City Hall** (Darling Street, 021-461 7084. *Open* during business hours and for concerts. *Admission free*) was built in 1905 in a blend of Italian

Renaissance and British colonial styles. It has been carefully restored and is now the home of the Cape Town Symphony Orchestra, which holds weekly concerts there. After his release from jail in February 1990, a crowd of 100,000 people waited for up to seven hours to hear Nelson Mandela's first speech from the balcony. It began: *"Amandla! Iafrika! Mayibuye!"* (Power to the People!).

Walk along Darling Street until you come to Adderley Street. To your right is the **Heerengracht**, a truly dull area of 1960s concrete apartment houses. One of the few mixed-race areas of Cape Town was demolished to create this monstrosity. Turn left up **Adderley Street**, the city's main shopping street with several charming small arcades and grand colonial and art deco buildings. The **Standard Bank** is on the left; peer inside at the magnificent 19th-century banking hall.

Also on the left, toward the top of the street, are the somber, plain gray **Groote Kerk** (see page 55) and the Cape Dutch **South African Cultural History Museum** (see page 60), in front of which stands a statue of Jan Smuts in battle dress. To the right, by Government Avenue, is **St. George's Cathedral** (see page 59).

From here, walk up leafy, pedestrian **Government Avenue►►►**, where squirrels play around the benches under the avenue of trees. A little way up on the left are the redbrick and white stucco **Houses of Parliament** (see page 56). To the right is the **South African Library** (see page 60).

Well-shaded Government Avenue is the historic heart of Cape Town

Above: Company's Garden began life as a market garden. Right: De Tuynhuys is now home to the office of the State President

Just beyond is the entrance to **Company's Garden** (top of Adderley Street. *Open* daily 7AM–sunset. *Admission free*). In 1652 Jan van Riebeeck and the Dutch East India Company laid out a 45-acre vegetable garden to supply merchant ships heading East with fresh fruit and vegetables. Only 8 acres of South Africa's first market garden survive, transformed by Sir Herbert Baker into a lush English park with lawns, shady trees, elegant walkways, and manicured flower beds. Opposite the entrance, **De Tuynhuys** was built in 1700 as a Company Guest House to accommodate any overflow of dignitaries from the Castle. Altered over the centuries, it has been restored to its 1795 Regency appearance and is now the office of the State President.

At the top of the garden is an open plaza. On your left are the **South African National Gallery** (see page 61) and the **Jewish Museum** (see page 56). Directly ahead is the **South African Museum and Planetarium** (see page 61). Continue to the top of Government Avenue, where you will see **Bertram House** (see page 54) on your right. Cross the street and walk under the pillars up Hof Street to reach the strawberry pink **Mount Nelson Hotel**, the oldest and plushest in central Cape Town (see page 258), where you can indulge in tea with smoked salmon sandwiches while resting your aching feet.

If you wish to continue, return along **Long Street** (see page 57) and **Greenmarket Square** (see page 55).

Cape Town Environs

Cape Flats 52B1

For township tours contact One City Tours (tel: 021-387 5351); AC Tours (tel: 021-797 7247 or mobile 082-568 8325); Day Trippers (tel: 021-531 3274). Admission charge: expensive

The wide, marshy plain of the Cape Flats—site of Cape Town's townships—lies inland from Table Mountain. The first township in South Africa was founded 3 miles from Cape Town in 1901. It was later moved because it was considered to be too close to the center of town, and the people were resettled in **Langa**, which survives today. The infamous **Crossroads** now has regular streets and drains and is probably the most congenial of the huge settlements, but it was for many years a massive squatter camp where terrified residents lived under the daily threat of the bulldozers.

The most astounding of the three main townships in the area is **Khayelitsha**, which sprang from nothing to become a shanty city of over 1 million people in the space of a very few years. Other local townships include Bonteheuwel, Heideveld, Guguletu, Nyanga, and Mitchells Plain.

Shanties on the Cape Flats offer a markedly different view of Cape Town

▶ Groot Constantia 52A1

About 9 miles south of the city center. Take the M3 to the Constantia exit and follow the signs (the turnoff is on the left)
Museum (tel: 021-794 5067). Open: daily 10–5. Admission charge: moderate

One of the oldest estates in South Africa, founded in 1685, this was the home of Governor Simon van der Stel, who planted the first vines. A century later, it was taken over by the Cloete family who created a range of world-famous dessert wines, Constantia Frontignac, Pontac, and Steen. Sadly, the grand age ended with the phylloxera outbreak in the 1860s and the estate was sold to the nation in 1885 by a near-bankrupt family. Since then, it has been used as an experimental station and museum, but from 1975 onwards, there has been significant replanting and Constantia wine is steadily regaining both quality and reputation.

At the entrance is a small museum showing the history of the manor. The elegant Cape Dutch house itself,

Divine wine
Napoleon is said to have demanded nothing but Constantia wine during his exile on St. Helena; Bismarck was a patron; Jane Austen recommends its "healing powers on a disappointed heart"; and King Louis Philippe of France liked it so much that he bought the whole vintage in 1833.

designed by Louis Thibault, was destroyed by fire in 1925, but has been carefully restored to the original plans, with high walls, flagged floor, heavy wooden ceilings, and dark green shutters. It is beautifully furnished in sturdy late 18th-century style. Behind it, the old cellars, with their magnificent pediment by Anton Anreith (1791), contain a fascinating small museum of wine. The modern cellars include a cellar tour, wine tasting and shop, while the Jonkershuis (old stables) contains an excellent restaurant (see page 264).

▶▶▶ Kirstenbosch National Botanical Gardens

52A2

Rhodes Drive, Newlands (tel: 021-761 4916), about 6 miles from city center.

Open: daily, Apr–Aug 8–6, Sep–Mar 8–7. Admission charge: moderate. Guided walks Tue and Sat.

In 1895, Cecil John Rhodes bought this estate and bequeathed it to the nation. In 1913, Henry Harold Welch Pearson, Professor of Botany at the University of South Africa, founded the National Botanical Gardens which grew rapidly to become one of the world's most important botanical collections. Most of the 1,310-acre estate, stretching up the eastern flank of Table Mountain, is local *fynbos* and coastal forest, but there are 89 acres of delightful formal gardens, with rich collections of flowers and trees, a fragrance garden and Braille trail for the blind, a pond, a herb garden, and specialist collections of pelargoniums, restios, proteas, cycads, and ericas. Concentrating on the indigenous flora of southern Africa, the gardens contain some 6,000 of South Africa's 22,000 plant species, while a further 900 grow in the wild areas. Several walking trails, lasting from 45 minutes to six hours, lead into the woods and up the mountain. There is a strong educational and scientific program, concentrating on the conservation of many rare and endangered species. A pleasant restaurant offers teas, coffees and lunches and a garden shop sells plants, souvenirs and books. Musical concerts are held in the gardens every Sunday during the summer. Allow at least half a day to explore.

Green history
The Kirstenbosch Gardens contain a living history of the Cape region, starting with the remains of a wild almond hedge planted by Jan van Riebeeck in 1660 to protect the cattle from marauding Khoikhoi. There is an avenue of fig and camphor trees (from China and Japan) planted by Rhodes during his tenure, and Professor Pearson, founder of the gardens, is buried among his first collection, in the Cycad Amphitheatre.

69

Anton Anreith's magnificent carving adorns the old cellars at Groot Constantia

Robben Island
48A2

6 miles off the Green Point coast
Half-day trips on Tue, Wed and Sat. Apply to the Commander, Public Relations, PB Robben Island 7400 (tel: 021-411 1006). Boat trips (expensive) from the V&A Waterfront circle the island but do not land

Measuring only 1¼ by 2 miles, Robben Island takes its name from "*robbe,*" the Dutch word for seals. There is still a thriving colony of Cape fur seals, but the island is far more infamous for its past inhabitants: high-ranking exiles, Islamic holy men, political dissidents, robbers, pirates and murderers. In the 19th century it held black leaders captured during the Frontier Wars; from the 1960s inmates included high-profile political detainees such as Nelson Mandela, who spent 27 years here. The last political prisoners left in May 1991. The prison itself has recently closed, leaving the island as a wildlife sanctuary and place of pilgrimage for South African nationalism.

►► Simon's Town
48A1

25 miles south of Cape Town
Tourist Information, Court Road (tel: 021-786 3046)

Named after Simon van der Stel, Governor of the Cape from 1691 to 1699, this little port became the Royal Navy headquarters in 1814 and was taken over by the S. A. Navy in 1957. Today it is a rather quaint seaside town with charming Victorian houses. The governor's residence (built 1777), later a court and prison, is now the delightful **Simon's Town Museum** (Court Road, tel: 021-786 3046. *Open* Mon–Fri 9–4, Sat 10–1. *Admission charge* inexpensive). Other places to visit are the **South African Naval Museum** (Masthouse, West Dockyard, tel: 021-787 4635. *Open* Mon–Fri 10–4); and the **Warrior Toy Museum** (St. George's Street, tel: 021-786 1395. *Open* Sun–Thu 10–4. *Admission charge* inexpensive) with a collection of dolls, toy soldiers, model cars, boats, and trains. At The Boulders, outside town, is a colony of jackass penguins, one of only two on the African mainland.

Convict island
The first-ever European attempt to colonize the Cape Peninsula was in 1615, when eight British convicts were left on the shore. They crossed to Robben Island and remained there until rescued by a passing ship some months later. With the arrival of the Dutch 40 years later, Robben Island became a high-security prison which it remained for nearly 350 years.

70

Below: splendid Victoriana along the main road in Simon's Town. Bottom: jackass penguins strut for the tourists at The Boulders

$\mathcal{D}$*rive* The Cape of Good Hope

A spiny ridge of mountains tails south along the Cape Peninsula to tumble into the sea in a riotous confusion of rocks at Cape Point. The scenery is spectacular, the beaches idyllic, and many of the charming small towns offer an enticing blend of good food, interesting shops and plentiful history. Allow at least one full day.

Cape Town to Muizenberg From the city center, take the M3 (De Waal Road) to Muizenberg. There are turnoffs *en route* for **Kirstenbosch** and **Groot Constantia** (see pages 68–9).

Herbert Baker once wielded his architect's pencil in trendy **Muizenberg** (Tourism Information tel: 021-788 1898), the favorite resort of the Randlords. There are still numerous fine houses including the cottage in which Cecil Rhodes died in 1902, kept as a museum/shrine (Main Road, tel: 021-788 1816. *Open* Tue–Sun 10–1, 2–5). Now the town is a bit tired and shabby, but nothing can spoil its lovely, safe, shallow beach, lined by rows of colorful changing booths. Away from the shore, the Venetian-style **Natale Labia Museum** (Main Road, tel: 021-788 4106. *Open* Tue–Sun 10–5, closed Aug), built as the Italian Ambassador's residence, is now a

Kalk Bay, one of many small towns with delightful beaches along the Cape Peninsula

satellite of the South African National Gallery (see page 61).

Kalk Bay to Cape Point A little farther down the coast, **Kalk Bay** ("lime bay"), was named after the kilns in which shells were burned to produce lime. It is a busy fishing port—home of the brightly painted False Bay fishing boats—with silvery heaps of fish auctioned in the harbor. The main road has a variety of antique and junk stores, craft shops and eateries. Soak up the atmosphere, climb up to the deep caves pitting the mountain slopes and try surfing on nearby **Danger Beach**.

Continue south along the coast-hugging M4 to **Fish Hoek** (Tourist Information tel: 021-782 1112), a popular if somewhat elderly resort which has the distinction of being the only teetotal town in the country—a stipulation laid down by Lord Charles Somerset in 1818. He also declared free fishing rights for all. **Peers Cave**, a rock shelter nearby, is named after the man who discovered 15,000-year-old "Fish Hoek Man." This is the best place on the peninsula to see whales; they come in close to calve.

Cape Point divides two oceans

Continue down the coast, through **Simon's Town** (see page 70) to the farthest tip of the peninsula and the somewhat bleak 19,150-acre **Cape of Good Hope Nature Reserve** (tel: 021-780 1100. *Open* daily 6AM–6PM. *Admission charge* moderate). The accepted meeting place of the Atlantic and Indian Oceans is Cape Point which has also always been the psychological if not physical end of Africa (the most southerly point is actually Cape Agulhas, see page 94). There are drives, places to picnic and swim and the possibility of seeing wild animals in their natural surroundings. The east coast sheers abruptly off the cliffs into the warm waters of the Indian Ocean's False Bay; to the west the land slopes downward more gently in a series of ridges to wind-blown beaches and dunes pounded by Atlantic waves.

Chapman's Peak Drive Heading north for home, take the N65 along the Atlantic coast to **Kommetjie**, a quiet seaside village with a popular surfing beach. The water, famously, is freezing, but a shallow tidal pool provides safe swimming for children. From here, the beautiful 4-mile **Long Beach**, unsafe for swimming but popular with horse riders, leads up to **Noordhoek**, where you join the **Chapman's Peak Drive** to Hout Bay. Built between 1915 and 1922,

CAPE TOWN (KAAPSTAD)

Mouille Pt

Table Bay

GREEN POINT

SEA POINT

Signal Hill 350m

Clifton

Camps Bay

Bakoven

Twelve Apostles

1055m

Table Mountain (Tafelberg)

Kirstenbosch National Botanical Gardens

Llandudno

World of Birds

Sandy Bay

Hout Bay (Houtbaai)

Hout Bay

Duikereiland

Chapman's Peak 592m

Chapman's Point

Noordhoek

Chapman's Bay

Kommetjie

Ocean View

Witsandbaai

Scarborough

Sun Valley

Silver Mine Nature Reserve

Fish Hoek

False Bay (Valsbaai)

Simon's Town (Simonstad)

The Boulders

Krom

Miller's Point

Cape of Good Hope Nature Reserve

Smitswinkelbaai

Hoek van Bobbejaan

De Gama Monument 1497

Dias Monument 1436

Cape of Good Hope (Kaap die Goeie Hoop)

Cape Point

GOODWOOD

N1

N7

WOODSTOCK

PINELANDS

OBSERVATORY

MOWBRAY

N2

RONDEBOSCH

KENILWORTH

LANSDOWNE

CONSTANTIA

PLUMSTEAD

HEATHFIELD

Zeekoevlei

RETREAT

Cape Flats (Kaapse Vlakte)

Tokai

Strandfontein

Lakeside

Muizenberg

Kalkbaai

Groot Constantia

0   5   10 km

0   5 miles

this winding 6-mile drive is not only a magnificent feat of engineering, but offers continuous spectacular views with plentiful vista points, picnic areas, climbs and mountain walks.

Hout Bay to the city Dominated by the towering peak of The Sentinel, little **Hout Bay** was named after the wood (*hout*) harvested for shipbuilding. Traditionally a center of crayfish and snoek fishing, it is a lively seaside town filled with vacation cottages, fishermen, a thriving marina and several popular restaurants. The local **museum** (4 Andrews Road, tel: 021-790 3270. *Open* Tue–Sat, 10–12:30, 2–4:30. *Admission charge* inexpensive) has an excellent display of *strandloper* (beachcomber) culture. From the harbor, Drumboat Charters (tel: 021-438 9208) and Circe Launches (tel: 021-790 1040) run boat trips to the seal colony and seabird sanctuary on **Duiker Island**. In the summer thousands of Cape fur seals can be seen along with the rare bank cormorant—found only on the coast of South Africa and Namibia. Nearby, the **World of Birds Sanctuary** (Valley Road, tel: 021-790 2730. *Open* daily 9–5. *Admission charge* moderate) is one of the largest bird sanctuaries in South Africa, with over 3,000 birds from around 450 varieties flying free in walk-through aviaries designed to replicate their natural habitats.

Beyond Hout Bay, the coastline becomes one long ribbon development, with houses clustering ever more thickly as you head back into the city. Lovely undeveloped **Sandy Bay** is the local nudist beach. **Bakoven**, named after a large cave shaped like a baker's oven, has two small beaches, safe for children and popular with snorkelers. **Camps Bay**, tucked in at the base of the Twelve Apostles, has a wide beach with lawns and a good selection of cheap and cheerful restaurants. The sea here is very cold and has a strong backwash, but it is popular with families. Surfers use Glen Beach in the adjoining cove. **Clifton** is *the* place to be and to be seen. The water is freezing, but people still flock to its four overcrowded beaches. **Sea Point** is closer to the city center and not quite so fashionable, but is young, lively and trendy with a slightly bohemian tinge.

Camps Bay and the Twelve Apostles on the Atlantic Coast

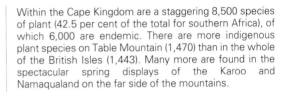

■ **The world is divided into six "floral kingdoms," distinct botanical habitats from tropical rain forest to tundra. The smallest (35,000 square miles) and, for its size, the richest is the Cape, which stretches from the Cederbergs in the Western Cape to Port Elizabeth in the east, always within 125 miles of the coast.** ■

Small is beautiful
The largest of the floral kingdoms, the Boreal, stretches much of the way across the northern hemisphere and covers 42 per cent of the earth's land surface. The Cape kingdom covers just 0.04 per cent— a mere 35,000 square miles.

Above: proteas in bloom at Kirstenbosch. Below: quiver trees in the Karoo

Within the Cape Kingdom are a staggering 8,500 species of plant (42.5 per cent of the total for southern Africa), of which 6,000 are endemic. There are more indigenous plant species on Table Mountain (1,470) than in the whole of the British Isles (1,443). Many more are found in the spectacular spring displays of the Karoo and Namaqualand on the far side of the mountains.

Fynbos This magical array of Cape plants and flowers is known overall as *fynbos* (literally "fine bush"), a group of evergreen fine-leafed plants which thrive in poor, sandy soil and harsh conditions, with hot dry summers and cold wet winters. From a distance, this heathland vegetation seems less than inspiring, with low, scrubby plants rolling on across the hills, few bushes standing higher than a person's knee. It is only when you look closely that you begin to see the infinite variation in species. Three-quarters are found nowhere else and many are so specialized that they survive in only one valley.

Fynbos is made up of three main plant families—reeds, proteas, and ericas—along with several smaller groups of legumes and bulbs. The most common are the wind-

pollinated reeds (*restios*) which here replace grass as general ground cover. Hardy and unpleasant grazing, they survive the weather and wildlife, but are harvested by locals for thatching. Proteas (*proteaceae*) are the national flower of South Africa. Most familiar are the king proteas, with their heavy, furry black and pink heads, but there are an infinite number of species, ranging from spiky red flowers to a great mass of minute florets and even inconspicuous, low-lying pincushions. Ericas (*ericaceae*), related to the European heathers, are the only true *fynbos* plant to trans-late happily to the gardens of the world, although other local species, such as freesias, pelargoniums, campanu-las, lobelias, and the subtropical gladioli and strelizias have become popular with gardeners and florists alike.

Spring color Mesembryanthemums and daisies (*aster-aceae*) dot the mountains and coast with color, but really come into their own in Namaqualand, where spring sees magnificent sheets of vibrant pinks, oranges and purples cloaking the landscape for miles on end. The Karoo also flowers in spring, but here there is a more subtle cover with tiny yellow and purple flowers gently tinting the soft gray of rock and shale.

Subtropical forest Until about 3 million years ago, the Cape is thought to have had a milder climate and to have been covered by lush subtropical woodland. This survives a little farther north, along the hills of the Garden Route (Knysna Forest and Tsitsikamma National Park, see pages 100–101) and through into KwaZulu-Natal. Here, the mountains foster a totally different range of species, of which the most dramatic are the huge, hard yellowwoods and stinkwoods, from which most Cape Dutch furniture is made. Lurking in the undergrowth below these giants are some of the most extraordinary plants in South Africa, the cycads, said to be unchanged since the Jurassic period (150–200 million years ago), when dinosaurs roamed the earth.

Orange-breasted sunbird in a bloom-ing Protea pityphla

Flower hunting
No one has yet attempted to produce a layman's guide to Cape flora, although there are numer-ous huge tomes on special-ist aspects, such as proteas. The Kirstenbosch Gardens (see page 69) are an essential first stop, but to see the mass of flowers in all their glory, visit in winter (Jul/Aug) for *fynbos*, and spring (Sep/Oct) for the desert flowers. Most of the desert plants are heliotropic, and keep their faces turned toward the sun, so are best seen through the midday heat, driving with your back to the light. Expect long traffic jams at the height of the season. A telephone hot line, Flowerline (021-418 3705), operates from Apr 1 during office hours and Jul 10–Oct 13, Mon–Fri 8:15–4:30, Sat–Sun 8:30–4.

The Breë River Valley Area

Earthquake
On September 29, 1969 a massive earthquake, measuring 6.5 on the Richter scale, reduced much of Tulbagh to ruins. Many early buildings, like Thibault's Drostdy (1806), were totally destroyed. One of the biggest restoration programs ever undertaken in South Africa swung into action. Over the years buildings had been altered and extended, windows blocked up and gables rearranged. The earthquake-shattered plasterwork allowed the Tulbagh Restoration Committee to reconstruct the original pattern of building. In Church Street alone, 32 small whitewashed, gabled homesteads have been carefully restored. The results are remarkable.

The Oude Kerk Museum, Tulbagh, carefully restored after a disastrous earthquake

Ceres 48B2

80 miles northeast of Cape Town, off the N1.
Tourist Information, John Steyn Library, corner Voortrekker and Owen Streets (tel: 0233-61287)
Named after the Roman goddess of fertility, Ceres is all about fruit. Tour the huge **Ceres Fruit Growers and Ceres Fruit Juices Co-operative** (tel: 0233-23121) to see fruit dried, squeezed, processed and packaged, or pick your own at the **Klondyke Cherry Farm** (Nov–Jan; tel: 0233-22085).

In early days the town was often cut off by winter snow, but in 1848, Andrew Geddes Bain built Mitchell's Pass after which it became an important stop *en route* to the diamond fields. The **Transport Riders Museum** (8 Orange Street, tel: 0233-22045. *Open* Mon–Fri 9–1, also Tue–Fri 2–5; Sat 9–12 noon. *Admission charge* inexpensive) traces the transport riders' part in local history.

About 50 miles north, **Kagga Kamma** (PO Box 7143, North Paarl 7623, tel: 02211-638 334, fax: 02211-638 383) is a private game reserve, home to some of South Africa's last traditional Bushmen (San).

▶ Tulbagh 48B2

About 100 miles north of Cape Town
Tulbagh Publicity Association (tel: 0236-301348)
Parts of remote rural Tulbagh seem to be an almost perfect 18th-century town. Church Street is particularly charming, while the old church is the focal point of the **Oude Kerk Volksmuseum** (4 Church Street, tel: 0236-301041. *Open* Mon–Sat 9–1 and 2–5; Sun 11–12:30 and 2–4:30. *Admission charge* inexpensive). This complex of four restored buildings houses a collec-

tion of furniture and costumes, and displays on the 1969 earthquake (see panel opposite) and the subsequent restoration work.

The Oude Drostdy (2½ miles from Tulbagh, tel: 0236-300203. *Open* Mon–Sat 10–1 and 2–5. *Admission charge* inexpensive) is now a museum, with an unexpected collection of early gramophones as well as the usual Cape Dutch furniture.

►► **Worcester** 48B2

65 miles northeast of Cape Town.

Breë River Valley Tourist Information, PO Box 91, Worcester 6850 (tel: 0231-70945). Worcester Tourist Information, 75 Church Street (0231-71408).

This sprawling, largely modern market town is "capital" of the country's biggest wine-producing district (see pages 86–7, 92–3). It is also home to the vast **KWV Brandy Cellars** (Church Street, tel: 0231-20255. Tours in English and Afrikaans Mon–Fri 9:30, 11, 1:30, and 3:30; Sat 9:30 and 11. *Admission charge* moderate), where 120 copper pot kettles distill the famous KWV 10- and 20-year-old brandies.

Allow plenty of time to visit the splendid **Kleinplasie Open Air Museum►** (off Robertson Road, tel: 0231-22225. *Open* Mon–Sat 9–4:30, Sun 10:30–4:30. *Admission charge* moderate). Recon-structed dwellings and farm buildings are accu-rately furnished according to dates between 1690 and 1900 and there is an exhaustive explanation of the lifestyle and agricultural techniques of pioneer farmers. The area hums with traditional activities, from baking and tobacco rolling to distilling *witblitz*, the local firewater (on sale, with tastings, in the museum).

Next door to the Open Air Museum, the **Kleinplasie Reptile World** (off Robertson Road, tel: 0231-26480. *Open* 9–5. *Admission charge* moderate) has over 80 species of snakes, lizards, turtles, and crocodiles. There are three satellite museums in the town: the Cape Dutch **Beck House** (1841), furnished as a late 19th-century townhouse, and **Stofberg House** (1920s), which covers the history of Worcester, are both on Baring Street (*Open:* Mon–Fri 8–1, 2–5. *Admission free*). The **Hugo Naudé House** (Russell Street. *Open:* Mon–Fri 9–4:30, Sat 9–12:30. *Admission free*) is the former studio of the South African pioneer painter. It now houses the munici-pal art collection, including several works by Naudé himself.

The **Karoo National Botanical Garden** (Roux Street, tel: 0231-70785. *Open* daily 8–5. *Admission charge* moderate) has 356 acres of natural semidesert vegeta-tion, 25 acres of landscaped gardens full of quiver trees, aloes and vygies, and greenhouses filled with extraordi-nary stone plants.

Rolling tobacco at the Kleinplasie Open Air Museum, Worcester

77

Other stops
The Breë River Valley is an important fruit- and wine-producing area, prolifically fertile and festooned with orchards, vineyards and wheatlands. It has small reserves of plants and birds and there are successions of pools, rapids and waterfalls, ideal for trout fishermen, canoeists, mountaineers and nature lovers. Several other towns in the region are worth a stop. They include Robertson (famous for its muscatel grapes and wines and popular as a base for climbs into the Langeberg range), McGregor, Rawsonville, Bonnievale, Ashton, and the spa towns of Montagu and Goudini. Most have a small museum and wine route.

The vast empty plains of the Great Karoo

Groot- (Great) Karoo

 Beaufort West *49D3*

30 miles northeast of Cape Town
Central Karoo Tourist Information, PO Box 56, Beaufort West 6970 (tel: 0201-51160)

This is the Karoo's largest town, with streets shaded by pear trees, and a small **museum** (Main Street) displaying awards presented to Dr. Christian Barnaard, the first man to perform a heart transplant.

The **Karoo National Park** (off the N1. Tel: 0201-52828; reservations tel: 012-343 1991. *Open* daily 5–10, reception 7:30AM–8PM. *Admission charge*: moderate), starting 2½ miles south of Beaufort West, encompasses 113,965 acres of virgin Karoo veld and the Nuweveldberge (Nuweveld Mountains). It is remarkably fecund for a semidesert with 64 species of mammal including mountain zebra, black rhino and huge herds of springbok; 194 bird species, including 20 breeding pairs of black eagles; and 59 reptile species. The park has a small museum (*Open* daily, 8–12:30, 1:30–6), restaurant, basic accommodations and hiking and 4x4 trails.

▶▶ **The Swartberg** *49D2*

High and gnarled, the Swartberg (Black Mountains), known to the San as the Cango (Water) Mountains, formed an almost impenetrable 125-mile barrier to the interior until the arrival of the great Victorian road builders.

Of the seven passes in the area, the most dramatic is the 15-mile Swartberg Pass, crossed by a road built by Thomas Bain using convict labor (1881–8). It has wide panoramas on the southern slopes, but the northern face plunges into a spectacular ravine, ending in a cauldron of rock at Eerstewater, near the charming village of Prince Albert. At the top is a remote valley, Gamkaskloof (once called "Hell"), settled for nearly 200 years by a group of farmers who were totally isolated before the road arrived in 1962. Also worth driving is the shorter Meiringspoort Pass on the road from De Rust to Beaufort West.

The Karoo
Aptly named "the land of thirst" by the Khoikhoi, the Karoo is a vast arid wilderness peppered with flat-topped *koppies* of hard doleritic rock trapping thousands of fossils, from enormous trees to strange amphibious creatures with mammalian features. Its hardy little desert plants curl unnoticed into the grayish dust, bursting into life in spring when their magnificent blossom splashes the landscape with pure color. The desert is divided into the markedly more fertile Little Karoo, around Oudtshoorn, separated from the sea by the Langeberg and Outeniqua Mountains, and the vast expanse of the Great Karoo beyond the Swartberg to the north (see also page 112).

Klein- (Little) Karoo

►► Cango Caves 49D2

*18 miles north of Oudtshoorn on the R328
(tel: 0443-227 410)
Open: daily 9–4, 8–5 in
Dec and Apr school vaca-
tions. Access to caves on
guided tours only, every
hour on the hour. Admis-
sion charge: moderate*

The San lived in the
entrance to this huge limestone system under the
Swartberg Mountains, but
they never penetrated far
inside. A local farmer,
Jacobus Van Zyl, led the
first lantern-lit expedition
into the heart of the caves
in 1780, discovering the
first of three sequences of
caverns adorned with stalactites and all manner of fantas-
tical dripstone formations. The largest of the chambers is
a stunning 350 feet across and 53 feet high. The entire
system remains at an even temperature of 64°F.
There are three levels of tours available: easy half-hour
strolls that take you through two of the caverns; more
comprehensive one-hour tours into eight chambers; and
full-scale adventure tours, requiring you to wriggle
through narrow passages and climb steep pipes, for
which you should be reasonably fit but do not need to
have any previous experience.

*Dripstone drama in
the Cango Caves*

► Cango Crocodile Ranch and Cheetahland 49D2

*About 6 miles north of Oudtshoorn, on the Cango Caves
Road R328 (tel: 0443-225 593/6)
Open: daily 8–6 (restaurant open until late). Admission
charge: moderate.*

This farm has everything: over 300 crocodiles, a snake
park, lions, cheetahs and jaguars for thrills; meercats,
wallabies, tortoises, pygmy hippos and warthogs for
comedy; cute and cuddly miniature horses and goats; and
a deer park for elegance. Nearby are the Cango Ostrich
Farm (see page 81) and the Cango Angora Rabbit Farm
(tel: 0443-291 259).

▒ Matjiesfontein 48C2

About 160 miles east of Cape Town

James Logan (see panel) found the dry, crisp Karoo air
good for his weak chest. In the late 19th century, he
founded Matjiesfontein as a resort and health spa,
attracting similarly afflicted guests including Lord
Randolph Churchill and the Sultan of Zanzibar. During the
Boer War, it became the headquarters of the Cape
Command, then a military hospital. Not much has
changed in the last 100 years. Recently restored, and now
called the Lord Milner (see page 259), the hotel is a
monument to Victoriana and is said to be haunted by
armies of jolly, party-loving ghosts.

Logan's luck
James Logan arrived from
Scotland in 1877, eventu-
ally settling in the Karoo
where he bought a farm,
Tweedside, and gradually
added land until he owned
over 120,000 acres. A
model and prosperous
farmer, Logan had the first
private residence in South
Africa with electricity,
pioneered water and
sewage treatment, and
made a second fortune
from his hotel and restaurants. His third fortune
came from selling water to
the railroads: a locomotive
consumed 55,000 gallons of
water in crossing the
Karoo and any dependable
supply was invaluable. He
died in Matjiesfontein on
July 30, 1920.

Oudtshoorn's ostrich
feather millionaires
built themselves
palatial homes

Pear power
In 1916, a Karoo farmer
invented a new alternative
to gas, brewed from prickly
pears. To prove it worked,
he invited writer Lawrence
Green to accompany him
on a drive from Cape Town
to Bulawayo (described in
Green's book, *Karoo*).
Sadly the venture failed
when the farmer inhaled
poisonous fumes from the
fuel and died. Karoo farmers went back to turning
prickly pears into a liqueur,
which they say is particularly good poured over ice
cream!

▶▶▶ Oudtshoorn   49D2
314 miles east of Cape Town
Klein Karoo and Oudtshoorn Tourist Information,
corner Baron van Rheede and Voortrekker Streets
(tel: 0443-226 643/222 221)
Diamonds may have been the treasure of Kimberley, but
ostrich feathers were the wealth of the Little Karoo. From
the 1880s, sweeping ostrich plumes and feather boas
were the height of ladies' fashion. Designers could not get
enough and the arid Karoo proved to be perfect breeding
territory. In 1905, the feathers plucked from just six birds
fetched R12,000. By the time the railroad arrived in 1913,
the district was awash with millionaires. Ordinary little
Oudtshoorn was transformed into a boomtown filled with
spectacular mansions. Oudtshoorn's "feather palaces"
were large, ornate and lavish beyond your wildest dreams.
Most were swirling sandstone art nouveau, with circular
turrets, iron railings and—the colonial variation—corru-
gated-iron roofs. The ceilings and cornices were
embossed papier-mâché, while the walls and windows
were bright with stained glass and vividly glazed tiles.

With World War I the market crashed and for a time
Oudtshoorn was bitterly poor. In the late 1930s ostriches
again came to the rescue, when the first show farm was
opened and the tourists arrived. Today the trade is thriving, but this time feathers, though still valuable, are not
the crucial product. International demand for low-fat,
almost cholesterol-free ostrich meat is soaring. Supple
ostrich leather is increasingly popular for seriously expensive designer shoes, bags, belts, and accessories. Even
the eggs fetch a good market price, both for eating and—
halved or carved—as souvenirs.

The town has two excellent museums. **The C. P. Nel**

Museum (Baron van Rheede Street, tel: 0443-227 306. *Open* Mon–Sat 8:30–1, 2–5. *Admission free*) occupies the old Boys' High School, a building designed in 1907 by leading "feather" architect Charles Bullock. The core of the compelling collection was donated in 1953 by C. P. Nel, a prominent local businessman. It tells the history of Oudtshoorn, ostriches and the feather trade, and should not be missed. **The Dorpshuis** (146 High Street, tel: 0443-223 676. *Open* Mon–Sat 8:30–1, 2–5. *Admission free*) is a carefully restored offshoot of the C. P. Nel Museum. Built by Charles Bullock for J. H. J. Le Roux in 1909, it is one of the finest of the "feather mansions." Lavishly appointed, it still contains most of its original furnishings.

There are three ostrich show farms in Oudtshoorn offering a full range of tours and facilities. **Highgate** (off the Mossel Bay Road R328, 6 miles from the town center. Tel: 0443-227 115. *Open* daily 7:30–5—tours last up to two hours. *Admission charge* moderate) was one of the first ostrich farms in the valley (1887). It was also the first to turn ostriches into a tourist attraction in 1937, setting the agenda for all tours. There you could—and still can—investigate every aspect of the birds' life: see them being born, reared and plucked; handle a baby, sit or ride on an adult and watch an ostrich Derby, with "professional" jockeys on board; buy the eggs, eat the fillet and wear the shoes. At the **Safari Ostrich Farm** (off the Mossel Bay Road R328, 3 miles from the town center. Tel: 0443-227 311. *Open* daily 7:30–5. *Admission charge* moderate) there is a restored feather baron's mansion, Welgeluk (1910), and the tour includes an explanation of how ostrich products are made, from feather dusters to handbags. The **Cango Ostrich Farm** (about 9 miles north of Oudtshoorn on the Cango Caves Road R328. Tel: 0443-224 623. *Open* daily, 8–5. *Admission charge* moderate) is smaller and simpler than the other two and has no racing, but does have a wine cellar and butterfly farm.

There is a tourist train, the **Ostrich Express** (tel: 0443-223 540), which shunts up the valley to Calitzdorp.

Ostriches
There are about 300,000 ostriches in the Oudtshoorn area, on around 350 farms. The female lays up to 15 eggs per clutch, each weighing the equivalent to 24 hen's eggs. They take six weeks to hatch. The young are fawn colored, while adult males are black and white and the females chocolate brown. They take two years to reach maturity, when they weigh about 220 pounds. The birds run in herds of 100–150 birds and are plucked every nine months, losing over 2 pounds of feathers each time.

The lap of honor in an ostrich race

Whale ahoy!

Of the world's 80 species of cetacean (sea mammals), 39 are found around South Africa. Migrant herds of southern right whales reappear in the seas off the Overberg every winter from May/June to November. You may also see porpoises and dolphins and, occasionally, Brydes and Sei whales. The best places to see them are at Stony Point, near Betty's Bay, Kleinmond, Onrus, Walker Bay in Hermanus, and at Koppie Alleen in the De Hoop Nature Reserve. With luck and patience, you can get to within 55 yards. Whale hot line, tel: 0283-21475 or 22629.

Whales and tourists dominate life in Hermanus

The Overberg and South Coast

The Overberg ("over the mountain") is the end of Africa, the segment of the south coast on the far side of the Hottentots Holland Mountains from Cape Town. It was one of the first areas beyond the bay to be colonized. Cut off by the mountains, the isolated Overbergers developed their own distinctive food, use of language and a strong sense of independence, heavily influenced by missionaries at Genadendal (which has an excellent mission museum in Herrnhut House), Elim, and Zuurbraak.

There are several pleasant resorts: **Gansbaai**, an unspoiled fishing village with safe swimming; **Betty's Bay**, a vacation village backed by magnificent mountains and site of the superb 495-acre **Harold Porter National Botanical Garden▶** (tel: 02823-29311. *Open* daily 8–6. *Admission charge* moderate); and **Kleinmond**, between Hermanus and Betty's Bay, where you can find within a 3-mile radius every type of natural habitat in the whole Western Cape—sea, beach dunes, rocky shore, tidal estuary, wetlands, freshwater rivers, caves, strandveld, and *fynbos*.

Cape Agulhas and Environs see pages 94–5.

▶   **Hermanus**   *48B1*

62 miles east of Cape Town
Tourist Information, 105 Main Road (tel: 0283-22629)
Fashionable Hermanus was founded early in the 19th century by Hermanus Pieters, who earmarked its green cliffs and freshwater stream as excellent summer grazing. But it was fishermen who settled it in the 1850s, and since the 1900s it has been a popular summer resort.

There are several fine beaches near by but the real draw is the whales. Hermanus is the only town in the world with an official "whale crier," who wanders the streets with a sandwich board and kelp horn. There are good viewing points for whales from the cliffs and the Old Harbour.

The harbor was the focal point of the early village; now it is the hub of a tourist town, part of a "living" **museum**

(Marine Drive, tel: 0283-21475. *Open* Mon–Sat 9–1, 2–5, Sun 12–4. *Admission charge* inexpensive), with exhibitions on local fishing and whaling. A sonar buoy catches the whales' song and transmits it live into the museum hall. In the square above is a lively craft market, while the Old School House is an annex to the museum with fascinating old photographs. There are hiking trails, including one through the mountain and coastal *fynbos* of the 3,573-acre **Fernkloof Nature Reserve**.

►► Swellendam 48C1

134 miles from Cape Town
Tourist Information (tel: 0291-42770).
The well-watered area around Swellendam, now rich in wheat fields, cows and fruit trees, once attracted great quantities of game, which in turn attracted the Hessekwa Khoikhoi. The first Europeans arrived in the 1740s, carving out farms along the Breë River. Many of their original homesteads still exist. By the early 19th century, Swellendam was a gung-ho eastern frontier village on the pioneering Kaapse Wapad (Cape wagon road). Named after Governor Swellengrebel and his wife Helena ten Damme, the town flirted briefly with independence before settling down as a charming country town with oak-lined streets, pristine Cape Dutch and Victorian houses and a particularly splendid Dutch Reformed church.

The **Drostdy Museum** (18 Swellengrebel Street, tel: 0291-41138. *Open* Mon–Fri 9–5, Sat–Sun 10–4. *Admission charge* inexpensive) is housed in the former seat of the *landdrost* (official representative of the governor). One of the finest such buildings (1747) in the country, it incorporated a residence for the *landdrost*, a courtroom and an office and now displays a fine collection of 18th- and 19th-century Cape furniture as well as art. The museum includes the old jail as well as two houses: Mayville (1853), an impeccably furnished Victorian house with a delightful cottage garden, and its neighbor, the Auld House.

The **Bontebok National Park** (entrance 4 miles south of Swellendam, tel: 0291-42735. *Open* 8–6—until 7PM Oct–Apr) is the home of the once rare antelope which has given it its name. To the north, the Marloth Nature Reserve climbs a flank of the Langeberg Mountains.

Swellendam's magnificent Dutch Reformed church

The West Coast and Cederberg

▶▶ **Cederberg** 48B3

About 137 miles north of Cape Town
Cederberg/Olifants River Valley Publicity Association,
PO Box 5, Clanwilliam 8135 (tel: 027-482 2024).
The 62-mile-long, north–south Cederberg Mountains take their name from the endangered Clanwilliam Cedar tree (*Widdringtonia cedarbergensis*), which grows uniquely in these mountains, at an altitude of 3,280/4,920 feet. With a protected wilderness area of some 175,450 acres, there are numerous opportunities for hiking, walking, climbing and riding, with magnificent views and sandstone formations such as the dramatic Wolfberg Arch. There are clear pools for swimming in the rivers, San rock paintings up to 6,000 years old, rare and wonderful flora and fauna, from the snowball protea to the Clanwilliam yellowfish and red-fin minnow and a mass of colorful bird life plus a healthy local leopard population. Pick up your hiking permits and maps, and obtain information about the wilderness area from the Algeria forestry station or write ahead to the Cederberg Wilderness Area office (see panel).

The two nearest towns are **Clanwilliam** (Tourist Information tel: 027-482 2024) and **Citrusdal** (Tourist Information, Sandveldhuisie Country Shop, Church Street, tel: 022-921 3210). Clanwilliam is famous for its health-giving rooibos tea (see panel opposite), Citrusdal for its oranges. The area between was named Olifants River Valley by early explorers because of the huge herds of elephants roaming it. Today it is all very different, a honeycomb of neatly manicured citrus groves and well-kept vineyards.

Tours and hiking
For specialist tours of the region, contact Cederberg Travel, PO Box 25, Clanwilliam 8135 (tel: 027-482 2444) or Eco Explorers, PO Box 21246, De Tyger 7502, Cape Town (tel: 021-929 361). Obtain hiking permits and information, from Cederberg Wilderness Area, Private Bag X1, Citrusdal 7340 (tel: 022-921 2289).

►► **West Coast** *48A2/A3*

West Coast Publicity Association, PO Box 139, Saldanha 7395 (tel: 02281-42088).

Dominated by the icy, plankton-rich Benguela Current, the Atlantic West Coast is a region of huge kelp beds and abundant seafish, crayfish, abalone, seabirds and seals. Known to those who like nicknames as the "Lobster Coast," after the prolific Cape rock lobster *(Jasus lalandi)* found along these shores, the area was once a key whaling station. It is still a crucial commercial fishing ground for both deep-sea fish and shellfish, although it is now struggling desperately against rampant overfishing.

Although the water is bitterly cold, the dry climate, cool sea breeze and easy access from Cape Town make this a popular vacation area, centered on **Langebaan** (Tourist Information, Municipality Building, tel: 02287-22115) where water sports on the sheltered lagoon are the main attraction, with waterskiing, fishing, board-sailing, diving, swimming and yachting on offer. The lagoon is part of the 49,500-acre **West Coast National Park** (tel: 012-343 1991), famous wetlands whose offshore islands offer predator-proof nesting sites for an estimated three-quarters of a million seabirds of 200 different species, including swift terns, Cape gannets, crowned cormorants, African black oystercatchers, migrant curlew sandpipers and other waders, and small colonies of jackass penguins. In the spring, the whales arrive.

Saldanha Bay (Tourist Information, Oorlogsvlei, tel: 02281-42088) is named after Portuguese Admiral Antonio de Saldanha, who never actually came here, though he anchored in Table Bay in 1503. The name was mistakenly moved on the map! The huge natural harbor is famous for its mussels and as a major port, processing iron ore from mines 534 miles inland (for tours, tel: 02281-357 295). Two other claims to fame include a vast and mysterious deposit of oyster shells and the great guano rush of 1844, when some 300 ships descended on the bay to "mine" the rocks and islands for fertilizer.

St. Helenabaai (Tourist Information, Municipality Building, tel: 02283-61043) and **Elandsbaai** (Tourist Information, Church Street, tel: 0265-31126) have world-famous surf.

A little way inland, the delightfully named **Darling** (Tourist Information in the museum, tel: 02241-3361) marks the start of the flower lands, a blaze of color throughout the spring (see pages 74–5). The **Butter Museum** (Pastorie Street) has a wide array of butter-making utensils. The Moravians, Catholics, and Dutch Reformed Church were all active in the area in the early 19th century and several local villages—Ebenhaeser, Eselbank, Goedverwacht, Mamre, Rietpoort, Vergenoeg, Wittewater, and Wupperthal—began life as missions.

Rooibos
Rooibos ("red bush," *Aspalanthus linearis*) is an indigenous plant of the Cederberg. The colored population were the first to drink it as a tea, but by the mid-19th century it was being drunk more widely. In 1904, Benjamin Ginsberg started trading seriously, and by 1930 full-scale cultivation was under way, centered on Clanwilliam. Now common throughout South Africa, with small quantities exported, it is brewed and presented like ordinary tea, looks a dark, reddish brown—and is terribly healthy. It is free of tannin and stimulants, rich in vitamin C, relaxing and contains antiallergenic agents.

85

Saldanha Bay survives on deep-sea Atlantic fishing

The Winelands

▶▶   **Franschhoek**   *48B2*

50 miles northeast of Cape Town.
Tourist Information, Huguenot Road (tel: 021-876 3603)
In 1688, Governor Simon van der Stel granted the valley to a small group of French Huguenots. The French tradition lives on in the surrounding sea of vines, in farms with names like La Provence, Bourgogne and Mont Rochelle, in the French surnames of many current Afrikaans-speaking residents, and in the exceptional number of good restaurants.

Today, Franschhoek is basically all about wine (see pages 92–3), but take time to visit the **Huguenot Museum** (Lambrecht Street, tel: 021-876 2532. *Open* Mon–Sat 9–1 and 2–5, Sun 2–5. *Admission charge* inexpensive). Housed in the curious Saasveld, a replica of a Cape Town house built by Louis Thibault in 1791, it contains a fascinating collection of Huguenot memorabilia which ranges from family trees and bibles to estate deeds and furniture.

Next door is the **Huguenot Memorial**, a large, unlovely edifice by Coert Steynberg, erected in 1938 to celebrate the 250th anniversary of the Huguenots' arrival. Above the town, the winding **Helshoogte** (Hell's Heights) **Pass** offers superb views back across a fairy-tale valley.

The Huguenots
Like other early Protestants, French Huguenots were persecuted by the Catholic church, their darkest moment coming on St. Bartholomew's Day, 1572, when 10,000 were massacred in Paris. Shortly afterwards, Henry of Navarre took the throne. While he was forced to convert to Catholicism, he remained sympathetic and signed the Edict of Nantes allowing religious freedom. It was revoked by Louis XIV in 1685 and thousands of Huguenots fled France. Most were skilled artisans and were of real benefit to their host countries, creating a range of industries from tapestry to wine, while France went into a long period of industrial decline.

Coert Steynberg's Huguenot Memorial, Franschhoek

► **Paarl** *48B2*

34 miles north of Cape Town on the N1.

Tourist Information, 216 Main Street (tel: 021-872 3829). Open: Mon–Fri 9–5, Sat 9–1, Sun 10–1

Paarl is the largest of the local towns, and a busy working center. It gains its name from the Paarl Rocks, three huge, smoothly rounded granite domes, 500 million years old, on the hill above the town. They are said, with a little imagination, to glisten like pearls after rain, but the mountain was known more aptly to the Khoikhoi as Skilpad (Tortoise

Mountain). The surrounding area is a nature reserve with walking trails and scenic drives. On the hilltop is the **Taal Monument** (1975) a huge sculptural homage to the Afrikaans language by Ian van Wyk (tel: 021-863 2800. *Open* daily 8–5).

In town, be prepared for a hike; Main Street is over 7 miles long! A more manageable 1¼-mile stretch around the tourist office contains many of the town's finest historic buildings. A walking guide is available. The **Paarl Museum** (303 Main Street, tel: 021-872 2651. *Open* Mon–Fri 10–5, Sat 10–4. *Admission charge* inexpensive, free on Wed) occupies a Cape Dutch house and former Dutch Reformed parsonage (1787). The rooms are filled with beautifully embroidered Victorian fashions, silver, ceramics, furniture, and cooking utensils. Real attempts are being made to provide a full history of Paarl with documents and photographs, a display on the Group Areas Act and regular temporary exhibitions. For the **KWV Wine Cellars** and winery tours, see page 93. Displays in the **Afrikaans Language Museum** (Pastorie Lane, tel: 021-872 3441. *Open* Mon–Fri 8–5; weekends by appointment) include the first printing press of the first Afrikaans newspaper. **Le Bonheur Crocodile Farm** (Babylonstoren Road, 4 miles from Paarl, tel: 021-863 1142. *Open* daily 9:30–5. *Admission charge* moderate) offers crocs live, on the plate and as fashion accessories.

► ► ► **Stellenbosch** see pages 90–1

▶ **Wellington** *48B2*

5 miles north of Paarl

Tourist Information, 104 Main Road (tel: 021-8734604)

Originally named Wagenmakersvallei (Wagon Maker's Valley) little Wellington was the northernmost of the early Cape settlements, where people transferred their goods to wagons for the long trek north. Its name was changed in 1840, in honor of the British Duke of Wellington. It has a wine route, fine historic houses and a small **Museum** (Church Street, tel: 021-873 4710. *Open* Mon–Fri 8–1, 2–5. *Admission free*) containing early Dutch implements, earlier local relics and—bizarrely—ancient Egyptian artifacts.

Paarl is the uncrowned capital of the Cape Winelands

Afrikaans
The earliest European settlers in South Africa were Dutch. Over the years, their language evolved into Afrikaans, soaking up a number of French, German, and English words from later settlers, Malay terms from the slaves and a little smattering of local African languages. It was recognized as an official language in its own right in 1925. Afrikaans and Dutch are still very closely related; the Dutch understand it easily but say it is comparable with an English person listening to a simple form of Shakespearean English.

■ **South Africa may not be the best-known producer in the world thanks to sanctions, but it has the oldest wine industry outside Europe and the Mediterranean. The first grapes were planted in 1655 and the first pressing took place in 1659.** ■

The country is currently the world's eighth largest wine producer, with about 3.3 per cent of the global market. It has some 306 million vines, producing about 500 million bottles of wine as well as table grapes, sultanas, grape juice, fortified wines, spirits, and industrial alcohol. The industry supports 300,000 jobs. Sudden international acceptance and marketing possibilities have produced a frenzy of activity, with over 400 new wines hitting the shelves in 1995 alone. But there is a problem—they simply cannot produce enough to satisfy demand. Many good vineyards sold their entire 1995 vintage within three weeks, and locals are complaining as favorite wines simply disappear into more lucrative foreign markets. Plans are afoot to double the acreage under production, but it will be several years before the new vines mature.

The winelands There are increasing numbers of vineyards in the Orange River valley (Northern Cape) and the Northern Province, but most are concentrated in a small area of the Western Cape, from the Swartland in the west to the Overberg in the east. There are 50 official growing regions, of which the most important include Constantia, Stellenbosch, Paarl, Worcester, and the Klein Karoo. Together they make up the winelands, a landscape of soaring, rugged mountains, steep-sided valleys combed with emerald-green, razor-straight lines of vines, and embellished with thickets of oak and gracious, whitewashed Cape Dutch homesteads.

The grapes The whites include global favorites such as Chenin Blanc (Steen), Chardonnay, and Sauvignon Blanc, as well as the more specialist Muscatels or Moscadels (also known to local winegrowers as Hanepoot), Colombard, Gewürztraminer, and Bukettraube. Look for the two unrelated Rieslings (European Weisser Riesling and local Cape Riesling). Among the reds are Cabernet Sauvignon, Merlot, Gamay, Pinot Noir, Shiraz, Cinsault (also known as Hermitage) and a local hybrid grape called Pinotage (Pinot Noir and Cinsault).

Top: the year begins for the wine-growers with the grape harvest. Above: elegantly carved show casks in the KWV cellars

The wines Much of the actual wine production is handled by a series of growers' cooperatives, all of which are, in turn, members of the giant KWV. The results include many unexceptional, pleasant table wines. There are virtually no bad wines, although local taste tends to

Vines cover most of the land round Stellenbosch

Boschendal, founded in 1685, is one of the oldest wineries in South Africa

veer more towards sweet, fruity wines than is common in Europe. The real gems are the tiny estate-bottled vintages (known as estate or boutique wines) normally sold only in South Africa and, even then, only available in small quantities. Many of these are superb, with full-bodied, slightly smoky reds and lightly scented whites oozing fruity undertones. For foreigners unfamiliar with the names and even in some cases the grape varietals, the wine list becomes an intensely pleasurable adventure. Even French vintners are having to admit reluctantly that South Africa's whites are superb.

The vineyards The larger vineyards produce at least half a dozen wines including whites, reds, sparkling, dessert, and fortified wines. Stellenbosch's Rustenberg estate has been producing wine for 300 years, while from the recently restored Klein Constantia vineyards, which produced some of the earliest and most famous wines in the Cape, comes exceptional Sauvignon Blanc. Meerlust, between Cape Town and Stellenbosch, has been in the Myburgh family for seven generations; it specializes in Pinot Noir and the Bordeaux-style Rubicon. Boschendal is known for Pinot Noir and Sauvignon Blanc, Backsberg for Pinotage and Chardonnay, Villiera for Merlot, and L'Ormarins for Shiraz. Most estates offer tastings, though some charge a small fee (see pages 92–3).

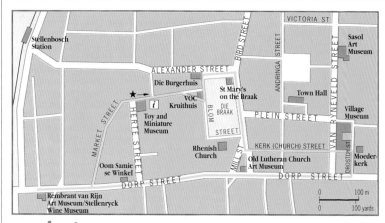

Walk Stellenbosch

Governor Simon van der Stel was not a modest man. In November 1679, he visited the Eerste River valley and founded the Cape Colony's second town, naming Stellenbosch after himself (he is also responsible for Simon's Town on the Peninsula). Although it is now home to a major university and is one of the centers of the wine industry, Stellenbosch remains a picture-perfect town of whitewashed cottages and elegant town houses, with oak-lined avenues set around a village green. Some of it is an illusion: careful reconstruction and restoration has repaired the ravages of three major fires, and the suburbs contain their fair share of hideous 1950s garages and super-

markets. The center is charming but full to the brim with tourists. The best way to see the town is on foot. This walk marks the high points; the tourist office publishes a walking tour guide giving details of the many old buildings you will see *en route*.

Start at the Tourist Office, housed in an old Cape Dutch rectory which also contains a small **Toy and Miniature Museum** (corner Market and Herte Streets. *Open* daily 9:30–5; closed 30 minutes for lunch).

Walk up Market Street. At the top, the **VOC Kruithuis**, the Dutch East India Company arsenal (1777), has a small military museum (Bloem Street, tel: 021-887 2902. *Open* Mon–Fri 9:30–1, 2–4:30).

Turn left for **Die Burgerhuis** (Bloem Street, tel: 021-883 3584. *Open* office hours), a private Cape Dutch home built in 1797 by Antonie Fick. It became the parsonage in 1839 and was restored and opened to the public in 1960. Although it now contains offices, it also has some fine Cape Dutch furniture.

Straight ahead, **Die Braak** (meaning "fallow land") was once a military parade ground but is now a combination village common and parking lot. In the northeast corner is the pretty

Stellenbosch has many of South Africa's finest Cape Dutch houses

Anglican church of **St. Mary's on the Braak** (1852). Surrounding it are a bevy of delightful Georgian and Victorian houses. Walk across the common and turn up Church Street to reach the jewel in the crown of Stellenbosch.

A whole block has been included in the **Village Museum** (37 Ryneveld Street, tel: 021-887 2902. *Open* Mon–Sat 9.30–5, Sun 2–5. *Admission charge* moderate), with four period houses restored and furnished to illustrate architectural development and changes in fashion between 1709, 1780, 1800–20 and the 1850s. Future plans include a further two houses to be furnished in style up to 1929. The detail is impeccable, down to the cottage gardens, and the progression from sturdy wooden furniture and flagged floors to fustian Victoriana is fascinating.

Turn on to Drostdy Street, then right along **Dorp Street**, one of the longest streets of old houses surviving in the country. Everything is here, from Dutch gables to Georgian pediments and Victorian ginger-bread balconies.

Shopping at Oom Samie's is a step back in time

Toward the bottom is **Oom Samie Se Winkel** (82/84 Dorp Street, tel: 021-887 2612. *Open* Mon–Fri 9–6, Sat 9–5). It is not often that a store becomes a tourist attraction in its own right, but the architecture, layout and stock of this glorious Victorian shop appear not to have changed for 100 years. Just some of its delights include souvenirs, African masks, toys, spices and dried fruit. There is a dusty, atmospheric wine shop specializing in rare vintages, and a tea garden, while an oak-beamed pub does stronger duty next door.

Farther along the road, the H-shaped Cape Dutch house, Libertas Parva, contains **Rembrandt Van Rijn Art Museum** (corner Dorp Street and Aan-De-Wagenweg, tel: 021-886 4340). In the cellar is the **Stellenryck Wine Museum** (tel: 021-887 3480). Both museums: *Open* Mon–Fri 9–12:45, 2–5, Sat 10–1, 2–5. Retrace your steps and turn left into Market Street to reach the Tourist Office.

❏ Stellenbosch lies 30 miles east of Cape Town. Tourist Information, 36 Market Street, Stellenbosch 7600 (tel: 021-883 3584). *Open* Mon–Sat, 8–5, Sun 8–4:30. Guided tours leave from the tourist office at 10, 11, 12 noon and 3. For guided walking tours, contact Stellenbosch Historical Walks (tel: 021-883 9633). ❏

Touring the wineries

Fruits of the vine

No less than 12 districts of the Western Cape have wine routes, totaling literally hundreds of properties. These pages cannot provide a comprehensive guide, or even a coherent route. Instead, a few of the most rewarding visits have been included, whether for the quality of the wine or the tour, or for the setting and architecture of the vineyard. Every property listed offers tastings and sales; most also have restaurants, tea gardens or picnic baskets. For organized tours, contact Vineyard Ventures (tel: 021-434 8888).

Backsberg (Klapmuts/Simondium Road, Paarl, off R45, tel: 021 875 5141). *Open* Mon–Fri 8:30–5:30, Sat 8:30–1). A famous, award-winning estate, owned by the Back family, specializing in classic reds; there is a small museum of early wine-making equipment and an audiovisual self-guided tour of the cellars.

Boschendal (off Hellshoogte Pass Road, between Franschhoek and Stellenbosch, tel: 021-874 1034. *Tastings* Mon–Fri 8:30–4:30, Sat 8:30–12:30; Nov–Apr, Sat 8:30–4:30, Sun 10–3. *Vineyard tours* Mon–Fri 10:30 and 11:30, Sat 10:30. *Manor house Open* daily 11–5). Among the area's oldest wineries (1685), this has become one of South Africa's

❑ **Tasting** You may be offered up to a dozen different wines at a tasting. Start with the dry whites and work through to the heavier reds, leaving fortified wines and spirits till last. Sniff the bouquet, take a small mouthful, swill it round your mouth and—if you are strong willed—spit it out. Rinse your glass and mouth with water between each wine. Appoint a nondrinking driver and pace yourself or you will be seriously light-headed by the end. Most vineyards are happy to provide soft drinks for drivers and minors. ❑

preeminent producers of red wines. Combine a vineyard tour with a trip around the superbly restored Cape Dutch manor, filled with magnificent 17th- and 18th-century furniture, Ming porcelain and Dutch East Indies Company glass.

Chamonix (Uitkyk Street, off the R45 to Cape Town, Franschhoek, tel: 021-876 3241. *Open* any reasonable time. There is a guest house if you wish to stay). Originally part of La Cotte, one of the early Huguenot estates, this has been a separate property only since 1990, but has already produced several award-winning wines. It also bottles its own spring water, and has a stud farm breeding American pinto horses.

Fairview (Suider-Agter Road, Paarl, off the R101, tel: 021-863 2450. *Open* Mon–Fri 8–5:30, Sat 8–1). Owned by the Back family, this fine but less illustrious vineyard offers a good family outing. The additional attractions are a herd of 500 Saanen goats, some of which live in a tower, and a thriving cheese-making operation. Milking is at 4PM daily, except in kidding season (Jul–Sep).

L'Ormarins (off the R45 to Cape Town, Franschhoek, tel: 021-874 1026. *Tastings* Mon–Fri, 9–4:30, Sat 9–12:30. *Cellar tours* Mon–Fri 10, 11:30 and 3, Sat 11). This was the very first wine estate in the Franschhoek valley, the property of a Huguenot settler, Jean Roi. In 1969 the estate was bought by the multi-millionaire philanthropist, Anton Rupert, since when it has leapt to prominence, producing some of the country's finest wines. It has a truly magnificent Cape Dutch homestead.

KWV Wine Cellars (Kohler Street, Paarl, tel: 021-807 3007. English-language tours: Mon, Wed, Fri at 11 and 3:45, Tue, Thu 9:30 and 2:15. Also regular tours in Afrikaans and German.) This formidable cellar is not only the heart of the Cape industry but the largest winery in the world. It can store up to half a million gallons of wine and 75,000 gallons of fortified wine at any one time, and has the five largest vats in the world, fashioned from giant sequoia wood.

KWV was set up to handle South Africa's surplus wine. This vast co-operative, with nearly 4,900 members, now controls virtually all wine production and, with affiliates, the sale of about 80 per cent of all alcohol except beer in South Africa. The KWV label is reserved almost exclusively for wine sold abroad, much of which is mass-produced

Boschendal manor is home to one of the country's finest wines

from the "wine lake." KWV admits that most wines with its labels are undistinguished. It no longer has any surplus to spare; in fact, with other countries such as Australia buying up South African wine to bottle as their own, KWV is actually running short.

Van Ryn Brandy Cellar (Vlottenburg, near Stellenbosch, tel: 021-881 3875. *Open* Mon–Thu, tours 10:30 and 3, Fri 10:30; extra tours 12 Dec–13 Jan, telephone for details. *Admission charge* moderate). There is an audiovisual presentation on brandymaking, tours of the distillery, cellar and cooperage, and of course, a tasting.

❏ **Contacts** Brochures containing details of all the wine routes are available from local tourist offices. Alternatively, you can phone the Wine Route offices: Constantia (021-794 5128); Stellenbosch (021-886 4310); Paarl (021-872 3605); Wellington (021-873 4604); Franschhoek (021-876 3062); Worcester (0231-28710); Klein Karoo (04439-2556); Robertson (02351-3167); Swartland (0224-21134); Tulbagh (01236-301001). ❏

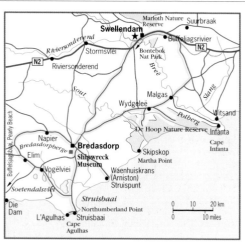

Drive Swellendam to Cape Agulhas

Known as the Coast of Flowers, this area is far more than a garden, with calm, sandy beaches and treacherous underwater rocks, vacation homes and historic missions. Distances are not huge but the route involves some backtracking and gravel roads. Allow one–two days.

Leave Swellendam on the N2 toward Cape Town, then turn left for **Bredasdorp** (Tourist Information, Dirkie Uys Street, tel: 02841-42584). This sleepy little town (founded 1838) is the "capital" of a region almost totally dependent on wheat and sheep farming. The **Shipwreck Museum** (Independent Street, tel: 02841-41240. *Open* Mon–Thu 9–4:45, Fri 9–3:45, Sat 9–12:45 plus in Dec–Mar 2–3:45, Sun 11–12:30. *Admission charge* inexpensive) catalogues the history of maritime disasters in the area, displaying figureheads, coins and furniture salvaged from vessels wrecked off the coast. On the edge of town, the **Heuningberg Nature Reserve** produces spectacular displays of fiery Bredasdorp lilies in April and May.

Take the road through Napier and turn left for **Elim**, an almost forgotten colored village which grew up around an early 19th-century Moravian mission (1824). Because of its isolation, the architecture has been left

The Cape Agulhas lighthouse marks the southernmost point in Africa

❑ On May 30, 1815 the *Arniston*, a British troop carrier sailing from India to England, was forced onto the rocks at Waenhuiskrans and broke up; only six of its 378 passengers survived. Among the dead were four boys on their way back to school. A memorial erected by their grieving parents stands on the cliff top, and the ship itself can sometimes be spotted at low tide. It is one of 412 wrecks strewn along the Cape coast. ❑

intact, with whole streets of thatched "Karoo" cottages. The villagers' main income is from dried flowers, cut in the local *fynbos*; you can visit the drying sheds.

Leaving Elim, head for Struisbaai and L'Agulhas. Named the "Cape of Needles" after its murderous rocks, **Cape Agulhas** (29 miles south of Bredasdorp. Tourist Information tel: 02846-620) is the southernmost tip of Africa, marked by a small plaque, where a compass needle points due north, with no magnetic variation. The real drama is out to sea, where 124 wrecks lie within a 50-mile radius, their crews drowned between 1673 and 1990 by what Rudyard Kipling called the "dread Agulhas roll." **L'Agulhas** itself is one of a series of beach resorts stretching from Pearly Beach in the west, through Buffelsjagsbaai and Die Dam to Struisbaai in the east. The swimming is safe and the angling excellent. The **Lighthouse**, built in 1849 and modeled on the Pharos lighthouse of Alexandria, Egypt, is the second oldest in the country and the most southerly in Africa, its beam reaching 30 miles out to sea. The lighthouse, which still works, houses a **museum** (Main Road, tel: 02846-56078. *Open Tue–Sat 9:30–5, Sun 10–1:30. Admission charge* inexpensive).

Head back to Bredasdorp, then turn back to the coast for **Arniston** (15 miles south of Bredasdorp. Tourist Information, see Bredasdorp, above), officially called Waenhuiskrans— "wagon house cliff"—after an enormous cave nearby, said to be large enough to turn an ox wagon around inside. The cave (less than a mile from the village) can be explored at low tide, and there are numerous other caves, cliffs and rock formations in the area. The village is known as Arniston after a ship wrecked here in 1815 (see box opposite). Today it is best known as an attractive resort, with vacation homes and excellent fishing, as well as for its handful of delightful 19th-century fishermen's cottages.

Fishing boats drawn up on Arniston beach

Return yet again to Bredasdorp and head for the **De Hoop Nature Reserve** (30 miles east of Bredasdorp. Private Bag X16, 7280 Bredasdorp, tel: 02922-782). Stretching 3 miles out to sea, this is an important 89,000-acre conservation area incorporating rare lowland *fynbos*, dunes and wetlands. It is home to 86 species of mammal including the Cape mountain zebra, gray rhebok, caracal and leopard, and over 250 species of bird, among them the last breeding colony in the region of the rare Cape vulture. The reserve has basic accommodations, hiking trails, walks and drives.

Leaving the park, take the road north, crossing the Breë River on the **Malgas Pont** (a hand-operated pontoon bridge), the only working pont left in South Africa, through the Bontebok National Park to Swellendam.

❏ The right whale, *Eubalaena australis*, was so named because it was thought to be the right whale to catch—large, slow-moving and rich in oil. There are thought to be about 4,000 still alive today. Up to 60 feet long and 88 tons in weight, they have a smooth, rounded, mainly black body, with occasional white markings on the back and belly, no dorsal fin, and white, cauliflower-like callosities (knobbly dollops of tough skin) on the head and jaw, as distinctive as fingerprints. They live on plankton and krill filtered from the water. ❏

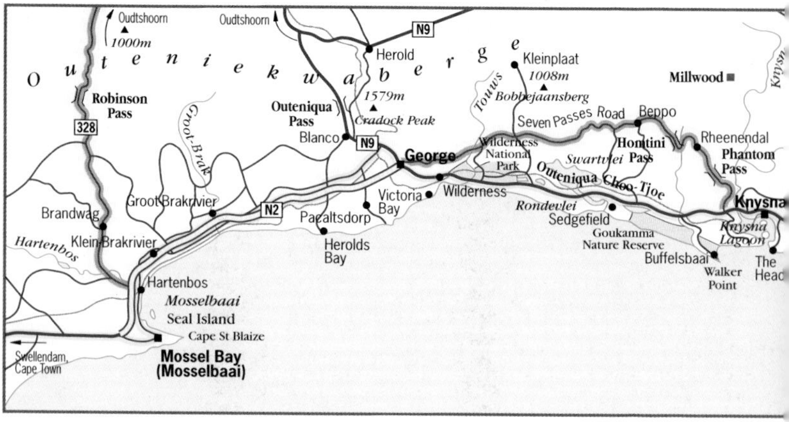

The map labels (reading within the map image): Oudtshoorn 1000m, Oudtshoorn, Herold, Outeniekwaberge, Kleinplaat 1008m, Millwood, Robinson Pass, 328, Groot-Brak, Outeniqua Pass 1579m, Cradock Peak, Blanco, N9, George, Wilderness National Park, Tou'ws, Bobbejaansberg, Seven Passes Road, Beppo, Hontini, Swartvlei Pass, Rheenendal, Phantom Pass, Groot Brakrivier, N2, Pagaltsdorp, Victoria Bay, Wilderness, Outeniqua Choo-Tjoe, Knysna, Brandwag, Klein Brakrivier, Hartenbos, Herolds Bay, Rondevlei, Sedgefield, Goukamma Nature Reserve, Knysna Lagoon, Buffelsbaai, The Heads, Hartenbos, Mosselbaai, Seal Island, Cape St Blaize, Swellendam, Cape Town, Mossel Bay (Mosselbaai), Walker Point

𝒟rive The Garden Route

One of South Africa's most popular tourist haunts, the Garden Route was so called for its landscape of green forests and fertile meadows. Officially it is the strip of the south coast from Mossel Bay in the west to Plettenberg Bay in the east, ranging inland to the Outeniqua Mountains. In practice, Captour include the whole coast from Cape Town to Port Elizabeth in their marketing campaigns. This is one of the busiest resort areas in the country and the forests and gardens have felt the pressure, giving way to roads and golf courses, hotels, vacation homes, trailer parks and campsites. Accommodations are plentiful, but sold out in peak season, so reserve in advance. Allow at least two days.

The route is easily followed, with the main N2 running the full length and on to Durban. Any stops are clearly signposted. If you have the time, follow the more picturesque old roads, which wind through the forests and villages, often on gravel. For the Overberg coast, from Cape Town to Swellendam, see pages 82 and 94.

Swellendam to Mossel Bay This section runs through several small villages (see map pages 48–9). **Heidelberg** (Tourist Information, tel: 02934-21917) was the site of the southernmost battle of the Anglo-

Boer War. **Riversdale** (Tourist Information, tel: 02933-32418) is home to the **Julius Gordon Africana Museum** (*Open* Mon–Fri 10:30–12:30, 3:30–5:30), with a fine collection of paintings by many top South African artists. Nearby, a turnoff to the right (B323) leads to **Stilbaai** (Tourist Information, Palinggat, tel: 02934-42602), a coastal resort with good fishing, boating and swimming. Its highlights are the prehistoric, but still working fish traps, and the town's fountain, full of tame eels. Watch them being fed at 11AM daily. Back on the N2, **Albertinia** (Tourist Information, tel: 02934-51572) is a mining community, producing yellow ocher, silica quartzite and kaolin. It also has an aloe factory extracting sap for use in cosmetics and medicines, and is the world's largest producer of thatching reed. A little farther on, there is **bungee jumping** off the Gourits River Bridge every weekend (tel: 021-724 516).

The whole section runs through fairly dull farmland, with wide, rolling wheat fields. Those with the time to spare should consider taking the mountainous inland route along the R62 through the Karoo villages of Barrydale, Ladismith and Calitzdorp to Oudtshoorn before heading south on the R328 over Robinson Pass to **Mossel Bay** (Tourist Information,

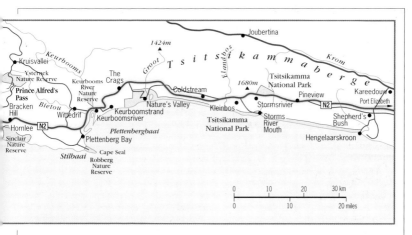

Market Street, tel: 0444-912 202). This is South Africa's fifth largest port, with booming local industry fueled by the oil and gas fields just off the coast. The massive Mossgas refinery and busy working harbor are interesting, but not really conducive to beach vacations. Nevertheless, the town is worth a visit.

The first European to show up here was Bartholomeu Dias in 1488. In 1500, a ship's captain left a letter under a local giant milkwood tree; a year later it was found by the Commander of the Third East India fleet. For the next 400 years, the tree became a post office for all passing sailors, and it now forms the heart of the **Bartolomeu Dias Museum Complex** (Market Street, tel: 0444-911 067. *Open* Mon–Fri 9–5, Sat 10–1. *Admission charge* inexpensive). The complex also includes collections of local and maritime history, with a life-size replica of Dias' caravel, a shell museum, Munroehoek (a group of 1830s houses), a Malay graveyard, and the Fountain, a spring used by Dias. A stone cross, the Padrao, donated by the Portuguese government, commemorates Vasco da Gama's visit in 1497. There are walks through the **Dana Bay Nature Reserve** to the St. Blaize Lighthouse and Bat Cave, used by early KhoiSan inhabitants, and boat trips to Seal Island (tel: 0444-3101).

The Portuguese Bartolomeu Dias rounded the Cape in 1488 and made shore in Mossel Bay

Around the bay to Knysna Follow the old coast road around the bay to **Hartenbos** (Tourist Information, tel: 0444-951 550), where the **Great Trek Museum** (*Open* Mon–Fri 9–12:30, 2–3:45, Sat 10–12:30) covers everything from wagon building to Zulu *impis*, entertainment and the role of women.

Rejoin the N2 for about 20 miles, then branch left (N12) for 6 miles to **George** (Tourist Information, 124 York Street, tel: 0441-744 000; Regional Tourist Information, tel: 0441-736 314). Founded in 1788 as a forestry outpost at the foot of the Outeniqua Mountains, George became a town in 1811, named after King George III of England. It grew up as an administrative center, living off the timber trade and hops. The huge **Dutch Reformed church** (corner of Meade and Courtenay Streets), built in 1842, has a magnificent yellow-wood ceiling and pillars and a pulpit which took two men a year to carve. By contrast the Anglican **Cathedral of St. Mark** (York Street), built eight years later, is tiny. The former **Drostdy** was a private residence and hotel before it became the local **Museum** (York Street, tel: 0441-735 343. *Open* Mon–Fri 9–4:30, Sat 9–12:30. *Admission charge* inexpensive) with local history and art, a display on the area's indigenous woods and timber industry, and mechanical musical instruments. The massive Slave Tree, in front of the

The Outeniqua Choo-Tjoe, a steamingly good day out

information office, has an old chain and lock embedded in the trunk, a souvenir of the bad old days. Once the site of local slave auctions, it is now said to be the biggest oak in the southern hemisphere.

Near by are two small beach resorts, **Herolds Bay** and **Victoria Bay**; a **Crocodile Farm** (Pacaltsdorp Road, tel: 0441-734 302. *Open* daily 9–5, feeding at 3. *Admission charge* moderate); as well as the wonderful little **Outeniqua Choo-Tjoe** steam railroad, which runs between George and Knysna through the beautiful Wilderness National Park (see page 235.) Head north from here on a side-trip to Oudtshoorn and the Klein Karoo (see pages 79–81).

Return to the N2 and continue on for 5 miles to **Wilderness** (Tourist Information, Wilderness Station, tel: 0441-770 045). In 1877, the legend goes, a young Cape Town man, George Bennett, was given permission to marry as long as he took his bride to live in the wilderness. He bought a farm, named it Wilderness, and triumphantly brought his bride home. Today this is one of the prettiest towns on the Garden Route, tucked behind high dunes along the Touws River estuary. The swimming and beaches are excellent and there are opportunities for canoeing, windsurfing, and fishing on the lakes.

Between Wilderness and Sedge-field, the Wilderness National Park (tel: 0441-877 1197) protects a sensitive wetlands area from encroaching development. In its 6,455 acres are five rivers, four lakes, two estuaries and 17 miles of southern Cape coastline, and it is surrounded by a further 25,000 acres of lakes. This is a popular area for bird-watchers, anglers and hikers, home to 79 of South Africa's 95 species of waterfowl, as well as the elusive Knysna loerie and many kingfisher species. Kingfisher Ferries (tel: 0441-877 1101) run guided walks and boat trips through the park.

The next stop along the N2 is cozy **Knysna** (Tourist Information, 40 Main Street, tel: 0445-21610), the largest and most beautiful of the coastal resorts, curled around the hilly shores of a huge lagoon (5 square miles), its narrow access to the sea guarded by The Heads, two large sandstone cliffs (656 feet and 380 feet high) and a coral reef. The lagoon is perfect for water sports, while several companies run boat trips, fishing charters and diving, on both wrecks and nearby coral reefs (ask the tourist office for details). The lagoon is home to 200 species of fish, including a rare seahorse, provides excellent fishing, and is a major source of oysters.

Plettenberg Bay, a gentle curve of tawny sand

**Knysna to Tsitsikamma National
Park** The **Knysna Museum** (Queen
Street, tel: 0445-825 066. *Open*
Mon–Sat 8:30–5) is made up of four
houses: wooden Millwood House
(*c.*1880) and Parkes Cottage (1890)
both have displays on the history of
Knysna, including memorabilia of its
founder, George Rex; the corrugated
iron **Parkes Shop** (1890) deals with
the Knysna timber industry; the **Old
Gaol** (1858) was the first public building erected in the town, to house
convict laborers on their way to
Prince Alfred's Pass. Its bell was
used both as a fire alarm and to signal
the arrival of the mail. It now contains
angling and maritime museums and

an art gallery. The **Knysna Oyster
Company** (Long Street, tel: 0445-
22168. *Open* Mon–Fri 8–5, Sat and
Sun 9–3) offers farm tours and tastings of oysters and mussels.

Knysna Forest is South Africa's
largest expanse of indigenous high
forest, home to rare reserves of
yellowwood, ironwood and
stinkwood trees, some up to 800
years old. It is a dark, eerie world
where antelope and birds flit through
the dense shadowy undergrowth and
monkeys trapeze across the giant
hardwood trees. It has only four
elephants, the last survivors of a
famous herd who used to roam the

Storms River mouth in the Tsitsikamma Forest National Park

fully functional 19th-century mine. There are many opportunities for guided walks in the area.

It is 20 miles from Knysna to **Plettenberg Bay** (Tourist Information, Kloof Street, tel: 04457-34065), one of South Africa's most fashionable beach resorts. Christened Baia Formosa ("beautiful bay") by the 16th-century Portuguese mariner, Manuel da Perestrello, this little town does indeed have a splendid setting, on a gently curving sandy bay backed by towering mountains. The Governor of the Cape, Baron Joachim von Plettenberg, renamed it after himself in 1779. The tip of the peninsula is now the Robberg (Cape Seal) Nature Reserve, with numerous walks and caves, while the cliffs offer excellent positions for whale or dolphin watching. Species seen along here include southern right, humpback, Brydes, minke, and killer whales. For the local whale hot line tel: 04457-33743.

A little way east of "Plett" is the start of the beautiful **Tsitsikamma Forest National Park** (tel: 012-343 1991) whose Khoikhoi name means "place of sparkling waters." Dedicated in 1964, it stretches 40 miles along the coast and 3½ miles out to sea, covering an extraordinarily rich variety of ecosystems, flora and fauna. Inland there is coastal forest, part of the great Knysna Forest belt, where ancient yellowwoods grow up to 165 feet high. On the coast, freshwater wetlands give way to dunes, crashing waves and shallow pools, coral reefs and plunging deep waters. At Storms River Mouth there are places to swim and snorkel and a restaurant and shop. For hikers, the Otter Trail (see page 236) runs right through the park.

Along the Garden Route there are numerous opportunities for water sports, from windsurfing to diving, as well as for tennis and golf and more adventurous activities including mountain biking, riding, or paragliding. Ask any regional tourist office for a brochure.

For Jeffreys Bay, Humansdorp and Port Elizabeth, see pages 116–117.

entire south coast. There are plans to introduce three youngsters in an attempt to revive the herd. The **Buffalo Valley Game Farm** (12 miles southwest on the Buffelsbaai road. Tel: 0445-22481. *Open* off season: Sun–Fri 11–3; peak season: daily 9–5 *Admission charge* moderate) is the only private game farm on the Garden Route with a wide variety of plains animals, antelope and birds, but no major predators. The **Millwood Project** (20 miles from Knysna) is an ongoing attempt to bring back the years of the Millwood Gold Rush, based on the abandoned Bendigo Mine. Equipment is being gathered together and restored to re-create a

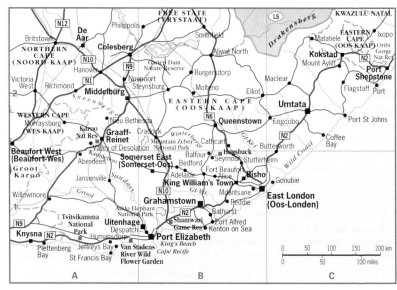

Eastern Cape The Eastern Cape is a patchwork province made up of numerous disparate cultures and eco-systems. It came into being only when the boundaries were rearranged in 1994. Until then, most of the area was simply an extension of the Western Cape, both geographically and politically.

In the far west, the Tsitsikamma Forest (see page 101) gives way to rolling scrub, while to the north are the eastern reaches of the Great Karoo. Around Grahamstown are lush green farmlands and montane forest. In the far east, the Wild Coast lives up to its name as one of South Africa's last undeveloped stretches of coast, the ragged cliffs and towering dunes broken by trailing river mouths and hidden coves of silver sand.

History This was a frontier land, inhabited initially by the Khoikhoi in the southwest, the Xhosa in the southeast and the San to the north. The Great Trek took the Afrikaners along the coast to the Fish River and ever farther out into the Karoo. They dispossessed the San and Khoikhoi, but left the more warlike Xhosa alone until 1780, when the Cape government extended its authority to the river and forced the two groups into direct conflict

EASTERN CAPE

Previous pages: the marina at Port Alfred

Human pawns
The 1820 Settlers were moved into the region (known as Albany) by the ruthless Governor, Lord Charles Somerset, chiefly as a way of breaking an expensive and irritating deadlock in the Frontier Wars. The sudden influx of 5,000 people was sufficient to force the hand of the Xhosa. Each settler family was allocated only 100 acres of land, scarcely enough to survive on. The settlers had a rough time for the first 50 years and many gave up farming, retreating to the towns.

Xhosa women selling vegetables in Peddie

in the first of a series of nine bloody Frontier Wars which lasted until the mid-19th century. Meantime, in 1806, the British took control of the Cape, and in 1820 5,000 British settlers arrived in the Grahamstown area. The Xhosa, who were already fighting not only the Boers but also the Zulus and their own offshoot tribe, the Mfengu, had to fight them too. Inevitably, the British with their superior firepower won the day, and the whole area became part of the Cape Colony.

The dramas continued however. Due to the intensity of missionary activity in the area, the black population gained a higher level of education than was the norm, and in 1916 the black University of Fort Hare was founded. The area became one of the most politically active in South Africa, providing the nationalist cause with many of its greatest leaders, including Nelson Mandela, Walter Sisulu and Steve Biko of the ANC, and Robert Sobukwe, founder of the hard-line PAC. During the apartheid years, two black homelands were formed in the eastern section of the province: the technically independent Xhosa territory of Transkei and the satellite Mfengu homeland of Ciskei.

A bright future Today, most of the region's towns look like charming toys. The Karoo is dotted with sparklingly clean Afrikaner villages, the coast lined with neat, Disneyesque waterfront estates. Bisho, once capital of Transkei and now state capital of the Eastern Cape, looks as though it is made of Legos, and even the tiny pastel-colored houses of the Xhosa hill villages appear to have just been taken out of the box. Only little Peddie, with its noisy street markets and blaring music, battered Coca-

Above: hardwood forest still coats much of the Hogsback. Left: stone leopards guard the main square of Bisho

Cola billboards and line of black taxis seems like the rest of Africa—or even real.

Though much less known than the Western Cape or KwaZulu-Natal, the Eastern Cape is just as rich in possibilities for the tourist. Almost every inlet along the Wild Coast has a small hideaway resort tucked unobtrusively along its banks, but as yet there are few towns or ribbon development of vacation homes, most people being deterred by the appalling dusty roads that bump down to the coast. But the beaches here are probably the best in South Africa and the real estate agents' boards are moving ever closer. This is the hot new area, partly because wealthy whites can now safely buy property in the former homelands.

The Garden Route extension to Port Elizabeth is being marketed, with the added bonus of the only good game parks in the south. At the same time, a whole new tourism industry is dedicated to following in the footsteps of Nelson Mandela. The future for this fledgling province seems bright.

The coelacanth

Over 350 million years old and thought to have been extinct for 65 million years, the coelacanth (*Latimeria chalumnae*) was rediscovered in 1938 when an East London fisherman landed one in his nets and showed it to museum curator Marjorie Courtenay-Latimer. It was about 5 feet long, weighed 125 pounds and was covered in deep-blue scales. Several other specimens have been caught since, and underwater photographs were taken in 1987.

This strange, predaceous fish has a deep, stocky body, and rounded, lobe-like fins. The first spine of the dorsal fin is hollow (the name means "hollow spine" in Greek). Because of the structure of the fins it is thought to be a "missing link" in the evolution of land animals.

Below: the coelacanth. Bottom: fishing off the rocks near East London

▶ **East London** 102B1

Tourist Information, Old Library Building, 35 Argyle Street (tel: 0431-26015)

East London on the Buffalo River (founded 1847) is the fourth largest port in South Africa. The city is not exciting architecturally, although there are some fine individual buildings such as the City Hall and St. Peter's church, but it is a highly popular resort with magnificent golden beaches stretching 25 miles along the coast in either direction. Nahoon and Eastern Beaches have some of the finest surf in South Africa. The old **Lock Street Gaol** (South Africa's first women's prison) is now a shopping center and the former fishing harbor a miniwaterfront development called **Latimer's Landing** (where the coelacanth—see panel—was landed in 1938).

The **Anne Bryant Art Gallery** (Upper Oxford Street, tel: 0431-342 209. *Open* Mon–Fri 9:30–5, Sat 9:30–12. *Admission free*) is an imposing Edwardian mansion containing a fair collection of South African art from the 1880s onwards. **Gately House Museum** (Terminus Street, tel: 0431-22141. *Open* Tue–Thu 10–1, 2–5, Fri 10–1, Sat–Sun 3–5. *Admission charge* inexpensive), once home of East London's first mayor, is furnished with fine Cape furniture. The impressive **East London Museum** (Oxford Street, entrance in Dawson Road, tel: 0431-430 686. *Open* Mon–Fri 9:30–5, Sat 9:30–12, Sun 11–4. *Admission charge* inexpensive) exhibits Xhosa culture, shells and stuffed animals. Star attractions are the world's only dodo egg and a stuffed coelacanth. If you prefer live animals, there is an **Aquarium** (Esplanade, tel: 0431-25151. *Open* daily 9–5; fish feeding at 10:30 and 3, seal shows at 11:30 and 3:30. *Admission charge* moderate) and a **Zoo** (Queen's Park, tel: 0431-21171. *Open* daily 9–5. *Admission charge* moderate). The **Calgary Museum** (Macleantown Road, tel: 0431-387 244. *Open* Wed–Sun 9–4. *Admission charge* inexpensive), 8 miles from town, has a collection of horse-drawn vehicles.

▶ **Alice** *102B1*

About 53 miles northeast of Grahamstown

Alice's claim to fame is **Fort Hare University**, the first black university in South Africa, founded in 1916 out of the mission-run Lovedale College. Nelson Mandela and many other nationalist leaders studied here. On campus, the **De Beer Centenary Art Gallery** (*Open* Mon, Wed, Fri 9–12, Tue, Thu 1–2) has an excellent collection of contemporary black art.

Bisho *102B1*

33 miles northwest of East London

Bisho was a satellite township to King William's Town before becoming the capital of Ciskei, then the Eastern Cape. The fledgling city consists of a sprawl of small grid housing, one vast pink cement office and shopping building, overlooked by stern stone leopards (locals say they smile when a virgin enters the square), and a casino.

▶▶▶ **Grahamstown** *102B1*

80 miles northeast of Port Elizabeth; 36 miles from the coast

Tourist Information, Church Square (tel: 0461-23241)

Founded by Colonel John Graham in 1812, Grahamstown began life as the military headquarters of the Cape Colony's eastern frontier, commanding a chain of small forts along the Fish River. Then, after many of the 1820 settlers abandoned their unprofitable farms for the security of urban life, the town took off and flourished, becoming for a time the second city of the colony. In the late 19th century, however, many of its inhabitants were lured north by the prospect of instant wealth in the diamond and gold fields, and the city withered. Today, it is a charming country town, with many delightful old buildings and several educational establishments, notably the prestigious Rhodes University, which has about 4,000 students.

▶▶ **Hogsback** *102B1*

90 miles northwest of East London

Tourist Information, (tel: 045-962 1050)

In the Amatola Mountains (Amatola means calf—the hills are supposed to look like a row of calves), Hogsback is a hill station, set in cool green forests with planted pine and eucalyptus on the high ground and virgin hardwood forest

Huberta

In 1928 Huberta, the happy hippo from St. Lucia, decided to go for a walk. Over the next three years she became a national celebrity, with the local press charting her progress on a 620-mile journey which took her to the Eastern Cape—the first hippo there for over 50 years. Sadly, Huberta was shot by a farmer in 1931 while she was dining on his crops. Now stuffed, she lives on amid her press cuttings in King William's Town's Kaffrarian Museum.

King William's Town is rich in ornate Victorian architecture

EASTERN CAPE

circling the lower slopes. It is perfectly designed for leisure, with tumbling waterfalls, cozy fireside bars, ideal walking and riding, and trout fishing in the dams and streams. A new Museum of the Struggle is under construction above Sandile Dam.

▶▶ **King William's Town** 102B1
37 miles west of East London
The settler town of King William's Town was an important military base during the Frontier Wars and has several 19th-century churches and other examples of colonial architecture. The excellent **Kaffrarian Museum** (3 Albert Road, tel: 0433-24506. *Open* Mon–Fri 9–12:45, 2–5. *Admission charge* inexpensive) has a large natural history section, as well as historic and contemporary displays on Xhosa culture. The **Missionary Museum** (Berkeley Street. *Open* Mon–Fri 9–5) explains the role of the missions in the development of South Africa.

Buildings of note The broad, tree-lined streets are filled with imposing public buildings and pleasing Victorian shops and houses. The heart of the town is triangular **Church Square**, originally the military parade ground between Colonel Graham's house and the officers' mess. In the center rises the spire of the Anglican **Cathedral of St. Michael and St. George**, which began life as a parish church in 1824 and became a bishopric in 1852. The Lady Chapel was finally completed in 1952. The Gothic Revival Methodist **Commemoration church** was dedicated in 1850 in thanks for the settlers' triumph after 25 grueling years. It has a fine organ and stained-glass windows. The **Drostdy Gate** was designed for military purposes in 1835 by Major Selwyn and built by the Royal Engineers in 1841 on the site of the old Drostdy. It now forms the pedestrian entrance to Rhodes University. There are numerous fine restored buildings in Hill and MacDonald Streets and in Artificers Square (corner of Bartholomew and Cross Streets), the artisan quarter where craftsmen were given plots to set up workshops.

Memorials The Settler Memorial Tower, now part of the City Hall, was erected in 1870, ahead of the rest of the building, to commemorate the 50th anniversary of the arrival of the 1820 settlers. Work on the main City Hall began in 1877. Overlooking the town, the **1820 Settlers Monu-ment** (Gunfire Hill, tel: 0461-27115) is an arts center opened in 1974, the official home of the Grahamstown Festival. The **Bible Monument** (Bedford Road) marks an occasion in 1837 when

the local British settlers presented a bible to some passing Voortrekkers as a token of friendship for the Dutch community. The War Memorial (Church Square) has an inscription specially composed by Rudyard Kipling.

Museums The Albany Museum (Somerset Street, tel: 0461-22312 for all sections. *Open* Mon–Fri 9:30–1, 2–5, Sat–Sun 2–5. *Admission charge* inexpensive), founded in 1855, contains several distinct sections. The **1820 Settlers Memorial Museum** specializes in the history of the British settlers of 1820 and later, with a good cultural history collection of domestic utensils, furniture and applied arts, and a large collection of 18th- and 19th-century South African art. It also has an excellent display on Xhosa life-styles and traditions. The **Natural History Museum** deals not only with animals, but with early humans in southern Africa. The **J.L.B. Smith Institute of Ichthyology** is a fish museum, with pride of place given to the coelacanth (see page 106). Away from Somerset Street are **Fort Selwyn** (Gunfire Hill), a small fort built in 1836, which saw several battles against Xhosa forces, and the **Observatory Museum** (Bathurst Street. *Open* Mon– Fri 9:30–1, 2–5, Sat 9–1. *Admission charge* inexpensive) which has displays on Victorian South Africa and the early diamond industry, and a working camera obscura on the roof.

Left: the Settlers'
Memorial,
Grahamstown.
Above: Grahamstown
Cathedral

Tour The 1820 Settler towns

Grahamstown is surrounded by a circle of small market towns, founded by the early Settlers from Britain. Together they form a very pleasant one–two day tour. The route forms a basic figure of eight with Grahamstown at the center. You can do a longer loop northward over the Hogsback to include Balfour, Seymour, Cathcart, Stutterheim, Bisho, and King William's Town (see page 107).

Southern loop Leave Grahamstown on the A67, heading south to Port Alfred. The first stop, after 25 miles, is Bathurst▶, named after the British Colonial Secretary in 1820. The town has several national monuments including the Anglican and Wesleyan churches, Bradshaw's water-driven wool mill and the settler fort. There is also an excellent **Agricultural Museum** (Trappes

The Bathurst pineapple is an unlikely but highly visible landmark

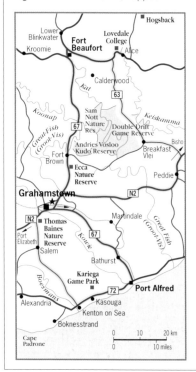

Street. *Open* Thu–Tue, 9–1, 2–4). On the top of Baillie's Beacon 1¼ miles from the town, a viewing telescope marks the spot from which the Settlers staked out their farms. You can still see the triangles fanning outward in the shape of the fields. The most obvious attraction is the 53-foot-high pineapple on **Summerhill Farm** (tel: 0464-250 833). You can climb it and do a farm tour with audiovisual performance about pineapples, the biggest crop in the area. The **Pig and Whistle Inn** (founded in 1831) is one of the oldest hostelries in the country.

Six miles on, **Port Alfred** (Tourist Information, Market Building, East Bank, tel: 0464-41235) is a tidy little coastal resort on the Kowie River estuary with a marina, boat cruises, canoe trips and fishing charters. The **Kowie Museum** has personal files on all the 1820 Settlers. Just off the coast is one of South Africa's most colorful reefs, with a range of sponges and corals (contact Kowie Dive School; tel: 0464-244 432).

From here, take the A72 west for 13 miles to the pleasant resort of **Kenton on Sea** (Tourist Information, Municipality Building, tel: 0464-81304) with good beaches and safe swimming. The 1,631-acre **Kariega Game Park** (8 miles from Kenton on Sea, on the Grahamstown road. Tel: 0461-311 049) has birds, game and hiking trails. Take the A72 back toward Port Alfred and turn left for Grahamstown, via the village of **Salem** and the **Thomas Baines Nature Reserve**.

Northern loop Leave Grahamstown on the N2, heading toward Bisho and turn left after 4 miles, via the 330 acre **Ecca Nature Reserve**. **Fort Beaufort** is 43 miles on, beside the Kat River. It has a local history museum and a Martello Tower of 1847; the officers' mess now houses a small **Military History Museum** (Durban Street. *Open* Mon–Sat 9–5), including several paintings by local hero, Thomas Baines. Nearby **Lovedale College**

(1841) has educated many of South Africa's great nationalist leaders.

Take the A63 east for 13 miles to **Alice** and **Fort Hare** (see page 107).

The road south from here leads through the **Double Drift Game Reserve**, one of several small parks which together make up a formidable wildlife preserve. At the intersection with the N2, turn right.

Peddie, named after Colonel John Peddie, began life in 1835 as an earth fort. In May 1846 the town, defended by a small white contingent and friendly Mfengu tribesmen, was attacked by an army of 9,000 Xhosa warriors. From the mid-19th century a town developed around the fort (no longer extant). It is now a lively, largely black community, brimming with music, fruit and vegetable stalls, and carts selling soft drinks. For a tiny taste of real Africa, stop here. Grahamstown is 36 miles west on the N2.

Peddie is one of the liveliest and most African of the small towns near Grahamstown

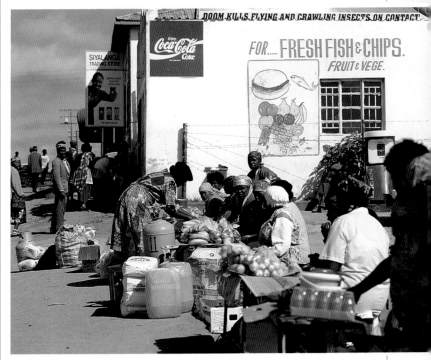

The Karoo

▶   Cradock

150 miles north of Port Elizabeth
Tourist Information, Civic Centre, tel: 0481-2383.
This quaint Karoo town in the upper Fish River valley was founded in 1813. The incongruous 1867 **Groote Kerk** (Stockenstroom Street) was modeled on London's St. Martin in the Fields. Local author Olive Schreiner (*The Story of an African Farm*, published 1883) lived here as a child; her house (Cross Street) is open to the public. The **Great Fish River Museum** has displays of local pioneer life. **Die Tuishuise Hotel** (see page 260) comprises nearly a whole street of impeccably restored and furnished houses.

▶▶▶   Graaff-Reinet

156 miles northeast of Port Elizabeth
Tourist Information Centre, Old Library, corner Church and Somerset Streets (tel: 0491-24248). All local museums: tel: 0491-23801. Open: Mon–Fri 9–12, 3–5; Sat 9–12, Sun 10–12, with minor variations
An architectural jewel, Graaff-Reinet is the fourth oldest town in South Africa, tucked into a horseshoe bend in the Sundays River, at the foot of the Sneeuberg Mountains. Founded in 1786 and named by the governor after himself and his wife, it remained a troubled frontier town for nearly a century. Much of its superb Cape Dutch architecture has been restored and the town is now the proud home of some 200 historic monuments (walking maps available).

The **Drosdty Hotel** (1806) was designed by Louis Thibault, but as the architect lived far away in Cape Town the local builders used their own initiative in, for instance,

Beyond the Valley of Desolation stretch the Plains of Kamdeboo

substituting a half-moon gable for the planned dome and bell tower. Behind the hotel, **Stretch's Court** is a complex of mid-19th-century Karoo cottages which were originally built for colored workers and emancipated slaves and are now used as hotel bedrooms. **Reinet House** (1 Parsonage Street), built in 1806–12 as the Dutch Reformed parsonage, is the local historical museum, while **Urquhart House**, next door, is furnished as a Victorian dwelling.

The early 19th-century **Old Residency** (Parsonage Street) is home to the Jan Felix Laegan Memorial Collection of firearms and the Middellandse Regimental Memorabilia. The **Hester Rupert Art Museum** in the 1821 Dutch Reformed Mission church has an excellent collection of contemporary South African art, and the **Old Library** (corner Church and Somerset Streets) contains Karoo fossils, San art, photography and costume. Other fine buildings include the Dutch Reformed church, the Town Hall, the John Rupert Little Theatre (Parsonage Street), built as the church of the London Mission Society, and the Graaff-Reinet Pharmacy (24 Caledon Street), preserved as a Victorian drugstore.

The Owl House, a strange concrete legacy of a tormented artist

To the south, the **Karoo Nature Reserve** (tel: 0491-23453) protects typical Karoo landscape and game, and has walks, hiking trails and an 8-mile drive up to the bizarrely twisted rock formations of the **Valley of Desolation**, with superb views across the Plains of Kamdeboo (particularly fine at sunset).

Thirty miles north of Graaff-Reinet, in the tiny Afrikaner village of **Nieu Bethesda**, is the **Owl House**▶▶ (*Open daily 9–5. Admission charge* inexpensive), home of artist Helen Martins (see panel), who decorated it inside and out with multicolored ground glass and "primitive" concrete statues of owls and camels, nativity scenes and mermaids. It is the epitome of imagination run riot—powerful, disturbing and exciting.

Mountain Zebra National Park   102B2

12 miles west of Cradock (tel: 0481-2427/2486)
Open: daily Oct–Apr 7AM–7PM, May–Sep 7:30–6.
Admission charge: moderate

This 16,150-acre sanctuary saved the distinctive Cape mountain zebra from extinction. There are over 200 here now, together with more than 200 bird species and many antelopes, including eland, blesbok, springbok, black wildebeest, red hartebeest, kudu, mountain reedbuck, grey rhebok, duiker, and steenbok, as well as the caracal (or lynx). There are driving routes, nature trails and day walks, while the Mountain Zebra Hiking Trail (16 miles) offers three days of hiking in the rugged Karoo landscape —the views alone are worth the effort.

Helen Martins
Brought up in the strict, isolated Dutch Reformed village of Nieu Bethesda, Helen Elizabeth Martins left home abruptly in 1915, married briefly and disastrously twice, returning to nurse her ailing parents in 1935. After their deaths, when she was about 50, she began to decorate the family home, the Owl House, covering every available surface (including chair seats) in boldly patterned ground glass, with huge sun motifs on the windows and ceilings. She also designed powerful naive concrete sculptures (actually made by colored helpers). She spent the rest of her life alone in dire poverty. In 1977, with her sight failing, she committed suicide by drinking caustic soda.

Cape architecture

■ **The most characteristic architecture of the Cape is the simple yet elegant style known as Cape Dutch which evolved over the 17th to early 19th centuries. Later, the British influence made itself felt in Georgian and Victorian buildings, some of the latter epitomizing imperial pomp.** ■

Above: wrought-iron gingerbread balconies in Swellendam. Below: elaborate 19th-century style in Grahamstown

Most early Cape Dutch buildings were farmhouses, simple rectangular structures with a wooden frame, wattle and clay infill, a steeply pitched thatched roof, central front door and symmetrically placed windows with heavy wooden shutters. The house often made up one side of a courtyard, with the barns, stables and servants' quarters on the other three. Most had white-washed walls and dark green paintwork (the only paint available to early settlers), a color scheme that became traditional. Inside, the hall led to just two rooms, one for sleeping, the other for living. Floors were of polished dung or mud inset with peach kernels. Furniture was basic: a solid box bed, dining table and chairs with woven gut seats. Few such houses survive in their original form outside museums such as those in Worcester (see page 77) and Pretoria (see page 163).

In time, as fortunes were made, the house began to sprout wings, becoming H-, T- or U-shaped, and acquired a small, raised veranda (*stoep*). The two largest rooms were in the front: the sitting room (*voerkammer*—front room) and the main bedroom. Behind, inter-connecting at first, but later leading off a central corridor, were a second public room (the *agterkammer*—back room), sometimes a study/office, further bedrooms and, right at the back, the kitchen. There were no indoor bathrooms until the mid-19th century. Before then, the lavatory was in an outhouse and the bath movable. These grander houses had ceilings and floors of highly polished yellowwood or stinkwood. The furniture became more varied and sophisticated, mirroring European fashion; the very wealthy imported everything.

It was the arrival of the gable that signaled the coming of age of Cape Dutch design. Based on the intricate gables fashionable in 17th- and 18th-century Holland, the typical Cape house had one large gable over the front door. Embellished with curved and curled edges, space for statues, the date of construction or the arms of the family, these provided an element of chic and individuality, elevating the house from cottage to mansion. The master archi-

Cape architecture

tect was Louis Thibault; the master sculptor, Anton Anreith. The Cape winelands (see pages 86–9) are littered with these beautiful houses, a number still owned by the original family and with some original furnishings.

By the end of the 18th century, design was shifting away from the rectangular farm to the square, two-story town house of Georgian England, with symmetrically positioned windows, a triangular pediment, and flat roof. The façade became more intricate, with pastel colors, pilasters and plaster garlands. Inside, traditional white walls gave way to elegantly painted *trompe l'oeil* columns and urns. Not many of these houses have survived urban progress, but there are a few outstanding examples such as the Koopmans de Wet House (see page 56) in Cape Town. In the country towns they became the model for the tiny square-built Karoo-style cottages, flat-roofed and with a small fanlight above the door, the interior quartered into four connecting rooms: sitting room, kitchen and two bedrooms. Many fine examples still survive in Karoo towns like Graaff-Reinet (see page 112) and even in the Bo-Kaap quarter of Cape Town (see page 54).

The last great shift before the modern era came in the mid- to late-19th century with the advent of neo-Gothic churches, the large-scale work of South Africa's first major architect, Sir Herbert Baker, and the prevalence of Victorian houses with steeply pitched roofs (many only pitched in front as the stunted trees did not provide sufficiently long timbers) and corrugated iron verandas sporting elaborate gingerbread trim.

Top: elegance in Graaff-Reinet.
Above: a typical simple rectangular house with a curved gable, in Tulbagh

Port Elizabeth and Environs

Port Elizabeth lies 470 miles east of Cape Town. A garrison was stationed here in 1799, but the real settlement came in 1820 with a large contingent of British immigrants. The recently widowed Acting Governor, Sir Rufane Donkin, named the port after his beloved wife. Port Elizabeth (or PE) is now South Africa's third largest port and fifth largest city. A massive redevelopment of the inner-city waterfront is planned. Meanwhile, there are several excellent beaches in the area, including King's (from the harbor to Humewood) and Humewood itself.

The main **Port Elizabeth Museum** (Beach Road, Humewood, tel: 041-561 051. *Open* daily 9–1, 2–5. *Admission charge* moderate) has several distinct sections. The museum itself has an interesting small collection of 18th- and 19th-century South African art, plus history, costume and marine exhibits. Far more fun, however, are the living satellites—a **Snake Park**, **Tropical House**, and **Oceanarium**. Here you see tropical vegetation dripping with slithering snakes, exotic birds, over 40 species of fish, including sharks, and—stars of the show—jackass penguins, bottlenose dolphins, and Cape fur seals. Dolphin and seal performances take place at 11 and 3 daily.

Elsewhere, the **Castle Hill Historical Museum** (7 Castle Hill, tel: 041-522 515. *Open* Sun–Mon 2–5, Tue–Sat 10–1, 2–5. *Admission charge* inexpensive) displays a fine collection of Cape furniture in PE's oldest surviving house, a former parsonage; the **King George VI Art Gallery** (Park Drive, tel: 041-561 030. *Open* Mon–Fri 8:30–5, Sat 8:30–4:30, Sun 2–4:30. *Admission charge*) has a collection of 19th- and 20th-century British and

A few early buildings have survived the redevelopment of bustling Port Elizabeth

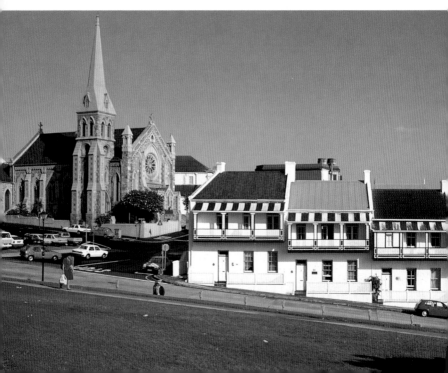

South African fine art, and the **Motor Museum** (Mowbray Street, Newton Park, tel: 041-351 300) is a small private collection of vintage and classic cars, dating back to 1901. **Tourist Information**, Donkin Lighthouse, Donkin Reserve (tel: 041-521 315); Satour, 23 Donkin Street (tel: 041-557 761).

▶▶ Addo Elephant National Park 102B1

45 miles north of Port Elizabeth (tel: 0426-400 556)
Enormous herds of elephants once roamed across the Eastern Cape, their migration routes leading right down the coast, from Natal to the Cape Peninsula. An animal without other predators, the elephant met its match in man, as towns cut across the ancient paths, forests were felled indiscriminately, the open grassland was planted with crops and the elephants themselves were shot—for sport and ivory, and as a pest. By 1931, the Eastern Cape was down to its last 11 elephants.

This 28,956-acre reserve was created solely to protect the tiny herd along with the last surviving Cape buffalo. Today, the population has risen to around 170 elephant, together with numerous other species including eland, kudu, red hartebeest, bushbuck, and Cape buffalo, 21 endangered Kenyan black rhino, and 185 species of bird. There are two walking trails, a rest camp, a restaurant and a store.

Jeffreys Bay 102A1

About 44 miles west of Port Elizabeth
Tourist Information, Oosterland Street
(tel: 0423-932 588)
Jeffreys Bay began as a trading store in 1849, named after one of the partners, Joseph Avent Jeffrey. The bay is an attractive area of meandering waterways and canals on the Kromme River estuary; it marks the end of the Garden Route. There are excellent beaches near here, with good swimming and internationally renowned surf. The region is also rich in shells, cataloged in the **Charlotte Kritzinger Shell Museum** (C. J. Langhoven Library, Diaz Road. *Open* Mon, Tue, Thu, Fri 9–1, 2–5, Wed 9–1, 3–6, Sat 9–12). Nearby is **Humansdorp** (54 miles west of PE. Tourist Information in the Municipal Parking Area, Bureau Street, tel: 0423-51361) which has a local history **museum** (Bureau Street, tel: 0423-910 625) as well as a restored watermill; you can even tour the local taxidermist's premises.

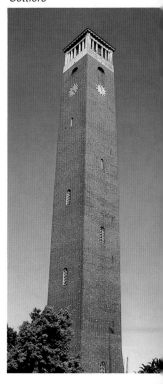

The Campanile, PE's memorial to the 1820 Settlers

Monumental glories
A walking guide to historic PE is available from the tourist office. Look for the original Fort Frederick (Belmont Terrace), which was built in 1799 and never saw a shot fired in anger; the 170-foot (204-step) Campanile Clock Tower (harbor entrance) with a carillon of 23 bells, built as a memorial to the 1820 settlers; the Horse Memorial (corner of Cape and Russell Roads), erected in honor of all the horses that died in the Anglo-Boer wars; and Sir Rufane Donkin's stone pyramid, erected in memory of his beloved Elizabeth, next to the Donkin Lighthouse.

Shamwari has been completely restocked with game

Rhino horn
The name rhinoceros comes from the Greek words *rhis* (nose) and *keras* (horn). The horns have no bony core but are made of heavily compacted fibers. They grow continuously but are restricted by wear and tear to about 2 feet (front horn) and 1 foot (rear horn). They contain no magical aphrodisiac properties, and are in fact made of exactly the same substance as human fingernails. This is a mild analgesic—which may be why we chew our nails in times of stress.

► **Shamwari Game Reserve**　102B1

45 miles east of Port Elizabeth, off the N2 (tel: 042-851 1196). The park runs a special train from Johannesburg. Open: only to overnight guests, with guided game drives (see page 260). Admission charge: moderate

Shamwari (the name means "friend") is a private game park covering some 34,600 acres, a mix of former farmland (20 per cent) and hunting preserve (80 per cent). The very landscape here was endangered; its five ecosystems include dense, low-growing valley bushveld—a mix of acacia scrub, milkwood and succulents—destroyed by sheep and goats, but thriving under elephant and rhino. Only small animals such as mongoose remained. More than 26 species, from black and white rhino, elephant and lion to the dung beetle and oxpecker have been reintroduced, and the reserve is carefully rebuilding an indigenous ecology, conducting scientific research and running breeding programs for rare and endangered species.

Tsitsikamma Forest National Park, see page 101.

Uitenhage　102B1

24 miles north of Port Elizabeth
Tourist Information, Sports Centre, Park Lane (tel: 041-992 4258)

Uitenhage began as a wool center but now has several car companies. Among a number of fine historic buildings, the **Old Drostdy Museum** (tel: 041-992 2063) includes a Volkswagen Motor museum alongside the local history and Africana collections, while the **Old Station** (tel: 041-922 8210. *Open* Mon–Fri 10–1, 2–5, Sat 10–12:30, Sun 2–5) is a perfectly preserved Victorian setting for a small railway museum. **Cuyler Manor Cultural Museum** (3 miles out of town on the PE road; tel: 041-922 0372. *Open* Mon–Fri 10–1, 2–5, Sun 2–5) has demonstrations of traditional farming, a mohair farm, and an annual prickly pear festival. The **Van Stadens Wildflower Reserve** (tel: 041-955 5649) is a 922-acre reserve and bird sanctuary on the eastern rim of the Van Stadens River gorge.

The Wild Coast

The great Kei River once marked the border of the Xhosa kingdom and later of the supposedly independent Transkei homeland. The region is markedly different from its neighbors; the endless ribbon of vacation homes comes to an abrupt halt and the few towns are quite obviously poorer. The only tourism here for many years took the form of getaway breaks on the Wild Coast and gambling weekends in the local casinos. And even this small number of visitors began to trail off as local feelings hardened into a strong antiwhite stance that regularly threatened violence.

These days, with Transkei reintegrated into South Africa, the area has opened up again, but the towns, particularly the capital Umtata, are still not always friendly and you do have to be careful. On the whole, there are few reasons for tourists to visit the towns. Instead, glory in the virgin hardwood forests, the flower-strewn meadows and, above all, the sea.

The Transkei's very poverty and isolation have produced unexpected benefits by protecting the local ecology from development. Here, if briefly, is a totally pristine stretch of magnificent coast, with gentle grasslands rolling down to wave-smashed cliffs, dunes as big as mountains, and snakelike river estuaries glistening in the afternoon sun. Dolphins play in the surf around the rusting hulks of long-wrecked ships and kingfishers dart, peacock-bright, through the twisted mangrove swamps. Occasional dusty potholed roads lead down to small, remote, friendly resort hotels, where you can wallow at ease, catch your own dinner, or enjoy sybaritic mounds of freshly caught oysters and lobster, crab and periwinkle, yellowtail and kingfish, just some of the 800-odd species found in these clear waters.

A hiking trail runs the full length of the Wild Coast. It takes about 14 days to walk the whole thing, but you can do a shorter segment (for information and permits, contact The Department of Agriculture and Forestry, P Bag X5002, Umtata 5100).

Prophecy of doom
In 1856 a young Xhosa medium named Nongqawuse had a prophetic vision while staring into a pool at the Qolora River mouth. In the vision the ancestors promised that if the Xhosa would destroy all their cattle and crops they would drive away the white men and provide the Xhosa with new and better animals and grain. The elders gathered, believed her, and the order went out. The cattle were driven into the sea and the granaries and fields set alight. The gleeful British forcibly shut the missionaries' aid stations, and some 25,000 people are thought to have died in the ensuing famine.

119

The Wild Coast car ferry across Kei River mouth

■ The Xhosa, Zulu and Ndebele—the latter are actually a breakaway Zulu clan—are all Nguni, a closely related cultural group whose languages are sufficiently similar for people to understand each other, albeit with some difficulty. They are spread across the Eastern Cape, KwaZulu-Natal, the borders of Northern Province and Mpumalanga. ■

The three cultures have a great deal in common. By tradition, all are pastoralist, the older boys herding cattle (which count as wealth), the younger boys looking after the goats, and the women growing maize, vegetables, and some fruit on small farms. In their youth, the men were warriors, becoming elders (forming the local council) when mature. These days, however, the old structure has all but vanished. Most men work away in the mines or factories, while the women rear the children, either separately in the villages or—increasingly—in the townships.

People The Xhosa come from the hills and coast of the Eastern Cape, around the area separated off under apartheid as the Transkei and Ciskei (see page 104). The many clans of the Zulu nation, unified under Shaka in the early 19th century (see page 30), live mainly in KwaZulu-Natal. The Ndebele, who fled north away from Shaka, live on the borders of the Northern Province and Mpumalanga, although a large number went farther still, crossing the Limpopo River into what is now Zimbabwe.

Religion The traditional religion is monotheistic, with one all-important god, who looks after the big things in life, leaving smaller tasks to an army of ancestors. Because of this, people revere and pray to their ancestors in much the way Catholics pray to the saints. Few Nguni see any real conflict with Christianity and many happily

A young Zulu dancer dressed for a performance

Three Ndebele women. The women are left to run their villages while the men work in cities or mines

The Nguni

practice both religions simultaneously. They still consult the *sangomas* (diviners) who act as mediums, interpreting the wishes of the ancestors, and the *nyangas* (traditional herbal doctors)—although they may try the better-safe-than-sorry approach by visiting a Western hospital too. There is still a belief in the evil influence of witchcraft. The only real difference made by the church has been in cutting down to some extent the number of wives each man takes in a polygamous culture.

Traditional life The life cycle is carefully marked as people progress from childhood to youth, marriage, and so on. Traditionally, female dress changes at each stage, while teenage boys are circumcized before they start training for adulthood. A boy must pay *lobolo* to the family of the girl he wishes to marry; this used to be in cattle, but today is more usually cash. Her parents must provide a dowry of useful household objects and clothes. Be it a wedding, the eve of battle or just a night out with the boys, every opportunity is taken to dance—energetically and competitively, with harmonizing song and rhythmic drums.

Decoration Western dress is becoming the norm, so that almost the only time you see the often magnificent traditional costume is during rituals and tourist pageants. Most people are very fond of personal adornment and bright color. All the Nguni used animal skins and beads of ostrich shell, seashells and seeds until multicolored glass beads were introduced by the early 19th-century missionaries. These have now become an integral part of the culture, used not only for decoration, but as a clearly understood language. Illiterate Zulu girls write love letters to their boyfriends in beads, and a woman's exact status, clan and home village can be told from the patterning of her headband and necklaces. The Ndebele took the love of adornment one stage further, the women creating jazzy geometric patterns on both inner and outer walls of their houses, at first in natural earth colors, but later, after they were introduced to acrylics, in a dazzling array of blues and greens, pinks and purples. Sadly this too seems to be dying out, although Ndebele designs are very popular on plant pots and souvenirs.

Beer
Beer, which is brewed by the women, has ritual and social connotations. Maize and sorghum are wrapped in wet sacks until they sprout, dried in the sun, ground into flour, boiled to a thin porridge, then strained through a woven grass tube and left to ferment, a process that takes up to 10 days. The sediment is given to the ancestors. Traditionally the beer is drunk from a communal clay or woven pot. A bowl placed face-down as a lid shows there is beer available; if it is faceup, visitors know that drinks are off!

Xhosa people still sometimes whiten their faces in the traditional way

Gemsbok silhouetted against the desert sunset in the Kalahari Gemsbok National Park

The Free State, Northern Cape and Northwest Province In the center of South Africa, on the high plains of the Free State, mile upon mile of maize and wheat coat the endless prairies, punctuated by nothing but an occasional windmill or isolated farmhouse. To the north and west is an enormous expanse of almost empty semi-desert stretching from the Karoo through the rust-red dunes of the Kalahari to merge with the even more terrible Namib desert, one of the thirstiest places on Earth. Together, they make up a truly massive area of windblown sand extending from the Northern Cape to southern Zaire—the largest continuous stretch of sand in the world. Like the Sahara, the desert is expanding.

It is a harsh, bleak, wonderful environment of strange, wind-carved rock, red-gold sand and weird succulents and stone plants. Thousands of shallow round or oval pans, ranging in size from a few hundred yards to several square miles, trap tiny amounts of rain and dew in their

FREE STATE, NORTHERN CAPE AND NORTHWEST PROVINCE

hard, gray clay. These lifesaving water holes support a surprising variety of life, from small reptiles to dramatically beautiful, drought-hardened antelope such as gemsbok and springbok. Where rivers or underground water feed the grass, there are some of Africa's largest remaining wildlife sanctuaries, such as the remote Kalahari Gemsbok National Park. Even people manage to survive here, from the last few desert-wise San (see page 132) to doughty Afrikaner farmers who bleed water drop by drop from boreholes deep underground to support scattered herds of cattle and game.

Game farming is increasingly popular in such difficult terrain. The squeamish should check before visiting them, however, as a staggeringly long list of people over all three provinces are eager to help you blast your animal of choice. Many of the private reserves are stocked specifically for hunting, and quite a few small towns list the local taxidermist as an attraction. The good news is

Orania

This small upper Karoo town began life in 1967 as a camp for workers on the Orange River Development Project. Since 1991 it has been owned by a private company, Vluytjieskraal Aandeleblok Bpk, in which each new property owner becomes a shareholder. Its most famous inhabitant is Betsy Verwoerd, widow of the former president and architect of apartheid; the leader of the project is her son-in-law, Professor Carel Boshoff. The community aims to become the focus of the *volkstad,* a new, whites-only homeland for the die-hard Afrikaner right. Nonwhites are only allowed in to make deliveries. Curious foreigners are not welcome.

The Griqua

The Griqua (the name is a simplification of "Xurikwa") originated in the Piketberg area, Khoikhoi people who were enslaved and became a subcaste of mixed-blood people. In the early 19th century some of them sought freedom, wandering north as herders and cattle raiders and calling themselves Bastaards. A freed slave, Adam Kok, former cook to the Governors of the Cape, was their leader. They settled around Klaarwater, where they drew in other displaced people of all races, from fragmented Tswana clans to army deserters. The surrounding area (now Griqualand West in the Northern Cape) succeeded in remaining independent until the 1860s, when diamonds were discovered in the area.

Right: the flowers of Crassula Marnierana *bloom in the desert*

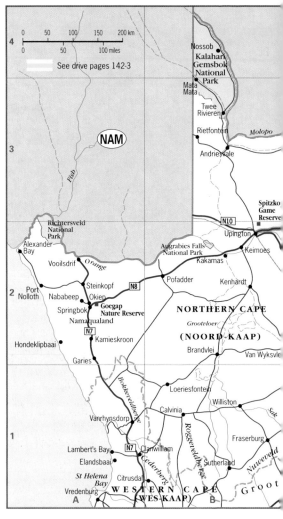

that it is expensive, carefully controlled, and carried out under strict supervision. Licenses for big-game hunting are only handed out when culling is strictly necessary.

The thread that binds—and feeds—the region is South Africa's largest river, the Orange (Gariep) River. It rises at Maluti in the Lesotho Drakensberg, flowing northwest for 1,400 feet to meet the Atlantic coast at Alexander Bay. The river basin covers 234,247 square miles (47 per cent of South Africa) and drains 22 per cent of all water in South Africa. The country's second largest river, the Vaal, is a tributary. The Orange River Development Project, founded in 1963 to provide hydroelectric power and irrigation, includes long tunnels and canals and two massive dams, the Gariep (Hendrik Verwoerd) and the Vanderkloof (P. K. Le Roux). From the central prairies, the river flows through the desert in a narrow strip of emerald green. The Orange River Valley is one of the major wine areas of South Africa, and also produces table grapes, sultanas, and much other fruit.

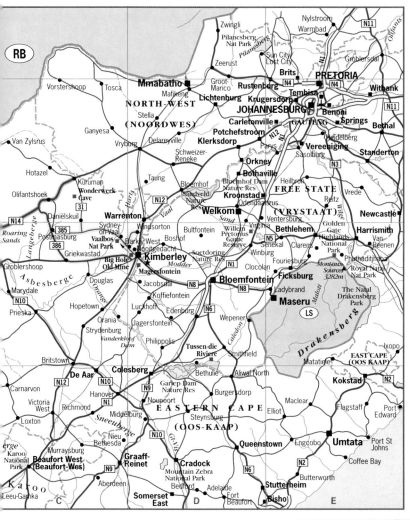

The real money, however, comes from underground. Diamonds were discovered here in 1869 and vast fortunes were made in the Kimberley area. There are still many working diamond mines in the region as well as increasing undersea harvesting of old river gravel. In April 1938, a borehole sunk on St. Helena Farm, near Welkom, drove through the lava walls of a vast underground treasure trove. Gold was found in quantities that staggered the world. By 1946, following the discovery of fabulous deposits on the farm named Geduld, at Odendaalsrus, it seemed that the Free State was the new El Dorado. The Free State goldfields currently produce more than a third of the country's output; the names of its mines daily echo around international stock exchanges, and its goldfields rival those of the Witwatersrand as the richest in the world. Local resources also include many other valuable minerals, from manganese and copper to uranium.

By appointment
Several of the most
magnificent buildings in
the President Brand
Conservation Area may be
visited by appointment
only. They include: the City
Hall (tel: 051-405 8911)
designed in 1934 by Sir
Gordon Leith, and now
housing the Tourist
Information Centre; the
twin-spired 1880
Tweetoringkerk (Charles
Street, tel: 051-430 4274);
the Supreme Court (corner
President Brand and
Fontein Streets, tel: 051-
447 8837); the 1929 Appeal
Court (corner President
Brand and Charles Streets,
tel: 051-447 2631); and the
Fourth Raadsaal (corner
President Brand and
Charles Streets, tel: 051-
447 8898), built in 1893,
with a magnificent Greek
Revival Council Chamber.

Free State

▶   **Bloemfontein**   125D2

247 miles south of Johannesburg
City Tourist Information, City Hall, Charles Street (tel:
051-405 8489). Open: Mon–Fri 8–4:15, Sat 8–12. Satour,
Sanlam Parkade, Charles Street (tel: 051-447 1362)
Some say Bloemfontein (Fountain of Flowers) was
named after a local Griqua (see page 124) leader, Jan
Bloem, others that it came from the flower garden
planted round the perennial spring by the first settler,
Johannes Brits. The city itself was founded by Major H. D.
Warden, British resident of the area between the
Orange and Vaal rivers. Following the Union in 1910,
Bloemfontein became—and remains—the judicial capital
of South Africa, an oddly provincial town with numerous
imposing public buildings and museums.

Conservation Area museums Many of the most
impressive buildings, clustered around President Brand
Street (walking tour maps available) now contain museums. The thatched-roofed, dung-floored **First Raadsaal**
(95 St. George Street, tel: 051-447 9609. *Open* Mon–Fri
10:15–3, Sat 8:30–1, 1:30–5, Sun 2–5. *Admission charge*
inexpensive) was built in 1848 as the first council chamber and school. It contains a small museum of the
Republic with a collection of carriages and wagons.
Highlights of the **National Museum** (corner Charles and
Aliwal Streets, tel: 051-447 9609. *Open* Mon–Sat 8–5,
Sun 1–6. *Admission charge* inexpensive) are a re-created
19th-century street and an extensive archaeological and
fossil collection, including the Florisbad skull, South
Africa's earliest example of *Homo sapiens*. The Old
Government Building (1908) is now home to the **National
Afrikaans Literary (Letterkundige) Museum** (corner
President Brand and Maitland Streets, tel: 051-405 4911.
Open Mon–Fri 8–12:15, 1–4, Sat 9–12. *Admission free*).
The opulent, Scottish baronial **Old Presidency** (corner
President Brand and St. George Streets, tel: 051-448
0949. *Open* Tue–Fri 10–12, 1–4, Sat–Sun 2–5. *Admission
free*) was built in 1885 on the site of the original Bloem
Fonteyn farm, as official residence of the presidents of
the Free State Republic.

*The First Raadsaal
Museum has also
done duty as a coun-
cil chamber, school
and community hall*

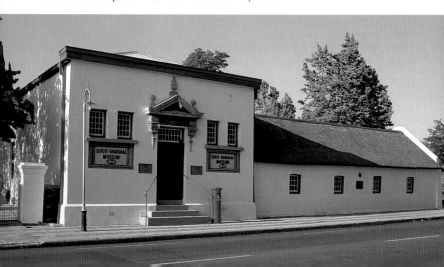

Emily Hobhouse
A staunch supporter of Afrikaner independence, Emily Hobhouse spent much of her life trying to conciliate between the British and Boers. In 1900, she began to raise money to alleviate the suffering in Boer concentration camps, eventually whipping up enough support to help improve conditions and force a settlement. After the war, she established a series of 26 spinning and weaving schools for Boer girls. Regarded as a local heroine, she is buried at the foot of the Women's Memorial. She never visited any black camps.

Left: tiled depiction of the Battle of Colenso. Below: memorial to Boer victims of the concentration camps. Both are in the Boer War Museum, Bloemfontein

Other museums Colonial **Freshford House** (31 Kellner Street, tel: 051-447 9609, ext 240. *Open* Mon–Fri 10–1, Sat–Sun 2–5. *Admission charge* inexpensive) is full of brass, stained glass and Victoriana. The **Oliewnhuis Art Gallery** (Harry Smith Street, tel: 051-447 9609. *Open* Mon–Fri 8–5, Sat 10–5, Sun 1–5:30. *Admission free*) was a neo-Cape Dutch homestead. **Queen's Fort** (Church Street, tel: 051-447 5478. *Open* Mon–Fri 8–4. *Admission free*), built in 1848, houses a small military museum.

The excellent **National Women's Memorial and War Museum**►► (Monument Road, tel: 051-447 3447. *Open* Mon–Fri 9–4:30, Sat 9–5, Sun 2–5. Guided tours by appointment. *Admission charge* inexpensive) gives a compelling (if one-sided) account of the Anglo-Boer War, with horrific details of prisoner-of-war and concentration camps (see page 39). In the grounds is a memorial to the 26,370 Afrikaner women and children who died in them.

Gardens Of Bloemfontein's gardens the finest are the lush 112-acre **National Botanical Garden**► (Rayton Road, tel: 051-431 3530. *Open* daily 8–6. *Admission charge* inexpensive) and rose-filled **King's Park**. The **Zoo** (King's Way, tel: 051-405 8483. *Open* daily, 8–6 in summer, 8–5 in winter. *Admission charge* moderate) is famous for its "liger" (a lion-tiger cross) and primates. Naval Hill includes the 476-acre **Franklin Game Reserve** (Union Avenue, tel: 051-405 8786. *Open* daily 8–5. *Admission free*). Nearby, in Hamilton Park, is the **Orchid House**► (Union Avenue, tel: 051-405 8124. *Open* Mon–Fri 10–4, Sat–Sun 10–5. *Admission free*).

Eastern Highlands

The Eastern Highlands are an area of great natural beauty and drama, where cold winters frequently blanket the higher reaches of the Maloti Mountains and the Drakensberg in snow. Traces remain of the various peoples who have lived here—in the San rock paintings, the scattered Sotho, Bakwena and Balokwa villages, and the tidy sandstone towns and churches of the Boers and British. For tourists, however, this area is all about the great outdoors, with a whirl of activities from bird-watching and game viewing to horseback riding, mountain biking, hiking and climbing, water sports and golf.

Several charming small towns with fine Victorian buildings of local sandstone make up the Highlands Route. Prosperous **Harrismith** (Tourist Information, Andries Pretorius Street, tel: 05861-23525) was founded in 1849. Nearby are the 2,471-acre **Mount Everest Game Reserve** and the 44,480-acre **Sterkfontein Dam Nature Reserve** (tel: 05861-23520. *Open* daily 6–10. *Admission charge* inexpensive) surrounding a lake. Stunningly situated beneath the Titanic, a huge ship-shape wedge of rock, **Clarens** (Tourist Information, 171 Main Street, tel: 058-256 1411) is a delightful village, founded in 1912 and named after the Swiss town where President Kruger died. The great local attraction is **Cinderella's Castle** (Naauport Street), a full-size fantasy lovingly constructed out of 55,000 empty beer bottles. It has various fairy-tale tableaux and, inevitably, a curio shop.

Bethlehem (Tourist Information, Civic Centre, Muller Street, tel: 058 303-5732) has a small local history museum, a particularly fine collection of Victorian buildings and several lakes nearby. **Fouriesburg** (Tourist Information, Fouriesburg Hotel, tel: 058-223 0207) was founded in 1892. Surrounded by flat-topped sandstone hillocks, many of them pierced by caves, it was a Boer stronghold in the Anglo-Boer War. An Asparagus Festival takes place here in September.

Ficksburg (Tourist Information, Town Hall, tel: 05192-2122) on the Caledon River border with Lesotho, began life in 1867 as a bulwark between disputed Boer and Sotho territory. The **General J. J. Fick Museum** (Town Square) sheds light on local history and the customs and life of the Sotho people. Caves in the nearby Imperani Mountains are adorned with San rock art, and the **Hoekfontein Game Ranch** (8 miles from town, off the R26 to Fouriesburg; tel: 05192-3915) is home to white rhino and hippo and offers ox-wagon rides. The district around the town produces 90 per cent of the cherries grown in South Africa, which it celebrates with a Cherry Festival held each November.

Sotho houses in Ficksburg

Gariep Dam 125D1

About 100 miles south of Bloemfontein (tel: 052 171-26)
The biggest stretch of inland water in South Africa lies behind this vast dam on the Orange and Caledon Rivers. The reservoir covers an area of 144 square miles when full and provides water for irrigation and hydroelectric power. The dam wall (1972) is 2,175 feet long and 297 feet high. Around the shores are huge expanses of grassland and Karoo vegetation dotted with rocky outcrops and massive boulders, most of it protected by the 27,768-acre **Gariep Nature Reserve** (tel: 052 172-26/108) and the 54,364-acre **Tussen-die-Riviere** (tel: 051 762-2803), which is a normal sanctuary in winter and hunting preserve in summer. Aasvoelkop, near the eastern boundary, preserves some San rock paintings. Both reserves offer accommodations, sailing, fishing and swimming.

The **Pellissier House Museum**, in nearby **Bethulie** (Tourist Information, tel: 051 762-2) is thought to be the oldest settler structure north of the Orange River.

▶▶ Golden Gate Highlands National Park 125E2

Approximately 224 miles south of Johannesburg and 186 miles northeast of Bloemfontein (tel: 058-256 1471)
In the upper valley of the Little Caledon River, in the foothills of the spectacular Maloti Mountains of Lesotho, this 28,665-acre reserve preserves a strange landscape of brilliant yellow, orange and red sandstone cliffs, high outcrops and caves, pummeled into bizarre shapes by water. Early San hunters were driven out of this area by the Sotho, who settled on the secure heights of the sandstone outcrop "fortresses." The reserve harbors a wide variety of animals and birds, including red hartebeest, black wildebeest, black eagles, and blue cranes. There are opportunities for hiking, trout fishing, and riding.

Highly colored sandstone cliffs in the Golden Gate National Park

The Berg Marathon
During the Anglo-Boer War, a British major, John Belcher, insulted the citizens of Harrismith by referring to "their" mountain, Platberg (5,700 feet.), as "that little hill of yours." They bet that he would not be able to reach the summit in 60 minutes. He took them on, won easily, and then donated a trophy for an annual race. The course consists of a 3-mile run, climbing 1,440 feet. to the top, followed by a run along the summit and down an old bridle path back to the town.

EASTERN HIGHLANDS

Jagersfontein   125D2

68 miles southwest of Bloemfontein
Tourist Information, Municipality (tel: 051 732-3)
A Victorian mining town, Jagersfontein has a number of attractive buildings, including four Herbert Baker specials. The main reason to come here is the **Mining Village**, an open-air museum on the rim of the local "Big Hole," nearly 1,640 feet in diameter and 1,640 feet deep. The 971-carat Excelsior diamond was discovered here in 1883.

▶   Philippolis   125D2

Tourist Information, tel: 051-773 0008
Philippolis is an oasis of white stucco and deep green trees in the immense, dry plain. Dating from 1823, it is the oldest town in the Free State, founded as a mission station for the Griqua people (see page 124). It has some interesting Karoo architecture, including a splendid Dutch Reformed church, Adam Kok's home (Voortrekker Street), his *kraal* (Justisie Street), and his *kruithuis* (arsenal) on a hill west of town. Emily Hobhouse (see page 127) established the first of her spinning and weaving schools here after the Anglo-Boer War. The **Transgariep Museum** covers all the town's fascinating history, and each April brings out its distilling kettle for a *witblitz* (moonshine) festival.

▶   Phuthaditjhaba   125E2

Previously known as Witsieshoek, **Phuthaditjhaba**, sprawling across the hills, was the capital of Qwa Qwa, the former homeland of the Bakwena and Balokwa tribes. It contains the Balokwa Museum covering local tribal history.

The **Qwa Qwa National Park** (tel: 058-713 4191) is a magnificent area of 52,000 acres crossed by richly green valleys and sparkling streams interspersed with gnarled sandstone cliffs. Within it is the **Basotho Cultural Village** (tel: 058-721 0300. *Open* daily—tours 10:30 and 2:30. *Admission charge* moderate). Though smacking slightly of the theme park, the village is fascinating, with a permanent exhibition of Sotho huts, from beehive-style thatch to brightly geometric clay constructions. There are demonstrations of Southern Sotho lifestyle, basketry, pottery, cooking and dance, as well as a cultural history museum and a restaurant.

Sandveld Nature Reserve   125D3

6 miles northwest of Bloemfontein; 6 miles from Bloemhof on the R34 (tel: 01802-31701)
Stretching down to the horseshoe-shape Bloemhof Dam, this is a 98,844-acre wonderland of Kalahari thornveld, with a 148-mile shoreline, softened by sandy beaches and shaded by giant camelthorn trees. White-backed vultures build huge, unruly nests in the high branches; below scuttle small mammals like aardwolf and antbears, porcupines and springhare. Gemsbok, wildebeest, white rhino, giraffe, and kudu also thrive here.

Welkom   125D3

Tourist Information, Stateway (tel: 057-352 9244)
Planned as a garden city, this industrial giant is a minescape of machinery, dumps, reduction works and

belching factories. Water pumped from the mines has collected as shallow pans which attract prolific bird life including flamingos. There is a museum (Tulbagh Street), but it is only worth coming here if you want an underground tour of a gold mine (ask at the tourist office).

Willem Pretorius Game Reserve   125D2

93 miles northeast of Bloemfontein off the N1 (the turnoff is between Winburg and Ventersdorp). (Tel: 05777-4003)
The Sand River and Allemanskraal Dam divide this 29,653-acre park into a densely covered, hilly northern section, which provides a perfect habitat for baboons, bushbuck, kudu, and duiker, and open grasslands to the south, teeming with springbok, wildebeest, blesbok, eland, impala, and zebra. White rhino and buffalo move freely through the park. On the summit of Beckersberg are a restored prehistoric settlement of dry-stone-walled huts and *kraals* belonging to the now-vanished Leghoya people, and a small site museum.

At nearby **Senekal** (Tourist Information, tel: 05848-2142) are the remains of a 250,000-year-old petrified forest. **Winburg** (Tourist Information, tel: 05242-3) is a Voortrekker town with a local history museum.

Zebra, springbok and wildebeest drinking

■ **Small, sharp-featured people, the San were dubbed "Bushmen" by the Dutch because of their extraordinary knowledge of and affinity with nature. Nomadic hunter-gatherers, they are thought to be the earliest aboriginal inhabitants of southern Africa, their lifestyle relatively little changed for some 40,000 years.** ■

The San roamed the animal-rich central plains, and left archaeological evidence of their passing—paintings and engravings—in lush, mountainous areas with plentiful water, such as the Drakensberg. Some of the most recent paintings depict soldiers on horseback wearing red and blue tunics, proving that the last of the San did not leave the area until after the arrival of the Europeans in the mid-19th century.

End of an era Most were long gone by then, however, pushed into the harsher fringes of the continent by the Nguni, who began to arrive around AD500. When the Voortrekkers began to compete—often violently—for the same water sources, many of the remaining San were killed, while some were taken prisoner and turned into servants and farm laborers. Yet others died of epidemic European diseases such as smallpox and even flu, to which they had no immunity. Most mingled with the Khoikhoi, Malays and incoming Nguni, and have slowly been absorbed into the general "colored" population. By the early 19th century, their independent lifestyle and tribal identity had all but disappeared. Today, the last few surviving groups skilfully scratch out a meager existence from the Kalahari sands. There are claimed to be some 60,000 San left across South Africa, Namibia, and Botswana, but relatively few are pure blood and living a traditional life.

Traditional life San huts consist of a domed framework of branches, covered in grass and reeds; in the dry season, when shade is more important than a waterproof covering, partly open shelters are made from reed mats bent over a frame. Always on the move, the San have few material possessions. Both men and women traditionally wear only a small "skirt" with front and back aprons of animal skin, hung from a beaded belt; these days it is as likely to be a loincloth or a pair of swimming trunks, while the

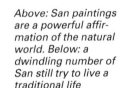

Above: San paintings are a powerful affirmation of the natural world. Below: a dwindling number of San still try to live a traditional life

San villagers at Kagga Kamma, near Ceres

women often feel more comfortable in Western dress when strangers are around. Both sexes wear elaborate beaded headdresses, necklaces, bracelets and anklets. Until the arrival of beads, these decorations would have been made of ostrich eggshell and seeds.

Tortoise shells are used as dishes; with one end filled in and the other corked, they also serve as containers and snuffboxes. Ostrich eggshells and dried springbok pouches are used as water containers, both for rations when on the move and for storage in the long dry season. The San have perfected a technique of skinning the animal without splitting the skin, then simply tying knots in the legs and head hole to make a watertight container.

The men hunt in groups, with bows and poison-tipped arrows, wooden clubs and spears. They also set snares, and track bee eaters in search of their favorite luxury—honey. The gathering, which accounts for most daily food, is done by the women, who search the veld for roots and tubers, berries and fruit. In the dry season, fruit such as melons are a vital source of liquid. Cooking was traditionally done in clay pots, although today the pan may well be an old tin can.

San art Above all, the San are famous for their art, which adorns many caves, overhangs or even particularly smooth slabs of rock, depicting local animals, the thrill of the hunt or a dance. The painters used natural dyes such as carbon, iron oxide or yellow ocher mixed with blood or animal fat; other pictures are engraved into the surface of the stone. The shapes are alive with movement and obviously executed with love.

Northern Cape

▶▶ Augrabies Falls   124B2

75 miles west of Upington (tel: 054-451 0050)
Open: Apr–Sep 6:30–10; Oct–Mar 6–10

The Khoikhoi called it *Aukoerebi* ("Place of Great Noise")
after the thunder of the Gariep River as it crashes foaming
down five flights of granite falls (totaling 184 feet) into a
magnificent 11-mile canyon. The Augrabies Falls are the
fifth largest in the world, made all the more dramatic by
the massive surrounding boulders and parched desert
landscape. The three-day Klipspringer Hiking Trail runs
along the canyon through the 38,092-acre **Augrabies
Falls National Park**, full of weird rock formations and
strange desert vegetation such as the quiver trees whose
lightweight branches were hollowed by the San to hold
their arrows. There are spectacular views along the rim
and some game, including rhino.

*The Augrabies Falls
are a spectacular
torrent of water
splitting the barren
desert rock*

Many roads in the district are gravel; drive slowly, and
reduce your tire pressure.
Augrabies is a malaria area,
so take precautions.

▶ Colesberg 125D1

*Tourist Information, tel: 051-
753 0777*

This classic Karoo town
halfway between Cape
Town and Johannesburg
grew up around a water hole
at the foot of the conical
Coleskop, used as a land-
mark by many early travelers. Its first settlement, a
mission, was forced to close
when local farmers decided
its San and Griqua followers
were a threat to security. A
white town (named after Sir
Lowry Cole, Governor of the
Cape, 1828–33), Colesberg
was founded in 1830. There
are still whole streets of
small Karoo block houses, as
well as grander Victorian
buildings, while the **Kemper
Museum** (Murray Street) is
one of the best small town
collections around, with a
fascinating photographic
exhibition on the Karoo
nomads.

▶▶ Kalahari
Gemsbok National Park
                                  124B4

*222 miles north of Upington.
(tel: 012-419 5365).
Open: daily 6AM–7:30PM in
midsummer, 7:30AM–6PM in
midwinter*

Far up in the northwest on the borders of Namibia and Botswana, this is a truly vast park in the harsh Kalahari desert; the whole area, of over 8.9 million acres, is one of the world's largest unspoiled ecosystems, set up in the 1930s to protect the magnificent gemsbok from poachers. Much of the park is located in Botswana but about a quarter, 2.4 million acres, is situated in South Africa. Access and facilities, including accommodations and fuel, are easily available only from the South African side. There are just three roads in the whole vast area, two of them following the riverbeds in which the animals tend to cluster near the small amounts of available water. The wealth of game to be seen in this park includes thousands and thousands of wildebeest, hartebeest and springbok, together with over 215 bird species and a spectacular range of flora, from the creeping desert melons on the Kalahari dunes to fertile woodland and savannah wherever there is water enough to sustain life.

There are few or no gas stations or stores on the road north from Upington. Bring supplies.

The Eye of God in Kuruman is a real desert oasis and was a center of early missionary activity in South Africa

Kimberley see pages 137–9

▶ Kuruman   125C3

148 miles northwest of Kimberley
Tourist Information, corner School and Voortrekker
Streets (tel: 05373-21001)
Known locally as **Gasegonyana** ("Place of the Little Calabash"), Kuruman is a lush oasis in the dusty Kalahari, built around the Eye of God, a huge spring. Four million gallons of water a day gush from the dolomitic rock, never weakening even during the most severe drought. In 1821 Robert Moffat of the London Missionary Society set up shop here, and the little settlement was tagged the Fountain of Christianity. Moffat only made eight converts locally, but his daughter married David Livingstone, who used Kuruman as a base from which to explore the hinterland and spread the gospel. Meanwhile, Moffat translated the Bible into Tswana, printing it on his own press. The **mission** is now a museum, and the church (1838) is still in use.

The **Wonderwerk Cave** (25 miles from Kuruman, on the Daniëlskuil Road) was a San home until 1914, and it contains their etchings.

Too hot for comfort
Hotazel (38 miles northwest of Kuruman) was named by two young prospectors who stopped here on their travels in 1917. They proclaimed the farm was "hot as hell" and were so busy recuperating that they failed to notice that the land underneath was almost solid manganese. It turned out to be the richest deposit in the world.

▶▶▶ Namaqualand 124A2

Springbok is 347 miles north of Cape Town
Tourist Information, tel: 0251-22011

The northwest Cape is semidesert, harsh, dry and unremarkable for most of the year. With an economy based almost entirely on a few scattered copper and diamond mines, it is almost devoid of people. The only reasonably sized town is the region's capital, **Springbok**. In spring (mid-Aug to mid-Sep) the whole region is transformed by millions of brightly colored daisies, mesembryanthemums, aloes and lilies. The **Goegap Nature Reserve** (9 miles southeast of Springbok, tel: 0251-21880. *Open*: daily 8–6) is one of the most accessible places to see them, with 581 plant species, 45 species of mammal and 94 bird species.

In the far north, the 2-million-acre **Richtersveld National Park** (58 miles east of Alexander Bay, tel: 0256-831 1506. For guided 4x4 tours, contact Richtersveld Challenge, tel: 0251-21905) is a lunar landscape slashed by deep gorges, and a botanist's paradise—50 per cent of the plants found here are rarities. The Parks Board Office is at Sendelings-drift, on the Orange River.

▶ Upington 124B2

497 miles west of Kimberley
Tourist Information, Library Building, Mutual Street
(tel: 054-26911)

By local standards Upington is a metropolis, with two interesting monuments. One, at the police station, is to the early Camel Corps; the other, commemorating the donkeys used to open up the area, stands beside the **museum** (Schroder Street. *Open*: Mon–Fri 9:30–12:30, 2–5). Tour the **Orange River Winery** (tel: 054-25651) or **Spitskop Game Reserve** (tel: 054-22336), or visit **Cannon Island**, in the Orange River, with its vineyards and catfish farm (tel: 054-491 1223). Many Koranna (mixed-race Griqua and Tswana) retained their land against all the odds and still farm in nearby **Keimoes** (Tourist Information, Main Road, tel: 054-461 1016). **Kakamas** (Tourist Information, Voortrekker Street, tel: 054-431 0855) has a complex network of waterwheels, canals and irrigation tunnels (1898–1901).

Biggest and best
Upington collects statistics. It has the world's longest avenue of date palms (half a mile) and the longest runway in the southern hemisphere (3 miles), needed in the intense desert heat, used for land speed trials and as a possible emergency landing strip for the space shuttle. The winery is the second largest in the southern hemisphere.

In spring, the whole of Namaqualand bursts into bloom

Kimberley

The famous diamond town lies 608 miles northeast of Cape Town and 301 miles southwest of Johannesburg. In 1871 the first diamond was discovered at Colesberg Kopje. Prospectors rushed to the area and a tented town sprang up. Originally called New Rush, the village was renamed Kimberley in 1873, in honor of the British Secretary of State for the Colonies. During the Anglo-Boer War the town was besieged by the Boers for 124 days. Over 3,000 women and children sheltered in the mine tunnels, while the mine workshops were converted to make ammunition and a huge gun, Long Cecil. The **Honoured Dead Memorial** (Memorial Road), commissioned by Rhodes, has an inscription by Rudyard Kipling and commemorates those who died during the siege. At the base stands Long Cecil. Kimberley is now a city of around 200,000 people with several museums, although diamonds are the biggest draw. The mines still produce about 4,000 carats a day.

Kimberley's wealth paid for some beautiful buildings, such as the rococo **City Hall** (1899; Market Square), the **Dutch Reformed church** (1885; Hertzog Square) and the **Kimberley Club** (1882; Dutoitspan Road). Equally imposing are the mansions built by the diamond magnates, such as **Dunluce** (1897; 10 Lodge Road), the **Rudd House** (5–7 Loch Road) and the **Oppenheimer House** (7 Lodge Road). The **Diggers' Fountain** by Herman Wald, in the Oppenheimer Memorial Gardens, shows five miners holding a diamond sieve.

After John Weston made a nonstop flight of 8 minutes 30 seconds in 1911, the country's first flight school opened in Kimberley. The **Memorial to the Pioneers of Aviation** (Oliver Road, 2 miles from the airport; (tel: 0531-32645). *Open* Mon–Sat 9–1, 2–5, Sun 2–5. *Admission charge* inexpensive) consists of a monument, reconstruction hangar and replica Compton Paterson biplane.

Basics
Tourist Information: City Hall, Market Square (tel: 0531-827 298). *Open*: Mon–Fri, 7:45–4:30, Sat 9–11. For guided tours, contact Diamond Tours Unlimited, tel: 0531-814 006.

Cecil John Rhodes

Rhodes (1853–1902) came to South Africa in 1870 for his health. In 1871, he headed for the Kimberley diamond fields. By 1888, he had formed the De Beers Mining Company and controlled 90 per cent of the world's diamond production. He made a second fortune from the Transvaal goldfields and, in 1889, founded the British South Africa Company. In 1890, he became prime minister of Cape Colony, while the BSAC colonized Rhodesia (now Zimbabwe and Zambia). He died in Muizenberg, near Cape Town, but is buried in the Matobo Hills, Zimbabwe. Part of his fortune still funds the Rhodes Scholarships to Oxford University.

The Star of the West is one of the oldest pubs in South Africa

▶▶▶ The Big Hole and Kimberley Mine Museum   125C2

Tucker Street (tel: 0531-31557)
Open: daily 8–6. Admission charge: moderate
The hole really is big, the largest man-made excavation in the world, with a circumference of 1 mile and a surface area of 33 acres. It is now part of an open-air museum which vividly re-creates old Kimberley with over 40 lovingly restored buildings, from homes and dealers' offices, to shops, a church and Barnato's Boxing Gym, all carefully furnished in period, with photos and plentiful explanation. A diamond exhibition hall has replicas of some of the world's most famous diamonds, plus about 2,000 gleaming carats of the real thing, including the cut and polished Eureka diamond (see page 140).

A trolley runs from the town to the museum, the last vestiges of a route which began as a mule-drawn service in 1887. Near the main entrance, the **Jewel Box** has demonstrations of diamond polishing and goldsmithing, while the **Star of the West** pub (corner North Circular and Barkly Roads) oozes 19th-century atmosphere and is one of the most popular drinking spots in the city.

▶▶ Bultfontein Mine Tours   125D2

Molyneux Road, Kimberley (tel: 0531-29651/807 270)
Surface tours: Mon–Fri, 9 and 11 (no children under 8 years); underground tours: Mon–Fri by appointment; minimum age 16 years. Admission charge: moderate. Advance reservations essential
The first diamonds discovered here in 1869 were actually in the mud walls of the Bultfontein farmhouse, which was destroyed in the attempt to find more. Today there is a large hole where the house once stood. Bultfontein Mine is still operational, owned by De Beers. To see the hi-tech version of diamond mining, take the daily surface and underground tours.

The Duggan-Cronin Gallery   125D2

Egerton Road, Kimberley (tel: 0531-32645)
Open: Mon–Fri 9–5, Sat 9–1, 2–5, Sun 2–5, Admission charge: moderate
A. M. Duggan-Cronin was an avid photographer and recorder of "native" life in South Africa at the turn of the century, and the collection includes many fascinating if rather dubious photos. It is said that he traveled with a leopard skin for people to wear when posing.

▶ The McGregor Museum   125D2

Atlas and Chapel Streets, Kimberley (tel: 0531-32645)
Open: Mon–Sat 9–5, Sun 2–5, public holidays 10–5. Admission charge: moderate
Built as a sanitorium, this became a luxury hotel, where Cecil Rhodes lived and worked during the siege. Today it is a museum of Kimberley history and the ecology of the Northern Cape, with a fine collection of 19th-century furniture. **The Alexander McGregor Memorial Museum** (Chapel Street, tel: 0531-32645. Open Mon–Fri 9–5, Sat 9–1, Sun 2–5. Admission charge inexpensive), a satellite of the main McGregor Museum, contains displays about geology worldwide and the history of the Northern Cape, as well as a small costume collection.

Magersfontein Battlefield 125D2

20 miles from Kimberley, on the Modder River road (tel: 0531-22029)
Admission charge: moderate

On December 11 1899 a troop of 12,500 British soldiers led by Lord Methuen attacked a well-entrenched Boer force of 8,200 under General Cronje, in an effort to break the siege of Kimberley. The battle lasted 10 days, leaving 239 Britons and 87 Boers dead. It was one of the worst British defeats in the Anglo-Boer War. A small museum at the battlefield contains uniforms, weapons, documents, and photos.

► The William Humphreys Art Gallery 125D2

Jan Smuts Boulevard (tel: 0531-811 724)
Open: Mon–Sat 10–1, 2–5, Sun 2–5. Admission charge: inexpensive

Founded around a personal collection of 16th- and 17th-century Dutch and Flemish masters and British and French paintings, belonging to former Member of Parliament William Benbow Humphreys (1889–1965), this gallery is one of the best in South Africa. As well as the international collection, it has an innovative selection of South African art by both black and white artists.

The Big Hole
Diamonds produced: 14,504,566 carats (5,988 pounds.)
Ground excavated: 24,800 tons
Depth of hole: 705 feet.
Depth from surface to water: 571 feet.
Depth of water: 135 feet.
Original depth of open cast working: 787 feet.
Original depth of underground working: 3,598 feet.

The aptly named Big Hole in Kimberley was one of the world's richest sources of diamonds

139

■ **The story goes that in 1866 young Erasmus Jacobs was playing on his father's farm, near Hopetown, when he picked up a pretty pebble on the banks of the Orange River. A neighbor, Schalk van Niekerk, offered to buy the stone; thinking it worthless, the family gave it to him for nothing. Erasmus' plaything turned out to be the 21.25-carat "Eureka" diamond, the trigger for the Kimberley diamond rush.** ■

"Of course I thought when once on the field,
Every load of stone would yield,
But, I owned, after many a weary day,
That gravel is gravel, and clay is clay."
Longlands, 1908

Early days In 1869 Schalk van Niekerk bartered with a Griqua shepherd for a second, larger stone, later named the "Star of South Africa," weighing 83.5 carats. Diamonds were also found on two other farms, Bultfontein and Dorstfontein (now known as Dutoitspan), about 25 miles south of the Vaal River. By 1871, diggings had also been opened up on the De Beers farm, Vooruitzicht, and Colesberg Kopje. It was this small, rocky hill which was eventually to turn into the Kimberley Big Hole. Some 50,000 people streamed into the area from across the globe, living in tents and flimsy houses of wood and galvanized iron. There were not even the most basic facilities such as drains, disease was rife in the hot summer months, and the diggers had to pay up to 2.5 cents for one bucket of muddy water or 10 cents for a loaf of bread.

By the mid-1880s, the hills were flattened and the diggings began to hollow out the land. At 50–60 feet down, the last of the yellow oxidized earth began to run out. Disappointed diggers were preparing to move out when, to their astonished delight, someone discovered that the harder blue rock beneath (now named kimberlite) was even richer in gems. They had tapped into the volcanic pipe in which the diamonds had been born, in the center of the earth.

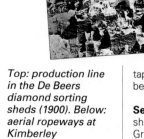

Top: production line in the De Beers diamond sorting sheds (1900). Below: aerial ropeways at Kimberley

Seeking a fortune The biggest problem was the ownership of the diamond fields. The whole area was known as Griqualand West and claimed by the Khoikhoi Griqua people, who had lived there for 70 years. It was also on the frontier, and the governments of the Orange Free State, the South African Republic and the Cape Colony all claimed so rich a prize. In 1880, the British simply annexed it and dared the others to complain.

Diamonds

There was also the problem of individual claims. Each new rumor led to a frantic rush to stake claims and obtain licenses. Early maps are a patchwork of tiny squares of land—eventually there were some 1,600 individual properties, each only 30 feet by 30 feet, in the Big Hole alone. As they dug farther into the earth, the dividing walls collapsed. There were often brutal fights over who owned the resulting heap of earth—and it became ever harder for prospectors to reach their workings or get the gravel out of the pits. Enterprising businessmen set up pulley systems which covered the diggings like a cobweb, making fortunes which they used to buy up small claims. Kimberley came to be dominated by a handful of key players like Cecil Rhodes, Charles Rudd, and Barney Barnato, who worked together in an increasingly powerful cartel, eventually merging to become De Beers Consolidated Mines. Today, under the Oppenheimers, De Beers still controls much of the world's diamond market, although South Africa's ranking has slipped to fourth.

The big one
The largest uncut diamond in the world, and the largest ever found at Kimberley, is the 616, found in 1974 at Dutoitspan Mine by Abel Maratela. It was named after its carat weight, which happened to coincide with the De Beers box number.

Below: the Cullinan diamond—530.2 carats

❏ **Sparklers** There are six common shapes for cut and polished diamonds. The round brilliant, oval marquise, emerald cut, and pear-shaped each have 58 facets, the oblong baguette has 25, and the square cut 30. The normal color range is from white to dark yellow, but defects in the crystal lattice can produce unusual colors. Known as "fancies," these are more expensive still. ❏

Left: rough diamonds in many shapes and colors. Below: De Beers' newest mine—Venetia, Transvaal

Tour Diamond Drive

Kimberley is the heart of South Africa's diamond trade, but many other places in the neighborhood still have commercial mines, while elsewhere diggers still scratch at the riverbanks under a blazing sun amid ocher sands and camelthorn trees. Allow one–two days for this tour.

Leave Kimberley on the R31 toward Barkly West. After 15 miles, turn right to Nooitgedacht and follow the dirt road for 5 miles. Here extraordinary

Many small operations, such as these near Barkly West, are still grubbing alluvial diamonds from riverbanks near Kimberley

pavements of 2,500-million-year-old Ventersdorp lava were polished by glaciers 250 million years ago, then covered in engravings by the San.

Return to the main road and continue for 5 miles to **Barkly West** (Tourist Information, tel: 053-531 0671). Once known as Klipdrift, this is the site of the Northern Cape's first diamond rush to Canteen Kopje in 1869. A cairn and small archaeological museum mark the spot. In 1870, the Klipdrift diggers declared independence from the Transvaal, only to be annexed by Britain in 1871. Two years later the name was changed in honor of the Governor, Sir Henry Barkly. Early records of the diamond

rush, and the many fossils and Stone Age implements discovered by the miners, are displayed in the **Mining Commissioner's Museum** (*Open* Mon–Fri 8–4:30) . There are further mementoes in St. Mary's church (1871). Numerous small diggings line the Vaal River in nearby Windsorton (take the R374 north for 20 miles). Return to Barkly West and continue west along the R31.

At Sydney-on-Vaal (17 miles on) the diamond boom tent town of **Sydney Village** (1896) offers opportunities for diamond panning. Also near by is the 64,250-acre **Vaalbos National Park** (tel: 0531-827298) with buffalo and both black and white rhino. From here, keep going along the R31 for 60 miles to Daniëlskuil (literally "Daniel's Den"). Mining began here in 1960 when a group of hopefuls found 26 diamonds in the first two hours.

Take the R31 south for 6 miles, then turn west on the R385 for 30 miles to **Postmasburg** (Tourist Information, tel: 0591-30343). Founded in 1892 as a trading center, Postmasburg found wealth in a meerkat burrow in 1918. The huge kimberlite pipe turned into a Big Hole (surface area of nearly 1 mile and depth of about 148 feet) which was worked until 1935. It is now filled with water and stocked with fish. You can still visit the West End Diamond Mine and ancient mine workings in the Gatkoppies (by appointment only): around AD700, the Khoikhoi were mining a glittering black iron oxide called specularite here, which they used for personal adornment.

Head north to Olifantshoek (Tourist Information, tel: 059512-2) on the R385 (33 miles) or via the N14 and R386 (44 miles, but a better road). The little town is named after the elephant whose tusks paid for the ground on which it stands. This is the gateway to the **Roaring Sands**. When disturbed air rushes through these 328-foot-high sand dunes, it produces curiously human moans. Below the surface is pure, sweet water.

From Olifantshoek, you can take the N14 west for 104 miles to Upington (see page 136) set amidst near desert, or east for 62 miles to Kuruman (see page 135). Alternatively, return to Postmasburg and head south to **Griekwastad (Griquatown)** on the R386 (60 miles).

Once "capital" of Griqualand (see page 124), this small settlement under the Asbesberge (Asbestos Mountains) was a mission station, founded by the London Missionary Society. The old mission house, birth-place of David Livingstone's wife Mary Moffat, is now the **Mary Moffat Museum** (Voortrekker Street. *Open* Mon–Fri 8–5). Griquatown is also famous for gemstones, including jasper and tiger's eye, a semi-precious stone so common here that the British Stone Fort on Prieska

Mary Moffat, missionary and wife of David Livingstone

Koppie (50 miles south) is built of it. For a full range, visit **Earth Treasures** (Moffat Street, tel: 05962, extension 121. *Open* Mon–Fri 7:30–5). Take the R64 back for 98 miles to return to Kimberley.

Northwest Province

Mafikeng and Mmabatho 125D3

Tourist Information, corner Carrington and Marshall Streets, Mafikeng (tel: 0140-843 040)

The African town now called Mafikeng ("Place of Stones") was known as Mafeking under the British protectorate in Victorian times. A small town much lauded as an example of British courage at its best, Mafeking was besieged by the Boers in 1899, a few days after the outbreak of the Anglo-Boer War. The British Commander, Colonel Robert Baden-Powell (who went on to found the Boy Scout movement) held out for 271 days before relief finally arrived, an event rapturously celebrated in the streets of London. The fort on Cannon Koppie has been restored, and the **Mafikeng Museum** (Old Town Hall, tel: 0140-816102) outlines a history of the area and all its people (tours to nearby historic sites can be arranged by the museum).

In 1977 Mmabatho, built on the outskirts of Mafikeng, became capital of the Tswana homeland of Bophuthatswana, a fragmented "state" with no less than 17 different parcels of land scattered through white South Africa. Mafikeng was incorporated into its former satellite in 1980. The 14,332-acre **Botsalano Game Reserve** (18 miles north of Mmabatho, tel: 01465-23649) has a wide variety of game, with a successful white rhino breeding program, amid acacia plains and dramatic outcrops of volcanic lavas.

▶▶ Pilanesberg National Park 125D4

14 miles from Sun City (tel: 011-465 5423)
Open: daily Sep–Apr 5:30AM–7PM, May–Aug 6AM–6:30PM. Admission charge: expensive

South Africa's third largest park, Pilanesberg sprawls over 338,540 acres around an extinct volcanic crater. The terrain is dry bushveld and Kalahari thornveld, with wooded ravines and grassy plains. Several farms were taken over in the 1970s. Operation Genesis, the largest animal translocation program in the world, then restocked the park with over 7,000 animals, including the "big five." There are also more than 300 bird species, as well as walk-in aviaries, a self-guided walking trail around Manyane Camp (which is also the information center), blinds near several dams, over 125 miles of gravel roads for game viewing, and regular hot-air balloon flights over the park.

▶▶▶ Sun City 125D4

About 115 miles northwest of Johannesburg, 25 miles from Rustenburg (tel: Sun City—01465-21000, The Palace—01465-73000)
Open: daily 24 hours, day permits available at the gate. Admission charge: expensive

---

Baden-Powell refusing to surrender Mafeking

Relief
The overembellished stories of the siege of Mafeking tapped a vein of heroic imperialism but had little to do with reality. Baden-Powell loved every minute, exaggerating the number of Boers from 5,000 in 1899, to 12,000 in 1937. Throughout the siege he made a marked distinction, in all matters, between white and black: healthy rations for the 2,000 whites were denied to the 5,000 Africans. Baden-Powell advised that "the toe of the boot" be applied to disapproving "grousers." Spin-offs from the siege include the Boy Scout movement and the British catchphrase "Mafeking has been relieved!"

This is a place to spend money—you could easily lose the shirt off your back in the 24-hour casino. But to do it in style, you need to stay at the Palace of the Lost City, a magnificently kitsch rich man's fantasy which is South Africa's nearest thing to Las Vegas. Re-creating Rider Haggard's turn-of-the-century novel *King Solomon's Mines*, Sun City is like the set of a film: the attractions include the Valley of the Waves, an inland sea complete with wave machine, beach and water-slides, the "volcanic" Bridge of Time which erupts every hour, and a Vegas-style Extravaganza of showgirls in feathers. The whole complex is trying to transform itself into a family destination (with gambling) and offers a kids' club, amusement park, petting zoo, and a host of sports, including two of the best golf courses in Africa (with live crocodiles in the water hazard at the 13th hole), and a lake offering water sports from windsurfing to parascending. There are rumors of a possible theme park with Disney-style rides.

The whole place could be ghastly, but isn't. The Palace is splendid, the other hotels comfortable, the gardens superb, the food delectable, the water warm and the weather (usually) sunny. Sun International answer critics' condemnation of this island of wealth amid an ocean of desperate poverty by financing regular social projects ranging from schools and clinics to entire housing developments. A significant number of shares, held by the former Bophutatswana government, are to be floated on the stock exchange.

Inland seas and brand new ancient ruins are just some of Sun City's attractions

Building to excess
The Palace of the Lost City complex cost R800 million and took 5,000 workers 19 months to build. Experts handcrafted the finishing touches including the massive painted dome. The mosaic in the Crystal Court is made from 30 different semiprecious stones, including jasper, malachite, and amethyst.

GAUTENG

Downtown Johannesburg from the Carlton Panorama

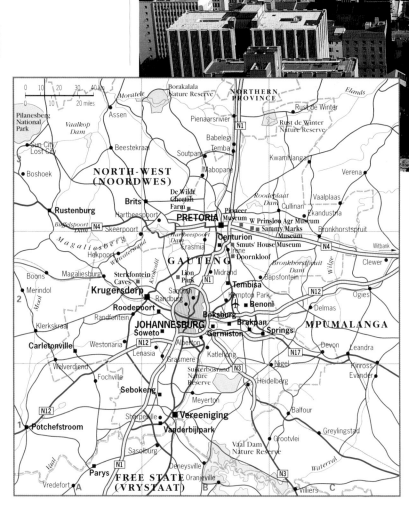

0 10 20 30 40 km
0 10 20 miles

Moratele
Borakalala Nature Reserve
NORTHERN PROVINCE
Elands

Pilanesberg National Park
Assen
Pienaarsrivier
N1
Rust de Winter
Rust de Winter Nature Reserve

Vaalkop Dam
Babelegi
Temba
KwaMhlanga

Sun City/Lost City
Beestekraal
Soutpan
Mabopane
Verena

Boshoek
NORTH-WEST (NOORDWES)
De Wildt Cheetah Farm
Roodeplaat Dam
Vaalplaas
Cullinan
Zkandustria

Rustenburg
Brits
Hartbeespoort
PRETORIA
Pioneer Museum
W Prinsloo Agr Museum
Bronkhorstspruit

Buffelspoort Dam
N4
Skeerpoort
Hartbeespoort Dam
Centurion
Sammy Marks Museum

Magaliesberg
Hekpoort
Erasmia
Smuts' House Museum
Irene
Museum
N4
Witbank

Boons
Magaliesburg
Sterkfontein Caves
GAUTENG
Doornkloof
Bronkhorstspruit Dam
Clewer

Merindol
Krugersdorp
Lion Park
Midrand
Bapsfontein

Moot
Randburg
Saxonwald
N1
Tembisa
Kempton Park
N12
Ogies

Klerkskraal
Roodepoort
Randfontein
Boksburg
Benoni
Delmas

Carletonville
Westonaria
JOHANNESBURG
Soweto
Alberton
Brakpan
Germiston
Springs
MPUMALANGA

Welverdiend
N12
Lenasia
Grasmere
Katlehong
N17
Devon
Leandra

Fochville
Suikerbosrand Nature Reserve
N3
Nigel
Kinross
Evander

Sebokeng
Meyerton
Heidelberg
Balfour

Sharpeville
Vereeniging
Grootvlei
Greylingstad

N12
Vanderbijlpark
Vaal Dam Nature Reserve
Waterval

Potchefstroom
Sasolburg
Deneysville
N1
N3
Villiers

Vaal
Parys
FREE STATE (VRYSTAAT)
Oranjeville

Vredefort
A
B
C

GAUTENG

Gauteng This word means "place of gold" in Sotho, and so does Egoli, the Zulu name for Johannesburg. A theme begins to emerge—for this is a region built, quite literally, on gold. Gauteng is the new name for a small area in central South Africa, once known as the PWV (Pretoria Witwatersrand Vereeniging). Pretoria is the calm, stately administrative capital of South Africa, and a place, like Washington D.C. or Canberra, populated almost entirely by civil servants. Vereeniging and the surrounding area, which includes the notorious township of Sharpeville (see page 43) is predominantly industrial, with very little to recommend it to the visitor. Between them is the area known as the Witwatersrand (Ridge of White Water), one of the country's main watersheds, under which lie unimaginably large reserves of gold, carbon, uranium, green diamonds, iron pyrites (fool's gold), chromite, silver, and platinum. Above these reserves tower the skyscrapers of Johannesburg, the social and economic powerhouse of the whole African continent. And beside that is Soweto, the political heart of black South Africa and now one of the largest cities in the country. The province, geographically the smallest in South Africa, has 43 per cent of South Africa's urban population; generates 36.9 per cent of the country's gross domestic product; accounts for 60 per cent of its manufacturing output; and contains 30 per cent of the world's known gold reserves.

Johannesburg

In 1886, an Australian prospector named George Harrison found the first gold on the Witwatersrand at Langlaagte Farm, Roodepoort; Johannes Joubert was sent north to investigate. Hot on his heels came the surveyor-general, Johannes Rissik, who had the responsibility of choosing a site for the new mining village that would inevitably appear. The fledgling town of Johannesburg, now known irreverently to locals as "the Big Naartjie" (tangerine), derived its name from these two men.

Gold has always been the pulse of this boomtown. From the air, the headgear of working mines and the tell-tale yellow mounds are clearly visible. In fact, with modern techniques to help, original dumps are being remined to extract the many trace minerals left behind by the early prospectors. The city center, built over exhausted tunnels, is steadily expanding upwards and outwards. In little over a century, it has grown into a massive conurbation covering 200 square miles, with more than 600 parks and 260,000 trees lining its streets. There are now fewer than 25 miles between northern Johannesburg and southern Pretoria, and with several smaller settlements in between, it seems likely that Gauteng is destined to become one giant city.

Greater Johannesburg is expanding rapidly as the rich move into closely guarded northern suburbs and more and more rural families flock toward Soweto

148

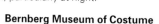

Johannesburg is exciting, restless and energetic, with bubbling street life and plenty of excellent restaurants, theaters, and other entertainment. To date, this is the only city in South Africa where the black Africans have moved into the center; the whites have moved out *en masse* to wealthy northern suburbs such as Sandton. In addition there is a considerable problem with crime. In 1994, nearly 2 million serious crimes were reported in South Africa, most of which took place in and around Johannesburg and Soweto. Murder is commonplace: on average, one person is murdered every 29 minutes (a figure that is five times the murder rate per capita in the United States). There are also frightening numbers of armed robberies, rapes and car-jackings. Be extremely careful, and do not walk around the streets on your own, particularly at night.

Bernberg Museum of Costume   150B4

Corner Jan Smuts and Duncombe Avenues, Forest Town (tel: 011-646 0716)
Open: Tue–Sat 9–1, 1:30–5. Admission free
This Victorian house, still containing most of its original furniture and decor, makes an ideal setting for a museum of fashion. Most of the dresses are 19th century, but there are displays showing the development of style from the hooped skirts of the 1750s to Dior's "New Look" of the 1950s.

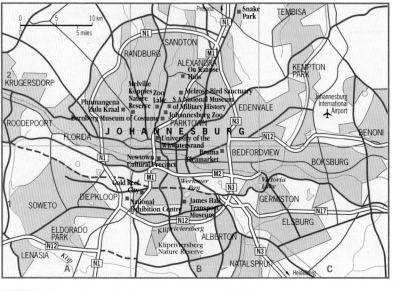

Bruma Fleamarket   149B1

Off Marcia and Allum Roads, near Eastgate Shopping Centre (tel: 011-786 0776)
Open: Tue–Fri 9:30–6, Sat 8:30–6, Sun 9–6.
Admission free

Billed as the world's only flea-market theme park, Bruma is the single largest tourist attraction in Gauteng, with 2.5 million visitors a year. It has over 300 stalls during the week, more than 600 on weekends and 15 restaurants. There are plenty of excellent souvenirs, and around-the-clock entertainment, from South African tribal dancers to Tanzanian acrobats.

Sandton shopping mall represents probably the greatest concentration of wealth in Africa

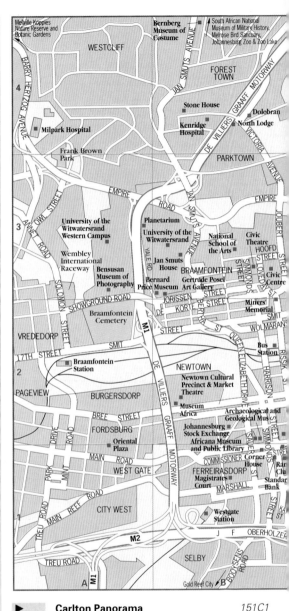

Touring Jo'burg
Johannesburg Publicity Association (first floor). North State Building, corner Kruis and Market Streets (tel: 011-336 4961; fax: 011-336 4965). *Open* Mon–Fri 8:30–5.
For organized tours, contact Springbok Atlas (tel: 011-493 3780); Welcome Tours (tel: 011-442 8905); Magari (tel: 011-453 5635). For walking tours, contact Historical Walks of Johannesburg (tel: 011-673 8409). For a personal guide, contact Gold Reef Guides (tel: 011-496 1400). To tour a working gold mine, contact Gold Mine Tours (tel: 011-498 7204; reservations essential). For tours of Soweto, contact Jimmy's Face to Face Tours (tel: 011-331 6109).

▶ **Carlton Panorama** 151C1

Commissioner Street, entrance at upper level of Carlton Shopping Centre (tel: 011-331 2892)
Open: daily 8AM–11PM
The 663-foot-high Carlton Centre is large, hideous and one of the most useful buildings in downtown Johannesburg. As well as being home to the luxurious Carlton Hotel, it has a huge shopping mall, several movie theaters, the local ice rink and an array of eateries. On the 50th floor, the Top of Africa Panorama offers superb views of the city and beyond. On a clear day you can see as far as the Magaliesberg.

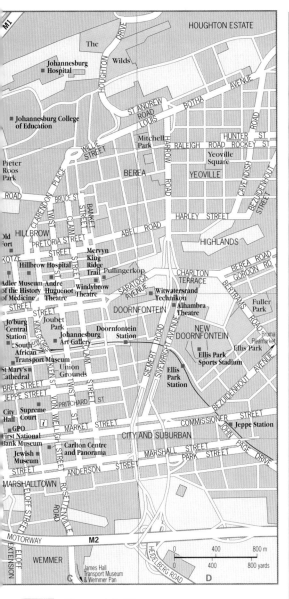

"An extended brickfield is the first impression: a prosperous powder-factory is the last..."
—John Buchan on Johannesburg, *The African Colony*, (1903)

A mini Manhattan—Johannesburg at night

► **Diamond Cutting**

Johan Erikson Diamond Centre (tel: 011-970 1369); Mynardts (tel: 011-334 8897); M-Cut (tel: 011-493 7367). Reservations essential; check times and directions

Although the diamond mines are elsewhere, Johannesburg is South Africa's major market and polishing center. Visit one of these establishments and discover how to turn a dull pebble into a real gem on a tour of a diamond cutting and polishing workshop. Learn how to pick out the quality, decide on the cut, polish, and even set the stones. The Erikson Centre has a small diamond museum; they all have stores.

GAUTENG

The Gold Reef City dancers are a top attraction

▶▶▶   **Gold Reef City**   149B1

Off Xavier Road (off M1), 5 miles south of the city (tel: 011-496 1600)
Open: Tue–Sun 9:30–5. Check newspaper listings for details of special events. Admission charge free after 5PM weekdays, moderate after 5PM weekends

A combination of open-air museum and theme park with a bewildering but jolly mix of ersatz and real entertainments, Gold Reef City is built around a famous gold mine (No.14 Shaft of the Crown Mines), and reconstructs the pioneering days of Johannesburg during the gold-rush era. There are regular demonstrations of pouring liquid gold into bullion, and you can take the elevator 720 feet down the shaft into what was once the richest gold mine in the world. Thirty thousand men toiled in unbearable conditions below the earth's surface to produce about 3 million pounds of gold during its working life. Above ground are several reconstructed Victorian streets that feature pubs, hotel, restaurants, an old-fashioned apothecary's shop, Chinese laundry, tailor, newspaper office, bank, brewery and early stock exchange. There are many live demonstrations, a number of fairly tame fairground rides and a Victorian funfair, souvenir shops, and plenty of places to eat and drink; visitors can also take a ride on the miniature railroad around the edge of the park.

Regular entertainments throughout the day include can-can dancers and the 16-member Gold Reef City International Dancers team, the only professional troupe of tribal dancers in the country, who perform both traditional and gumboot dances (developed because of the miners' heavy protective footwear).

▶   **Jewish Museum**   151C1

Corner Kruis and Main Streets (tel: 011-331 0331)
Open: 9–1, 2–5. Admission charge: inexpensive

South Africa has a large Jewish population. Some were drawn to the country in the late 19th century; many arrived from Eastern Europe in the 1920s. This museum covers the history of South African Judaism from the 1920s to the present, and displays many beautiful religious artifacts.

▶▶   **Johannesburg Art Gallery**   151C2

Joubert Park (tel: 011-725 3130)
Open: Tue–Sun 10–5. Admission free

In 1904, Lady Phillips, wife of randlord Sir Lionel Phillips, went to London and sold a 21½ carat diamond ring, returning home with three paintings by Wilson Steer. She spent the next five years wringing sufficient money out of wealthy friends such as Max Michaelis, Otto Beit, Abe Bailey, Julius Wernher and Frederick Eckstein to found an art gallery in Johannesburg. Sir Edwin Lutyens was commissioned to design the building, and the imposing classical gallery opened in 1915, with the building not yet complete. Further sections were added in 1940 and 1984.

The gallery has three distinct collections. The first is European, with works by masters such as El Greco, Picasso and Rodin alongside the inevitable minor Flemish portraits. The second includes works by many of South Africa's finest artists, such as Jackson Hlungwane, J. H. Pierneef, Irma Stern and William Kentridge. Finally, the gallery now houses the somewhat eccentric Brenthurst Collection of African Art, which comprises curios originally taken back to Europe by 19th-century missionaries, explorers, travelers and scientists; most exhibits are of Nguni, Sotho or East African origin. The complex has excellent gift and coffee shops.

Johannesburg Stock Exchange 150B2

Corner Diagonal and Pritchard Streets (tel: 011-833 6580) Open: for presentation video and slide show Mon–Fri 11AM
This was the second Stock Exchange in South Africa, founded in 1887. The first one was simply unable to cope with the sudden surge in business following the gold strikes. Consequently, the authorities chained off an open area between Commissioner and Market Streets and the trading floor went alfresco. This led to the expression "between the chains," still used in common parlance for stock trading. Guided tours paint a vivid picture of gold-rush Johannesburg and the fevered trading that made and lost fortunes. Today, trading takes place in slightly more restrained fashion in the modern Stock Exchange on Diagonal Street.

Capitalism and the arts —the Stock Exchange (above) and the Art Gallery (below)—key facets of city life

GAUTENG

▶ **Johannesburg Zoo and Zoo Lake**   149B2
*Hermann Eckstein Park, Jan Smuts Avenue, Parktown
(tel: 011-646 2000)*
Open: daily 8:30–5:30. Admission charge: moderate
It may be nothing like seeing them in the wild, but
Johannesburg Zoo is a good second-best. Surrounded by
impeccable gardens, the 136-acre zoo is home to around
300 species of animal, most of which are in danger of
extinction. It is also a center for conservation, scientific
research, and education. Across the street, Zoo Lake is
popular for picnics. Once a month, it hosts an open-air art
exhibition, "Art in the Park."

Minor museums
The **First National Bank Museum** (corner Market and
Harrison Streets, tel: 011-836 5887. *Open* Mon–Fri 9–4,
Sat by arrangement. *Admission free*) reveals the history
of South Africa's most important bank since 1838. The
Hector Schultz Museum (123 Francis Road,
Ravenswood, Boksburg, tel: 011-894 4535. *Open* by
appointment. *Admission charge* inexpensive) covers
South African tribal culture. The **James Hall Transport
Museum** (Pioneer Park, Wemmerpan, tel: 011-435 9718).
Open Tue–Sun 9–5. *Admission charge* inexpensive)
displays the history of land transportation in South Africa.
The **Ou Kaapse Huis** (Pretoria Avenue, Sandown, tel:
011-884 1054) would be familiar in the Cape, but is a rarity
up here in Johannesburg: a Cape-style house filled with
antique Cape furniture.

▶▶ **Museum Africa**   150B2
121 Breë Street (tel: 011-833 5624)
*Open: Tue–Sun 9–5. Admission charge:
moderate*
Several older, smaller museums scattered
across the city have been closed, and their
collections gathered under one roof to create
one of the finest and most imaginative
museums in South Africa. Museum Africa is
housed in an old market warehouse in the
recently revived Newtown Cultural Precinct.
The aim, eventually, is to tell the true, multicultural story of South Africa, from Big Bang
to the present.

The **Museum of South African Rock Art**
contains not only a magnificent collection of
original San paintings, but some of the clearest explanations on record of how these
powerful works were created. The
Johannesburg Transformations section
concentrates on a few key aspects of the
city's history, from local prehistoric settlements onward. There is a special exhibition
on gold, but more powerful are three inter-
linked sections describing township music,
the growth of the townships and squatter
camps, and South African politics over the
last 40 to 50 years.

Beyond these are two more traditional
displays. The original **Africana Museum**
collection, founded in 1934, includes a huge

*Museum Africa is
a magnificent
celebration of
Johannesburg, past
and present*

array of paintings, documents, photographs, prints, traditional African art and costume, from the Cape to the Zambezi. The **Bensusan Museum of Photography** contains hundreds of cameras spanning the period from the magic lantern to digital imaging and CD-ROM. Photographs include everything from pioneering classics by Fox-Talbot to a powerful local exhibition of South African life. Work is still in progress on the **Geological Museum**. Historically, geology is a subject dear to the hearts of many South Africans, who maintain an innate ability to look at rocks and summon up images of inestimable wealth. There are also constantly changing special exhibitions, workshops, and activities from music and dance to story-telling.

▶ **Newtown Cultural Precinct** 150B2

Breë Street (tel: 011-832 1641)

The old fruit and spice market buildings of Newtown have been given a new lease on life as the city's bohemian quarter, centered on the Museum Africa complex and the **Market Theatre**, itself once a market hall, built in 1911 and ennobled with an impressive *beaux arts* façade. The theater became renowned internationally for its courageous stand during the apartheid era; many of its powerful dramas, both black and white, were openly critical of the government. The surrounding precinct has a total of four theaters, an art gallery, numerous fascinating shops, places to eat, drink and listen to music, and a buzzing Saturday market. The **South African Breweries' Centenary Centre** (Becker Street, tel: 011-836 4900. *Open* Tue–Sat 11–6. *Admission charge* expensive) explores the history of brewing in South Africa, with opportunities to sample.

Rebirth

Newtown was once a multicultural district of slum housing, known as Farm Bloemfontein (1853), Brookfields (1887), and Burgersdorp (1896). In 1904, the inhabitants were evacuated and the area burned, supposedly in response to an outbreak of plague, after which it was renamed Newtown. During the 1970s, in line with the Group Areas Act, much of neighboring Fordsburg was demolished, and its Indian community moved out to Lenasia township. Now there are over 300 Indian-owned shops in the rebuilt area glowing with brilliant, gilded saris, incense, and tottering heaps of brass pots, and redolent of cumin and other delicious spices.

155

The Market Theatre, once a market hall

Sir Herbert Baker's Stone House

▶ **Parktown**   *150B3*

For guided walks, contact the Parktown and Westcliff Heritage Trust (tel: 011-482 3349, mornings only)
Johannesburg took three years to become the largest city in southern Africa, but it was a typical miners' town, rife with crime, alcohol, and prostitution. Parktown was one of the first "respectable" leafy suburbs created by the mining magnates as a suitable environment for their wives and daughters. There are still some fine mansions, including Sir Herbert Baker's home, Stone House, and Lord Alfred Milner's "kindergarten," Moot Cottage.

Phumangena Zulu Kraal   *149A2*

D. F. Malan Drive, Johannesburg (tel: 011-659 0605)
Open: Mon–Sat by appointment
For those who cannot visit Natal, this is an authentic Zulu village alive and well and living in Johannesburg with authentic Zulus living and working here. Have a Zulu meal, watch the regular dance displays and let the authentic *sangoma* (diviner) throw the bones and tell your fortune.

▶ **South African National Museum of**   *149B2*
Military History

Hermann Eckstein Park, Erlswold Way, Saxonwold (tel: 011-646 5513)
Open: daily 9–4:30. Admission charge: moderate
This is one of Johannesburg's most popular museums, set by a park near the zoo. It is colorful and ferocious with fighter aircraft from both world wars, tanks and artillery, swords, uniforms and medals, displays on the Namibian and Angolan wars, and a German one-man submarine.

▶ **South African Transport Museum**   *151C2*

Old Concourse, Johannesburg Station Complex, De Villiers Street (tel: 011-773 9118)
Open: Mon–Fri 7:30–3:45. Admission charge: inexpensive
This small museum houses a unique collection of model trains, as well as displays on South Africa's railroads, high-

ways, harbors and airlines. It also has a number of landscape paintings by the notable South African artist, J. H. Pierneef. The museum runs regular steam safaris to raise the funds that pay for its preservation program (see pages 234–5).

Train enthusiasts should also stop at the **South African National Railway and Steam Museum** (Randfontein Road, Krugersdorp, off R28, tel: 011-888 1154. *Open* 1st Sun of every month), which has a number of historic locomotives and other rolling stock.

▶ **University of the Witwatersrand**   *150B3*
    Museums

Founded in 1896 as a training institute for the diamond industry, "Wits" is now one of the largest and most highly regarded universities in South Africa and boasts no fewer than 26 small museums. The **Bernard Price Museum of Palaeontology** (Jorrison Street, Braamfontein, tel: 011-716 1111) is dedicated to the study of fossils. It contains a mass of tools and bones such as those of *Australopithecus africanus* and *Homo erectus*, found at various sites in South Africa including the Sterkfontein Caves (see page 159). The **Planetarium** (Yale Road, Milner Park tel: 011-716 3199. *Presentations* Fri 8PM; Sat 3, 8; Sun 4. *Admission charge* expensive, reservations essential) offers a wonderful way to identify the Southern Cross and explore the unfamiliar southern skies, where the crescent moon hangs upside-down. Then you can head out into the bush and see the real thing as you have never seen it before. With no artificial light to dim the eyes, the sky seems to have twice the number of stars. The Planetarium bookshop sells maps and charts.

A range of exhibits at the **Adler Museum of the History of Medicine** (in the grounds of the South African Institute for Medical Research, Hospital Hill, Hillbrow, tel: 011-725 1704. *Open* Mon–Fri 9–4) includes a dental museum, hospital optometry, a video room, a coach house, and reconstructions of a 19th-century pharmacy, surgery and African herbalist's shop.

Smaller university museums include **Jan Smuts Study** (tel: 011-716 3793), transferred in its entirety from his home, Doornkloof (see page 171) after his death; the **Zoology Museum** (tel: 011-716 2307) has butterflies, moths and shells; the **Adler Museum of the History of Music** (tel: 011-716 3733) has valuable and historical musical instruments and scores; and the **Gertrude Posel Art Gallery** (Senate House, Jorissen Street, tel: 011-716 3632) offers changing exhibitions of African art from the Standard Bank collection.

Randberg Waterfront, fun and shopping for all the family

Johannesburg Environs

Heidelberg 146B1

18 miles southeast of Johannesburg on the N3
Tourist Information, Library, corner Verwoerd and
Ueckermann Streets (tel: 0151-3111)

This small Victorian town, founded in 1861 by a general dealer, Heinrich Ueckermann, stands on part of Langlaagte Farm, site of the first Rand gold strike. It has a number of attractive old houses and several small museums. These include the **Museum and Cultural Information Centre** (tel: 0151-2892), which has a collection of art, antiques, and period household articles; the **Diepkloof Farm Museum** (AECI, Modderfontein, tel: 0151-2181); the **Motor Museum** (tel: 0151-6303), with a fine collection of veteran bicycles, motorcycles and cars; and, bizarrely, the **Dynamite Museum** (tel: 011-606 3206) with exhibits and photographs illustrating and explaining the role played by explosives and chemicals in general in the history of South Africa.

Nature Reserves 146B2 and 149B2

There are several game and nature reserves in the Gauteng area surrounding Johannesburg, of which the following are probably the most interesting. The 495-acre **Johannesburg Lion Park** (18 miles north of Johannesburg, tel: 011-460 1814. *Open* daily 8–4:30. *Admission charge* expensive) houses up to 60 lions. They are fed daily between 9 and 9:30. Other animals include gemsbok, impala, wildebeest, and ostrich. There is a Ndebele village and a small-animals area for children. The **Snake Park** (Halfway House, tel: 011-805 3116. *Open* daily 9–4; demonstrations Mon–Fri 11, 3; Sat 11, 2, 3, 4; Sun 2:30, 3:30, 4:30. *Admission charge* expensive) has a collection of mainly African snakes.

▶▶▶ Soweto 146B2

About 12 miles southwest of Johannesburg
To visit Soweto, contact Jimmy's Face to Face Tours
(tel: 011-331 6131/2)

From 1923, the Native Urban Areas Act tried to stop any more black people migrating to the cities and set up segregated "locations" away from urban centers. In the 1930s, the Johannesburg council bought Klipspruit farm with the intention of creating an African city for 80,000 people. The first areas of this South Western Township (Soweto) were set up in 1944, though most of it was built in the 1950s. It was unpopular from the beginning: it was too far from the jobs in the city, it lacked decent housing, and there was no provision made for even basic amenities such as water, electricity, or shopping within easy walking distance.

Today, it is the largest black city south of the equator, with anything up to 3.5 million people (there are an estimated 2 million squatters in the Johannesburg area). It is a mass of contradictions that seems poised to overshadow its wealthier, older parent; grand mansions and Mercedes dwell alongside cardboard shanties. Many of its young people are poorly educated, after the schoolchildren refused to learn in Afrikaans and

Township music
Marabi began in the shebeens in the 1920s. Fast and furious, it was played on any available instrument, from an organ to a can of stones, with anyone and everyone joining in the jam sessions. Never written or recorded, it ended when the slums were bulldozed in the late 1930s. In multicultural Sophiatown, however, it fathered other forms of music, including township jazz (heavily influenced by American big bands and swing), *kwela*, and *mbaqanga* (the earliest protest songs). From the mid-1970s, anti-conscription white musicians also began to use music as a form of protest.

boycotted their classes. Yet it is the most vibrant source of creativity in the country, pouring out art and music, theater and poetry in a dozen languages. It is troubled, violent, and optimistic. Above all, it is at the forefront of the revolution.

► **Sterkfontein Caves**   146A2

Take the R563 Hekpoort Kromdraai Road, Krugersdorp North (tel: 011-956 6342)

Open: Tue–Sun 9–4. Admission charge: inexpensive

These caves are southern Africa's treasure trove of fossils, and one of the world's most important prehistoric sites, discovered in 1896 by an Italian gold prospector on Sterkfontein Farm, near Krugersdorp. In 1936, Dr. Robert Broom discovered the first known adult cranium of the 2.5-million-year-old ape-man, *Australopithecus africanus*. At first, it was not recognized as a relative of the Taung baby, an infant skull found 12 years before by Dr. Raymond Dart, and was named *Plesianthropus transvaalensis* (known to locals as "Mrs. Ples"). Later reclassified as "AA," she has become a crucial pointer to man's origins, and one of many "missing links" between ape and man.

The caves contain six cathedral-like chambers, a deep underground lake (said by local Africans to have magic powers which cure all ailments, and blindness in particular), and the **Robert Broom Museum** of fossils.

Soweto has long outgrown Johannesburg to become South Africa's largest city

Gold

■ **Gold has been admired for its beauty since about 9000BC, but its use as currency is relatively recent. Even when 16th-century Spaniards were plundering Aztec hoards, gold coins were rare. In 1821, when gold became the yardstick for all currencies in the British Empire, nations had to build up bullion reserves. The value of gold skyrocketed and the search for more was on.** ■

"I tell you today that every ounce of gold taken from the bowels of our soil will yet have to be weighed up with rivers of tears..."
—Paul Kruger, ZAR President (quoted in *The Randlords*, by Geoffrey Wheatcroft)

For hundreds of years, people had known that there was gold in southern Africa—Arab traders were dealing with the inland tribes even in the 7th century. In 1853, prospectors found the first significant reserves in South Africa at Pilgrim's Rest, Mpumalanga (see page 183). That proved to be a thin seam, but it did generate a minor gold rush. By the time George Harrison struck it lucky in 1886 and discovered the Main Reef on the Witwatersrand, there were a lot of people with a great deal of optimism nearby, ready and able to start digging. Farms along the line of the reef were declared public property, ready for licensed claims, and a new city (Johannesburg) was laid out not far away. The God-fearing Boers, who had trekked north specifically to get away from the crowds, were bemused by the onslaught of the rough-and-ready miners and the accompanying wave of sin. The British, led by Cecil Rhodes, started eyeing the area for a takeover—which they eventually achieved in 1902 at the end of the Anglo-Boer War.

Pockets of wealth As in the diamond fields, the real wealth soon ended up in the hands of a privileged few, such as Cecil Rhodes and Barney Barnato, J. B. Robinson, Hermann Eckstein, and Lionel Phillips. But the prospect of wealth attracted countless others including black workers, who still travel literally thousands of miles from home to work underground. Until very

The Transvaal Gold Rush lasted for 30 years until the discovery of far richer seams on the Witwatersrand in 1886

recently, the mines were employing over half a million men from 10 southern African countries at any given time. They come from a multitude of tribes, so a common "pidgin," *Fanakalo*, was developed for communication. It is still used, but is no longer considered politically correct.

Lower yields Today, the mines stretch in a 310-mile arc from Evander in Mpumalanga, through the Witwatersrand and Johannesburg to Klerksdorp, and south to Welkom in the Free State. Johannesburg is still the focus of the industry, with seven Stock Exchange-listed mines, but the Free State goldfields currently produce more than one third of the country's output.

Since mining began, South Africa has produced over 37,000 tons of gold, but there is trouble ahead. In 1985,

the country was producing 43 per cent of the world's gold and was the world's cheapest producer; by 1995, production was down to 25 per cent of the global total and it had become the most expensive in the world. The 1995 output of around 540 tons was the country's worst performance since 1957. Some 140,000 workers have already been laid off and more are expected to follow. This situation is partly due to the economic facts of life in the new South Africa: after years of blatant exploitation, the workers are demanding better wages, housing, conditions and safety, and are striking if their demands are not met. There is also a technical reason. South Africa already has the deepest mines in the world, with shafts going down nearly 3,000 feet. It costs a great deal more to work that far underground and the veins of gold are getting ever deeper. Nevertheless, South Africa still owns some 40 per cent of the world's known gold deposits (30 per cent of them in Gauteng), and it will be a long time before the country needs to look for a source of income to replace that of gold.

Pure gold
Gold is pure, malleable, does not tarnish or corrode, is almost indestructible and can be finely molded and remolded without alteration. It is heavy, dense, and an excellent conductor of heat and electricity. The simplest version of placer mining is panning, which uses a large sieve to collect easily separated deposits from river gravel; sluicing, hydraulic mining and dredging are similar processes on a larger scale. In underground lode mining of quartz seams, an average 100,000 ounces of ore is required to produce one ounce of gold. Gold is also recovered as a by-product of copper.

Liquid gold being poured into an ingot at Gold Reef City

Pretoria

Born in a leisurely fashion in 1856 as a farming settlement on the Apies (Little Monkeys) River, Pretoria was roughly in the center of the newly colonized Transvaal region, so was chosen as the capital of the South African Republic. The president, Marthinus Pretorius, named it after his father, Andries Pretorius, leader of the Boer forces at the Battle of Blood River and a great Afrikaner hero. At the Union in 1910, the city became the administrative capital of the republic, and is likely to become the single capital of South Africa should the legislature, administration, and judiciary ever be merged into one city.

The city takes its role seriously, with many fine statues, 33 museums and four universities, including Pretoria University (the largest in the country), and the University of South Africa (UNISA), the world's largest correspondence university.

*Jacaranda in bloom
carpets the streets in
purple*

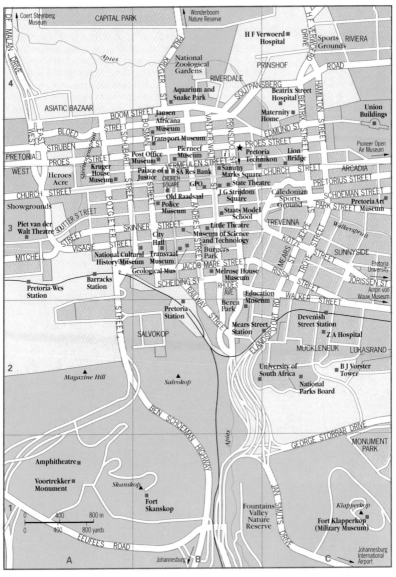

Almost totally white-collar, it was, until very recently, the only major city in South Africa where the majority of the population (estimated at 2 million) was white. Because of this fact it escaped most of the violence during the years of unrest, and is at present one of the few major cities without a significant crime problem. As a city, it is totally unlike its neighbor Johannesburg, and is mostly quiet, dignified and conservative. It could be dull, but as befits anywhere with a large diplomatic contingent, it has some of the best nightlife around, from theaters to clubs and restaurants. Until Johannesburg begins to deal with its problems, you may find this a far more pleasant place to stay.

The jacaranda city
The first two jacarandas were planted in Pretoria in 1888. Today, over 70,000 mature trees line the streets of the city, providing much-needed shade and greenery. Every October, they burst into flower, coating the city in purple blossom. The city celebrates with a jacaranda festival.

GAUTENG

Pretoria's forts
In 1896, following the abortive Jameson Raid (see page 37), the Transvaal government built four forts to defend Pretoria. Beautifully constructed of stone with meticulously executed brickwork, they were guarded by stout armor-plated doors, fitted with bomb-resistant casements, and armed with heavy artillery. Revolving artillery pieces could be mounted on the ramparts when required, but they were never needed, and the forts were only used to accommodate Lord Roberts' troops after the British occupation in 1900. Fort Klapperkop and Fort Schamskop are still intact; Forts Wonderboom and Daspoort are in ruins.

President Kruger as a lion, in the Coert Steynberg museum

Art Museums

The **Pretoria Art Museum▶** (corner Schoeman and Wessel Streets, Arcadia Park tel: 012-344 1807. *Open* Mon–Fri 9–4:30. *Admission charge* inexpensive) has works by a number of Dutch and Flemish painters, including Frans Hals and Van Dyck, as well as one of the most important collections of South African artists such as Maggie Laubscher, Irma Stern, and local residents Anton van Wouw and J. H. Pierneef. There are several museums in the artists' former homes and studios. **Coert Steynberg Museum▶** (465 Berg Avenue, Pretoria North, tel: 012-546 0404. *Open* Tue–Fri 8:30–1; Sun 11–4:30. Guided tours Tue–Fri 10:15, 11:15; Sun 11:15, 2:30 and 3:30. Closed Sat, Mon. *Admission charge* inexpensive); **Pierneef Museum** (218 Vermeulen Street, tel: 012-323 1419. *Open* Mon–Fri 8–4. *Admission charge* inexpensive); **Anton von Wouw Museum** (299 Clark Street, Brooklyn, tel: 012-346 7422. *Open* Mon–Sat 10–5. *Admission charge* moderate).

Church Square see Walk, page168.

▶ Kruger House Museum 163A3

Church Street West (tel: 012-326 9172)
Open: Mon–Sat 8.30–4; Sun 11–4. Admission charge: inexpensive
Paul Kruger, President of the Transvaal, is to the Boers what George Washington is to the Americans. He was a stubborn but deeply pious man who really believed that the Voortrekkers were the elect of God and had been led out of bondage to the Transvaal. He lived in this simple home, with its tin roof and broad veranda, from 1883 until 1900, and would sit on the doorstep and chat to passersby. When Pretoria surrendered to the British in 1900, he went into exile and died in Switzerland, in 1904. His home is now a shrine to one of the country's most remarkable figures. The carved lions beside the entrance were given to Kruger by Barney Barnato. Inside you can see the state coach, presidential train, the rooms furnished as they were when he lived here, the knife he used to cut off his thumb following a gunshot wound, and many gifts and tributes. He worshipped and preached in the Dutch Reformed church opposite the house.

▶ Melrose House 163B3

275 Jacob Mare Street (tel: 012-322 2805)
Open: Tue–Sat 10–5 (Thu until 8); Sun 12 noon–5. Admission charge: moderate
George Heys made a fortune out of operating stagecoaches and other vehicles in the Transvaal and, like all good capitalists, aspired to the life of a gentleman. The result was Melrose House, built in 1886, a delicate confection of gables and turrets, curlicues, wrought iron, marshmallow-pink walls and white stucco, set amid perfectly manicured gardens. The newly enriched Transvaal magnates never understood the meaning of restraint. Heys' new home lacked nothing, and many of its original furnishings are still *in situ*, including a fine collection of English-influenced 19th-century furniture.

In 1902, the house was requisitioned by the British and occupied by Lord Roberts, and later by Lord Kitchener.

The Treaty of Vereeniging, which ended the Anglo-Boer War, was signed on the dining-room table on May 31 1902.

Minor museums

The **Education Museum** (Van Boeschoten Avenue, Sunnyside, tel: 012-443 337. *Open* Mon–Fri 7:30–4. *Admission free*) covers education in the Transvaal since 1837. The **Correctional Service Museum** (Central Prison, Potgieter Street, tel: 012-314 1766. *Open* Tue–Fri 9–3. *Admission free*) describes the development of South Africa's penal system. The **Transport Technology Museum** (Forum Building, Bosman Street, tel: 012-290 2016. *Open* Mon–Fri 8–4. *Admission free*) includes exhibitions on meteorology and Antarctic expeditions.

The Paul Kruger House is still furnished much as it was when the President lived here

National Cultural History Museum   *163B3*

Corner Visagie and Struben Streets (tel: 012-323 3128) Closed for total reconstruction, reopening in 1997
With a collection of nearly 4 million items, this museum ran out of space. The Old Mint is being converted into a state-of-the-art museum, with displays on the human environment and people of South Africa from the Stone Age to the present, with temporary exhibitions on subjects from black music to the liberation struggle, South African silver and San rock art.

165

Sir Herbert Baker's Union Buildings are among the greatest highlights of British imperial architecture

Sir Herbert Baker
Born in Kent, Sir Herbert Baker (1862–1946) was one of the most influential of the colonial architects, scattering suburban England and small neo-Gothic churches across the world. He flourished when faced with the glory of the Empire, and undoubtedly his two greatest works are the Union Buildings, Pretoria, and the Rashtrapati Bhavan (Secretariat Buildings) in New Delhi (over which he had a feud with the other great colonial architect of the period, Sir Edwin Lutyens). Other particularly fine buildings include Rhodes' house in Cape Town, and South Africa House in London.

▶▶   **National Zoological Garden**   163B4

Corner Boom and Paul Kruger Streets (tel: 012-328 3265)
Open: daily 8–5. Seals are fed at 11 and 3, the carnivores at 3:30. Admission charge: moderate
Pretoria Zoo is wonderful. It has over 3,500 animals of 118 species, both indigenous and foreign, some of which, like the pygmy hippo, are extremely rare; more than 190 species of bird; an aquarium with 300 species of freshwater and saltwater fish; and a reptile park. The pens are seminatural, the surrounding gardens green and shady; a cable car up to the local *kopje* offers a bird's-eye view.

▶   **Transvaal Museum**   163B3

Paul Kruger Street (tel: 012-322 7632)
Open: Mon–Sat 9–5; Sun 11–5. Admission charge: inexpensive
Founded in 1893, this museum is dedicated to natural history and ethnography. The Austin Roberts Bird Hall contains the most comprehensive collection of birds south of the equator—all of them stuffed and in glass cases (there is a small Austin Roberts bird sanctuary, with the live version, in the suburbs of Pretoria). Roberts compiled the standard work, *Birds of South Africa*. Every bird here is accompanied by a recording of its song. The museum also contains a large collection of mammals, reptiles, shells and a skeleton of the extinct dodo, while the **Geological Survey Museum** (Paul Kruger Street tel: 012-322 7632. *Open* Mon–Fri 7:15–12:30, 1–4. *Admission charge* inexpensive) covers dinosaurs, fossils, and the geology and mineralogy of the world (with special emphasis on South Africa) and fascinating displays of precious and semi-precious stones.

▶▶   **Union Buildings**   163C4

Open: office hours. Tours can be arranged
(tel: 012-325 2000)
In 1910, following the Act of Union, Sir Herbert Baker (see panel) was commissioned by Jan Smuts to build a fitting administration office. Never one to stint on imperial

grandeur, he created a superb sandstone eagle of a building, swooping with outstretched wings over the city.

The site, Meintjieskop, once belonged to President Pretorius and reminded Baker of the acropolises of Greece. Two great office buildings with domed towers, representing the British and Afrikaner peoples, are linked in reconciliation by the curved colonnade of the amphitheater. Columned loggias were intended to lure ministers out to "lift up their eyes to the high veld." No room was made for South Africa's black population, save a planned "small partly open Council Place for Native Indabas (meetings), where, without coming into the Building, Natives may feel the majesty of Government." It was never built.

Since 1913, this has been the headquarters of the South African government. Nelson Mandela was sworn in as president and still has his offices here.

► **Voortrekker Monument and Museum** *163A1*

Monument Hill, 4 miles from the center of town (tel: 012-323 0682)
Open: daily, 9–4:30. Admission charge: inexpensive
Built in 1936, this 130-foot high granite block is intended to be uniquely African, symbolizing the indomitable spirit of the Voortrekkers, and harmonizing with the vastness, solitude, and mystery of the African landscape. Designed by Gerhard Moerdyk and apparently inspired by Great Zimbabwe, it looks more like a nuclear power plant. Outside, a symbolic *laager* protects the monument, while *assegais* (spears) at the gate represent the power of Dingane. A statue of the mother and child represents the spread of civilization, surrounded by the figures of Piet Retief, Andries Pretorius, Hendrik Potgieter, and an Unknown Voortrekker. This is hallowed ground for the Afrikaners, and the marble relief frieze of Voortrekker history surrounding the lower hall is poignant—if one can ignore the many references to "barbaric" blacks and the "shining light" of Afrikaner civilization. At noon on December 16—the Day of the Covenant (see panel)—a shaft of sunlight falls on the central inscription "Ons vir jou, Suid Afrika" ("We for thee, South Africa").

The Voortrekker Museum has maps of the trek, a tapestry version of the frieze, Voortrekker weapons, clothing, and other memorabilia.

The Covenant
On December 9 1838, following the massacre of Piet Retief and his companions (see page 33), a group of Voortrekkers led by Andries Pretorius took a solemn vow at Danskraal: that if God would deliver their enemies and allow them victory and vengeance, they would mark the anniversary as a holiday of thanksgiving every year forever more. On December 16, they fought the Battle of Blood River (see page 204), and won without a single fatality; the date remains a holiday in the new South Africa, a memorial perhaps to the 4,000 Zulus who lost their lives.

Below: a laager *of bas relief wagons protects the Voortrekker Monument. Bottom: tapestry depiction of a Voortrekker camp in the Monument Museum*

Walk Central Pretoria

This gentle walk covers many of the finest buildings in the city center. Start from the Tourist Office. Allow three hours. *See map on page 163.*

Turn right into Prinsloo Street and take the first right into Church Street, between **Sammy Marks Square**, named after the Randlord (see page 171), and **J. G. Strijdom Square**, dominated by a vast memorial to the former prime minister by sculptors Coert Steynberg and Danie de Jager. To one side is the **State Theatre** (tel: 012-321 9440), one of the finest theaters in South Africa, with five auditoria. Long-exiled black jazz musician, Hugh Masakela, is now its artistic director. **Church Street** runs right across Pretoria from east to west, a distance of 16 miles, and is one of the longest streets in the world.

Continue west along Church Street for three blocks to **Church Square►►** (for guided tours, tel: 012-201 3223), the focus of early Pretoria. In 1857, the Transvaal Republic's Vierkleur flag was hoisted here for the first time—and taken down for the last in 1902. The square housed the market and the city's first stores, with parking for ox wagons. Today, the wagons have been replaced by buses which belch smoke over the central garden and Anton van Wouw's statue of Paul Kruger (paid for by Sammy Marks but set up only in 1954).

There are many magnificent, early 20th-century sandstone buildings around the edge. The façades, at least, have survived the developers. They include the **Tudor Buildings**, built by George Heys (who also built

Melrose House, one of Pretoria's few surviving Victorian mansions

Melrose House); both the old and the new headquarters of the **South African Reserve Bank**; the **Old Mint**; the **Palace of Justice**, which was used as a military hospital during the Anglo-Boer War, and later became the Transvaal division of the Supreme Court; and the Italian-Renaissance style **Old Raadsaal**, seat of President Kruger's republican government. The last two buildings both have lavishly decorated interiors, with cut stone, brass, stained glass, and elaborate tiles jostling for prominence.

Continue west along Church Street. Three blocks farther on is the **Kruger House Museum** (see page 164), and two blocks beyond that is **Heroes' Acre**, the pantheon of Afrikaner greats. Those who lie buried in this cemetery include Presidents Kruger and Verwoerd, Andries Pretorius and, movingly, "Breaker" Morant—the Australian soldier and poet who was court-martialed and executed by the British in 1902 for supposedly murdering a Boer prisoner and a British missionary.

Retrace your steps along Church Street for four blocks, turn right into Bosman Street and take the first left to the **Police Museum** (Compol Building, Pretorius Street, tel: 012-353 6771. *Open* Mon–Fri 8–3:30; Sat 8:30–12:30. *Admission free*), a fascinating collection about the South African police force (from its own point of view).

Turn right into Paul Kruger Street, then left to visit the **Museum of Science and Technology** (Didacta Building, Skinner Street, tel: 012-322 640. *Open* Mon–Fri 8–4; Sun 2–5. *Admission charge* inexpensive), the only hands-on science museum in South Africa. Return to Paul Kruger Street and continue for another block. On your right is the **City Hall**, with a frieze by Coert Steynberg and statues of Andries and Marthinus Pretorius. On your left is the **Transvaal Museum** (see page 166). Straight ahead is Herbert Baker's magnificently overdone and quite impractical **Railway Station** (1910),

designed like an Italian Renaissance palace. This is the home base of both the Blue Train and Rovos Rail (see page 234). The surrounding area is the central focus of the black taxis, and offers a fascinating glimpse of township life. Do not walk around this area at night.

From the station, turn right along Scheiding Street and left onto Jacob Mare Street for **Melrose House** (see page 164). Behind the museum, the road leads into Burgers Park. Turn right to leave the park and left onto Van Der Walt Street, which leads north past the **Staats Model School**. Preserved as a typical Boer school, it is famous for being the place where Winston Churchill was imprisoned during the Anglo-Boer War. Continue down the street and back to the Tourist Office.

Opulent Church Square was the focus of historic Pretoria

GAUTENG

The Cullinan

Found in 1905 and named after Sir Thomas Cullinan, the Cullinan was the world's largest rough diamond, weighing 3,106 carats. It is thought to have been part of an even larger diamond broken up by weathering. The Transvaal government presented it to King Edward VII, who had it cut into nine major jewels. The 530-carat Great Star of Africa (the largest cut diamond in the world) is set in the Royal Sceptre; the 317-carat Lesser Star of Africa is in the Imperial State Crown. The other seven are the property of the British royal family.

170

Sammy Marks and his family still seem alive in their former home

Pretoria Environs

►   **Cullinan**   *146C3*

Premier Diamond Tours, 95 Oak Avenue, Cullinan, 25 miles east of Pretoria (tel: 012-734 0081)
Open: Mon–Sat, 10:30 for guided surface tours; reservations essential. No children under 10. Admission charge: moderate
The Premier Mine is one of the richest in the world, yielding an average of 2 million carats a year since 1902, including some of the world's most famous diamonds—the Cullinan (see page 141, and panel), the Centenary Diamond, and the Premier Rose. Mine tours include the Big Hole (100 acres in area and 1,640 feet deep), the 2,624-foot deep mine shaft, displays of uncut diamonds, and replicas of the most famous sparklers.

►   **De Wildt Cheetah Farm**   *146B3*

*Brits, 30 miles west of Pretoria on the R513
(tel: 01204-41921)*
Open: Tue–Thu 10, and Sat 8:30 and 2:15 for tours; booking essential. Admission charge: expensive
A research and breeding center for wild dog, brown hyena and cheetah, including the magnificent and rare king cheetah.

       Hartbeespoort Dam   *146B3*

About 22 miles west of Pretoria
The 75-mile-long, low ridge of the Magaliesberg is an attractive area with reddish soil and well-wooded valleys, but its history is one of conflict. Early white hunters were followed by Voortrekker pastoralists, leading to a series of savage encounters with the Ndebele in the late 1830s. Men began hunting for gold here long before the Witwatersrand deposits were discovered—and you can still see old diggings, stamp mills, and machinery. Anglo-Boer War forts dot the hills. In the foothills, the 4,000-acre Hartbeespoort Dam is a haven from city life, with boating,

angling, walking, swimming, and bird-watching. A mile-and-a-half-long cableway takes visitors to a viewing site over the dam wall, built in a narrow gorge on the Crocodile River in 1923.

▶ **Pioneer Museum** *146B3*

Take exit 3 off the N4 to Witbank (tel: 012-803 6086)
Open: daily 8:30–4. Admission charge: inexpensive
A delightfully imaginative museum, based around a restored Voortrekker cottage, with several other early buildings and a carefully reconstructed farmyard. There are plenty of hands-on demonstrations including candle-making, baking, and how to crack a bullwhip.

▶ **Sammy Marks Museum** *146B3*

11 miles from the city center off the R104, Old Bronkhorstspruit Road (tel: 012-803 6158)
Open: Tue–Fri 9–4; Sat–Sun 10–4 (Sep–Mar 10–5).
Admission charge: moderate
Randlord Sammy Marks (see panel right) designed his own house, Zwartkoppies Hall (completed in 1886). The somewhat eccentric and richly decorated mansion includes an imposing library, even though Marks was illiterate, and contains most of its original furnishings. There is an excellent tearoom in the rose garden.

▶ **Smuts' House Museum** *146B2*

Take the M1 south to Irene (tel: 012-667 1176)
Open: Mon–Fri 9:30–4:30; Sat–Sun 9:30–5. Admission charge: inexpensive
Jan Christian Smuts (1870–1950) was one of the great Afrikaner heroes and statesmen, commander-in-chief of the British forces in what was then German East Africa during World War I, and later prime minister of the Union. Doornkloof, a modest prefabricated farmhouse of galvanized iron and wood, was his home until his death, and still contains many of the original furnishings, two of his cars, and other memorabilia.

Tswaing (Soutpan) *146B3*

25 miles northwest of Pretoria on the R80 (tel: 01214-987 302)
Visits by prior arrangement only
A 200,000-year-old meteor crater (almost 1 mile in diameter and 1,640 feet deep), surrounding a small soda lake, is the site of South Africa's first environmental museum, with walking trails, archaeological sites (the area has been inhabited for 120,000 years), a traditional African village, and a craft market.

▶▶ **Willem Prinsloo** *146B3*
Agricultural Museum

8 miles from city center. Take exit 27 off the N4 to Witbank, or follow the R104 (tel: 012-734 417)
Open: daily 8–4. Admission charge: inexpensive
This is as much interactive theater as museum, with people in costume demonstrating a wide range of farm activities from plucking geese to working in a black-smith's shop. The museum also features an Ndebele house, a fully furnished farmhouse, and the largest collection of agricultural implements in the country.

Traditional Ndebele home in the Willem Prinsloo Museum

171

South African Art

South Africa has a long and distinguished tradition of white, mainly Afrikaner, art. There have been magnificent sculptors, from Anton Anreith to Coert Steynberg, and some fine painters from the early watercolorist Thomas Baines to the more flamboyant expressionist Irma Stern. Their themes are predominantly the landscape and people of South Africa, but their works are entirely rooted in Europe.

Above: jazzy masks have become a favorite tourist souvenir

The 20th century has also produced some fine black art, such as the sleek, tactile forms of Sydney Kumalo, Bonnie Ntshalintshali's magnificently complex confections of pure imagination, and many of the weavings and etchings issuing from the Rorke's Drift school. On the whole though, most of the black art that achieved public viewing was derivative, somewhat staid and generally unsuccessful in its attempts to emulate European media and styles.

Ethnic arts Exciting things were happening elsewhere, however. Since the first San artist picked up a flint and scratched the outline of an eland on a rock, Africa has of course had its own superb artistic traditions. From glass-beaded Zulu bridal veils and carved tribal fighting sticks, burnished clay cooking pots to intricately patterned Sotho baskets, South Africa was filled with art. But it wasn't something to collect and hang on a wall. Art imbued every aspect of traditional culture, but because it was black and "tribal," even the most creative works were dismissed as handicrafts or curios, and their artists condemned to oblivion and penury. All that is now changing. The First World is weary of its own inventions and is hunting through other cultures for inspiration. Like the art of the Australian aborigines or Native American, the ethnic arts of Africa are finally trickling into view in galleries and shops across the globe. For the first time, people are being invited to take a serious look at these creations of amazing beauty, and to gain some understanding of their creators' identity.

Above: Rorke's Drift weavers. Below: Awakening, *by Coert Steynberg*

Township images The townships spawned a different and very vibrant art, as vivid as jazz, its feet planted in a sense of black rather than tribal identity. Some of it is born of necessity. Penniless youngsters, too poor to afford toys, patiently squat on the street corners, constructing ingenious bicycles, cars and airplanes (complete with moving parts) from tangles of old wire. Bored security guards while away the long night hours by weaving *imbenge* (shallow baskets) from psychedelic telephone cable wires. Others have been more ambitious, creating innovative and exciting fine art that uses exclusively urban themes, progressing with the struggle from the day-to-day street scenes of "township art" to the brutal battering of "protest art," howling with the pain of oppression. With less left to protest against, it has become known as "transitional art," and there, for the moment, it stays, searching out a new identity in these days of multicultural harmony.

Repression repressed South Africa is fertile ground for creativity, for cultural sanctions cut it off from the mainstream and its talents were tempered by repression. The galleries of the world are expecting great things. There are still two separate traditions of art making in the country: the European, in love with the land, and the African, searching for spirituality. Both still hark back to colonialism and apartheid; it will be a long time before their scars fade and are forgotten. Meanwhile, like everything else South African, art is in great demand across the world, and those with artistic talent are likely to be successful.

Among those who have arrived are Robert Hodgins, a painter and graphic artist of figures and urban life; Jackson Hlungwani, a self-taught sculptor in wood of both religious works and symbolic animals; the Ndou brothers (Goldwin and Owen); sculptor Noria Mabasa; and painter and sculptor Malcolm Payne. Also be on the lookout for works by Willie Bester, David Koloane (cofounder of the first Black art gallery in South Africa), Penny Siopis, and William Kentridge.

Olive Pickers, *by Irma Stern*

Where to buy
Cape Town Primart Gallery, Warwick Square, Warwick Street, Claremont, Cape Town 7700 (tel: 021-644 440); Sanlam Art Gallery, 1 Strand Street, Bellville 7530 (tel: 021-947 3359).

Johannesburg Everard Read Contemporary, 11 Selby Road, Parkwood (tel: 011-880 9419); Goodman Gallery, 3b Hyde Square, Hyde Park, Sandton 2196 (tel: 011-788 1113); Newtown Galleries, Market Theatre Precinct, corner Breë and Wolhuter Streets, Newtown 2113 (tel: 011-838 1296).

Durban African Art Centre, 8 Guildhall Arcade, 35 Gardiner Street (tel: 031-304 7915); Coppin-Johnson Gallery, 150 West Street (tel: 031-377 538).

MPUMALANGA AND NORTHERN PROVINCE

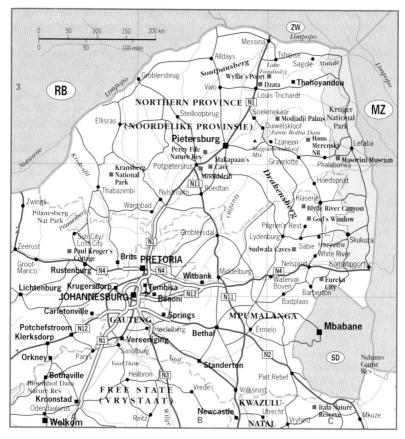

*Giant baobabs dwarf
the scrublands of the
northern lowveld*

Much of Mpumalanga ("the place of the rising sun") lies
in the northernmost section of the Drakensberg mountains, which run from the Swaziland border and taper
off as they near the Limpopo River. Considerably lower
than the Natal section (see pages 208–9), the peaks
nevertheless rear up to form a 7,544-foot rim around the
central plateau before the land plunges down over
the edge of the escarpment to the true lowveld. The
Limpopo, Olifants, and Crocodile Rivers, together with a
host of smaller streams, flow eastward to water the rocky
plains beneath.

The area is spectacularly beautiful, with numerous hiking
trails (tel: 013-764 1058/764 1392 for information), and
is an agricultural paradise, capable of supporting everything from tea to bananas, tobacco and nuts, lemons and
lettuces. Above all, however, it grows trees, mainly pine
and eucalyptus, and is home to the world's largest man-
made forest which covers 618,000 acres. When the early
underground mines were first opened, the local indigenous forests were decimated for building materials,
mine props and firewood. By 1876, a farsighted local
timber merchant, Joseph Brook Shires, was replanting
with fast-growing trees; about half of this timber is now
used for pulp and paper, one-fifth for the mines, and the
rest for telegraph poles and furniture. The eucalyptus has

MPUMALANGA AND NORTHERN PROVINCE

The baobab
The baobab, *Adansonia digitata*, is one of the largest trees in the world, not because of its height, which rarely exceeds 65 feet., but because of its enormous and slightly fleshy trunk. The tree favors a hot, dry climate and can live for at least 1,000 years. It has large white, waxy flowers in October– November and furry, gourd-shaped fruit in April–May. Numerous local legends abound: one says that the baobab once offended God, was uprooted and replanted upside-down; another that the flowers are inhabited by spirits and that anyone picking them will be eaten by lions.

Huge, hardy, horned cattle roam the Venda bush, policed by small boys

proved very damaging; each tree soaks up an enormous quantity of water, which drains the watershed and leads to severe drought on the plains below. Efforts are being made to change to more eco-friendly species, such as hardy Californian pine and mahogany.

The hot, arid area to the north and west feels like a different country. It used to be one. This was once the Boer Zuid Afrikanische Republiek (ZAR), known since the Union as the Transvaal. Most of it was not colonized until the mid- to late 19th century, and the hunters and farmers failed to kill off all the wildlife before it came under legal protection. The black tribes in the region are a mix of refugees from the Zulu Mfecane (such as the Ndebele and Shangaan) and people like the Venda, who are most closely related to the Zimbabwean Karanga-Rozwi group. Even the white "Vaalies" are considered a breed apart by the rest of South Africa. The descendants of the hardiest of pioneers, they are large, tough, rugby-playing, beer-drinking, hard-line conservatives, with a sentimental streak about 2 miles wide. The population is scattered widely, with few towns of any great size and huge farms roamed by wild horned cattle. The Northern Province survives almost entirely on farming, but has been hit severely by protracted drought and is in desperate need of new sources of income. In common with many other parts of the world, it sees tourism as its salvation.

Both the Northern Province and Mpumalanga have a number of thermal spring and spa resorts. The most popular are **Badplaas** in the highveld, where the hot sulphur spring emerges from the ground at a rate of 6,600 gallons an hour, **Warmbad** in the bushveld, **Tshipise** (said to be beneficial for diabetes), **Sagole**, and **Mphephu** in Venda territory bordering the Limpopo River. Badplaas, once known as *Emanzana* ("the healing waters"), and Warmbad, known in Tswana as *Biela bela* ("the water that boils on its own") are the most highly developed, and both have accommodations. Warmbad has a variety of

treatment facilities. Its springs have been in use since the Iron Age—and were long popular with wild animals who, like the settlers of the 19th century, liked to wallow in the warm, mineralized mud.

However, the single real focus of the entire region is the **Kruger National Park**, a vast stretch of protected land, quite literally the size of a country, stretching north along the Mozambique border. Around it cluster countless smaller reserves, infinite numbers of hotels, and tour companies offering every permutation from training as a game ranger to whitewater rafting. Currently, most of the activity is concentrated at the southern end of the park in Mpumalanga, but everyone has a vested interest in spreading the honey farther north. The park needs to control the number of tourists in any one area if it is to avoid overstressing the animals and refute the accusation of being a large zoo, while the Northern Province needs its share of tourist dollars. Even as Nelspruit builds its airport, tiny Pietersburg is converting its old airforce base into an international airport; the road north is being dramatically improved, and even little Hoedspruit is planning to use the local airforce base as an airport for nonscheduled services.

Meanwhile, the authorities are currently negotiating to create a massive new national park—Dongola—linking up with the northern end of the Kruger and running along the line of the Limpopo River, to include territory in Mozambique, Zimbabwe, and Botswana. Since the recent droughts, the territory is totally unsuitable for farming, and many farms in the area have already been abandoned. Villagers are being evacuated from most of the area, but a 112-mile strip around Messina will be fenced off and remain inhabited.

Kruger National Park

Geological saucer
Millions of years ago, the whole Transvaal area was completely flat. As the volcanoes settled down it became an inland sea, and a layer of mud and sand solidified and was turned into shale and quartz. A later eruption poured lava across the center, pushing it down and forcing up the sides to create a vast saucer. Since then, much of the soft shale has weathered away, leaving the hard granite outcrops exposed. The gold-bearing reefs discovered in the cliffs of Mpumalanga are the same geological strata as those found deep underground in Gauteng.

Northern Province

Kruger National Park, see pages 186–7

▶   **Letaba District**   *174C3*

Tzaneen (from *dzana*, a Karanga word meaning "to dance") is an attractive settlement on the Letaba River. Nearby the spectacular **Magoeboeskloof Mountains** climb 2,000 feet up the escarpment, through primeval forest, banana and tea plantations. Tours are available around the **Sapekoe tea plantations** (tel: 0152-305 3241). The Tlou people once made sacrifices to the spirits at **Debengeni Falls**, on the Ramadipa River, now a popular picnic site. Both the **Fanie Botha Dam** and **Ebenezer Dam** offer nature reserves, bird-watching, water sports, and angling. In the **Hans Merensky Nature Reserve** is the **Tsonga Kraal Museum** (tel: 015-386 8727), dedicated to the Tsonga and Shangaan peoples. **Moria** is the headquarters of the Zion Christian Church whose open-air Easter service attracts up to 2 million pilgrims.

The **Modjadji Forest** (17 miles northeast of Duiwelskloof, tel: 0158-21911 for permits) contains the world's largest concentration of a 50-million-year-old cycad, the so-called Modjaji palm (*Encephalartos transvenosus*). This is also the home of the rain queens (see panel), who have protected the forest for many generations.

In Modjadji, cycads as old as dinosaurs are guarded by the rain queen

▶   **Phalaborwa**
       174C3
70 miles east of Tzaneen
Tourist Information, next to the Kruger Park Gate
(tel: 01524-85860)
Phalaborwa's name derives from the Tsonga term *pala borwa*, which means "to smooth the bow"—after the sandpaper-like leaves of the *Ficus capreifolia* which grows commonly in the area. Millions of years ago a series of massive geological explosions forced millions of tons of magma up from the depths of the earth, bestowing the area with untold wealth in the shape of rich deposits of phosphate, copper, and iron ore. The **Masorini Open-Air Village** (in the Kruger National Park, tel: 01311-66509) is a reconstruction of an Iron Age village; archaeological findings reveal that the area was first mined in about AD800. Tours are available around the **Phalaborwa Copper Mine** (tel: 01524-802 342), one of the five largest opencast mines in the world. The **Foskor Museum** (Tambotie Street, tel: 01524-892 019. *Open* Mon–Fri 10–12:30, 2–4) charts the area's archaeological, mining, and ethnographic history.

At nearby **Hoedspruit** (Tourist Information, tel: 015-793 1678) it is possible to see wildlife close up in the **Moholoholo Wildlife Rehabilitation Centre** (tel: 01528-35236), with an ever-changing array of sick and orphaned animals; the **Cheetah Project▶** (tel: 015-793 1633), a breeding and research center for cheetah, king cheetah, and Cape wild dog; and the **Swadini Reptile Park** (tel: 015-795 5203).

Pietersburg   *174B3*

Tourist Information and museums (tel: 0152-295 2011). Satour, corner Vorster and Landdros Maré streets (tel: 0152-295 3025)

Capital of the Northern Province, Pietersburg is a rather dull town which is trying hard to be something more. It has four small museums: the Victorian **Irish House Museum**; the **Hugh Exton Photographic Museum**; the **Art Museum**; and the **Bakone Malapa Ethnic Museum**, which exhibits the history and culture of the Northern Sotho people. The town also has a **Bird Sanctuary** (on the R521. *Open* daily 7–6, entry on foot only) with some 280 species; a 7,900 acre **Game Reserve** (next to Union Park. *Open* 7–6); and a **Crocodile Ranch** (15 miles from the center of town; tel: 0152-291 1867).

Potgietersrus and Environs   *174B2*

Tourist Information, Voortrekker Street (tel: 0154-2244)

This is an attractive town, established in 1852 and eventually named after Piet Potgieter, who was shot in 1854 during the 30-day Makapansgat Siege, a retaliatory strike for the massacre of 28 Voortrekkers at **Mooiddrift** (marked by a monument). Nearly 2,000 Tlou tribesmen died of thirst and starvation in the huge **Makapansgat Caves**. Archaeological digs in the caves have turned up many plant fossils and remains of *Australopithecus africanus*. The **Arend Dieperink Museum** (Voortrekker Street, tel: 0154-2244. *Open* Mon–Fri 8–4. *Admission charge* inexpensive) follows local culture from prehistory to the pioneers. The **Potgietersrus Nature Reserve and Game Breeding Centre** (tel: 0154-491 4314) specializes in rare African species such as tsessebe (antelope) and pygmy hippopotamus.

Roving author
John Buchan (1875–1940), author of *The Thirty-Nine Steps*, lived and traveled in the Tzaneen area between 1901 and 1903. He set the novel *Prester John* in the region, and later expressed a desire to return and be buried here. There is a small memorial to him on the Georges Valley Road (R538) overlooking the Ebenezer Dam.

179

The Magoeboeskloof Mountains are carpeted by shining velvet tea plantations

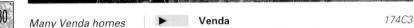

*Many Venda homes
still use traditional
thatch*

▶   **Venda**   *174C3*

Tourist Information (tel: 0159-41577)

In the southern foothills of the **Soutpansberge** (Salt Pan Mountains—named after a powerful brine spring on their western edge), the small town of **Louis Trichardt** (Tourist Information, tel: 015-516 0040) is named after the Voortrekker leader who opened up the area in 1836, before dying of fever, along with most of his party, on the Mozambique coast. The **Schoemansdaal Museum** (10 miles west of the town, tel: 015-516 2082. *Open* Tue–Sun 8–4) is a vivid reconstruction of early pioneer life.

Wyllies Poort, a narrow gorge of towering, lichen-covered cliffs, leads through the mountains to an intensely hot area of wide plains and high plateaux, pitted by deep valleys. It was settled in the 18th century by the baVenda, a small breakaway group of Karanga-Rozwi people from Zimbabwe, who survived there despite the impenetrable mountains, harsh climate and cattle-hostile tsetse fly. In 1979, it was designated the Venda tribal homeland, with its capital at **Thohoyandou**.

It is a land of ancient indigenous forests and lakes, magic and legend. Near mysterious **Lake Fundudzi** (see panel), on the Mutali River, is the sacred **Thathe Vondo Forest**, burial ground of the chiefs of the Thathe clan and forbidden to visitors. At **Dzata** is a ruined stone city similar to those of the Zimbabwe culture; the heads of Venda chiefs are turned to face the city after they die. There are **museums** of Venda history at Dzata and Thohoyandou. The many magnificent forests, waterfalls, and hot springs at Munwamadi and Sagole are well worth visiting; the sandstone caves at Sagole feature San paintings and the largest known baobab tree in southern Africa.

Messina (Tourist Information, tel: 01553-40221), near the Limpopo River and close to the Zimbabwe border, is South Africa's northernmost town and an important copper-mining center. Nearby is a baobab tree park with some exceptionally large specimens.

Mpumalanga

Barberton 174C2

27 miles south of Nelspruit
Tourist Information, Market Square, Crown Street
(tel: 013-712 2121)

On June 21 1884, Graham, Fred, and Henry Barber discovered a rich gold reef in Rimer's Creek. A few days later, the mining commissioner, David Wilson, visited their camp to verify the find and, after breaking a ceremonial bottle of gin over the rocks, christened the area Barberton. Over 1,400 fortune hunters rushed into the area and Barberton turned into a town of music halls, gambling dens, tin shanties, shops, and canteens. At the height of its importance in 1886, the town had a saloon for every 15 inhabitants, while the most famous of the many local prostitutes, Cockney Liz, danced on a billiard table every midnight, auctioning herself to the highest bidder.

Statue of Jock of the Bushveld

There was plenty of gold; but when the town received news of the gold strike on the Witwatersrand, the resulting exodus left Barberton almost uninhabited. Many of the original buildings are still intact, and you can visit several, including the 1886 **Stopforth House** (Bowness Street), the 1904 **Belhaven House,** and 1890s **Fernlea House** (both on Lee Road), while the **Museum** (in the Library) covers gold-rush history and local geology. Other buildings of note in Barberton include the Kaap Gold Fields Stock Exchange (the Transvaal's first stock exchange), the 1887 Globe Tavern, and the Lewis and Marks Building (all in Pilgrim Street), the Anglo-Boer War Blockhouse, and the 1884 Masonic Temple (on opposite corners of Lee and Judge streets).

Today, the town is most famous for the Barberton daisy, first exported to Kew Gardens in London in 1884, and now a staple of many gardens across the world.

Several small gold mines are still in operation in the surrounding De Kaap valley and it is possible to try your hand at panning for gold in the mountain streams. The **Fortuna Mine Trail** is a 1¼-mile walk through Barberton's indigenous tree park and the 1,968-foot tunnel of an old gold mine. High in the hills, 9 miles to the northeast of Barberton, is **Eureka City**, a ghost town which was originally built to house workers of the Golden Quarry Mine on the Sheba Reef, once the richest and most famous gold mine in the world.

Jock of the Bushveld
Percy FitzPatrick arrived from England when aged 22, and became a transport rider, accompanied always by his faithful dog, Jock. In 1907, he published the story of their adventures together and the book became an instant bestseller and local classic. It has never been out of print. A statue to the canine hero stands in front of the Town Hall in Barberton.

One of Africa's most dramatic views, the Three Rondavels in the Blyde River Canyon

►►► Blyde River Canyon 174C2

About 37 miles north of Graskop on the R532
Protected by a 64,248-acre nature reserve, this spectacular canyon (16 miles long and 1,150–2,624-feet deep) was gouged from the earth's crust by the humble Blyde River over a period of 60 million years. There are superb views at regular points along the rim, the finest of them overlooking the Three Rondavels, three conical minimountains bearing an uncanny resemblance to traditional thatched huts. The canyon floor is a true wilderness accessible only on foot with a two-day, 24-mile hiking trail running along the river. Human remains going back to the early Stone Age have been discovered within the canyon, and San cave art is abundant. Surrounding highlights include Marieskop, the highest peak in the district at 6,442 feet, a 656-foot tufa waterfall, and Bourke's Luck Potholes (see page 184). Astonishingly, the area is almost devoid of tourist development.

Echo Caves see page 184

Hazyview 174C2

262 miles east of Johannesburg
Tourist Information (tel: 013-737 7414)
This is one of the most convenient places to stay in Mpumalanga, with every available hilltop crowned by a small and usually delightful hotel. The town itself has little to offer tourists, aside from some lively roadside market stalls. The **Tsakani Silk Enterprise** (about 40 miles north, off the R40, tel: 013-55 3213. *Open* Tue–Thu, Mon–Fri during school vacations, tours at 10:30, 2:30; closed Aug 1 –Sep 15. *Admission charge* expensive) is a silk farm, offering tours of the production and weaving facilities.

Kruger National Park see pages 186–7

Nelspruit 174C2

205 miles east of Johannesburg
Tourist Information, Shops Promenade Centre,
Louis Trichardt Street (tel: 013-755 1988)
Capital of Mpumalanga, Nelspruit is an attractive small town in the Crocodile River valley, garlanded with bougainvillea and surrounded by citrus groves. Named after the Nel brothers who used the area as winter grazing for their cattle in the 1870s, the town developed around the railroad but is now a trading center for local farmers. Nearby are the **Lowveld Botanical Gardens**, and the **Crocgrove Crocodile Farm** (about 15 miles west on the R539, tel: 013-752 5531).

▶▶ Pilgrim's Rest 174C2

Tourist Information, opposite Royal Hotel,
Main Street (tel: 013-768 1211)
After Alec Patterson found the first commercial gold at Pilgrim's Creek in 1873, Pilgrim's Rest grew up as the adjacent miners' village. It is said to have been named by the first group of diggers, who called themselves "The Pilgrims" because they were always in search of spirits (reputedly they arrived complete with a wagonload of whisky!). There were rich pickings; the largest nugget found here weighed about 25 pounds. The miners did not stay for long, but the little town, with its houses of galvanized iron, has survived almost intact. A walking map leads visitors around the cemetery, shops and old houses, many of which are available to rent as vacation cottages. There are several small museums, including the Diggings Site, the Drezden Shop and House, and the typical wood-and-corrugated House Museum. (A single ticket, valid for all the museums, is available from the tourist office.)

Sabie see page 185

▶ Sudwala Caves 174C2

About 22 miles northwest of Nelspruit, off the R539
(tel: 013-733 4152)
Open: daily 8:30–4:30. Tours last 1½ hours.
Admission charge: moderate
The Sudwala Caves are thought to snake back more than 18 miles through the dolomitic Mankelekele in the northern Drakensberg. Tourists normally go no farther than 1,968 feet underground, yet even this section is spectacular, with giant chambers and twisted rock formations. Strange fossil algae such as stromatolites—the earliest identifiable forms of life—date the rocks back 2,000 million years, nearly half the age of the planet. Below the entrance is the open-air **P. R. Owen Dinosaur Park** inhabited by life-size replicas of numerous prehistoric creatures.

White River 174C2

Tourist Information, corner Peter Graham and Kruger
Park streets (tel: 01311-51599)
This small farming town grew up as a resettlement area for British soldiers after the Anglo-Boer War. Just outside town, **Rottcher Wineries** (Nutcracker Valley, tel: 013-751 3884) specializes in orange and ginger wines.

Shopping
The Kraal Kraft (9 miles north of White River on the White River road, tel: 0131-758 1228) is basically a superior souvenir shop and restaurant, but it also has a small museum, and a living African village. The White River Artists' Trading Post (Christie's Village Mall, Theo Kleynhans Street, White River, tel: 0131-750 1053) represents the work of around 60 local artists and craftsmen.

Refuge
In the 19th century, Somquba, son of the Swazi king Sobhuza I, stole a number of royal cattle, then fled. He and his followers hid in the Sudwala Caves while his brother, Mswati, laid siege outside. On several occasions, Mswati tried to smoke out the fugitives, but the caves have a natural ventilation system and they survived. Somquba was finally killed but survivors stayed on, led by his officer Sudwala, after whom the caves are named.

183

The beautiful Sudwala Caves, refuge for a royal thief

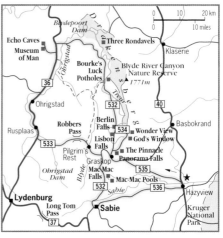

Drive Rim of the Escarpment

184

The scenery is stunning and the air cool and crisp, laden with the scent of a million wildflowers. Allow a minimum of one long day. Start at Hazyview, take the R40 north, then turn left on the R535 to the pretty market town of **Graskop**.

Leave Graskop on the R532 heading north, then turn right onto the R534, a 9-mile panoramic loop with tumbling views off the escarpment and across the lowveld to the Mozambique coast. There are four main viewing points, at **Panorama Falls**, **The Pinnacle**, **God's Window ►►** and **Wonder View**. God's Window has the most breathtaking views, and "played" the edge of the world in the film *The Gods Must Be Crazy*. As the road rejoins the R532, paths lead to two fine waterfalls, the 300-foot **Lisbon Falls** and 492-foot **Berlin Falls**.
The R532 continues north for about 31 miles to **Bourke's Luck Potholes** ► (tel: 013-769 6011. *Open* daily 7–5. Visitors' Centre 7:30–4:45. *Admission charge* inexpensive), which mark one end of the **Blyde River Canyon** (see pages 182–3). This is the confluence of the Treur and Blyde Rivers, a dramatic landscape of strange pools and cauldrons of rock, carved over the millennia by tempestuous water. The 100-foot potholes are named

after a 19th-century surveyor, Thomas Bourke, who found a great deal of gold here. Unfortunately, he worked for a big mining conglomerate and never reaped any of the rewards. The Visitors' Centre has a small museum, and walking trails for visitors with visual or physical disabilities. A little farther along the road you reach the first and most dramatic of several panoramas, with a magnificent view of the **Three Rondavels** and **Blydepoort Dam**.
The road wriggles along the rim of the canyon before looping south to join the R36. After about 6 miles a turnoff to the right leads to **Echo Caves**, a huge dolomitic complex of tunnels and caverns (the largest is 328 feet long and 148 feet wide) in the Molapong Valley. Tap the stalactites and they echo. The eastern end is open to the public, while the western end is home to millions of bats. A neighboring San rock shelter now houses the small **Museum of Man**, displaying archaeological finds from the caves. Return to the R36 and continue south for 23 miles. A turnoff to the left, onto the R533, leads over Robbers Pass to **Pilgrim's Rest** (see page 183).
Continue along the R533 toward Graskop for 10 miles, then turn right onto the R532 in the direction of

Sabie. After about 7 miles, you come to the **Mac Mac Falls** and, 1¼ miles farther on, the **Mac Mac Pools** on the Sabie River. Site of an alluvial gold strike in 1872, these delightful pools and falls were named by President Burgers, who looked at the 1,000-odd miners scratching for gold and was astonished to find that most of them were Scots. The water originally fell in a single stream, but was split by a dynamite blast in an attempt to reach the gold-bearing quartz on the bank.

Eight miles on, the town of **Sabie** (Tourist Information, Forest Museum, Fort Street, tel: 013-764 1241) was founded in 1871, when someone fired a stray bullet during a shooting

Left: the Mac Mac Falls. Below: Bourke's Luck Potholes, named after a successful prospector

party, chipped off a piece of rock and revealed a rich gold reef. Today, wood provides the lifeblood of the town: local forests supply half of all South Africa's needs. The **Forest Museum** (tel: 013-764 41243. *Open* Mon–Fri 9–4; Sat 9–1. *Admission charge* inexpensive) has a varied display on the timber industry, from chain saws to a model church made of matches. Little gray-stone **St. Peter's Church** was designed by Herbert Baker in 1913. The surrounding area has many stunningly beautiful waterfalls, while **Long Tom Pass**, on the R37 to Lydenburg, is one of the most spectacular mountain roads in South Africa. A disabled Long Tom field gun stands at the top as an Anglo-Boer War memorial. Take the R536 which runs along the Sabie River valley for 28 miles, back to Hazyview.

The Sabie River

There are several opinions on how this river got its name. One option derives from the Shangaan name Ulusaba ("River of Fear"). Some say it is haunted by black soldiers killed during tribal wars, whose bodies were thrown into the river without being ripped open to release the spirits. Others, more prosaically, suggest a healthy respect for the river's strong currents and large crocodile population. A more credible option comes from the Karanga word *save*, meaning "sand": this is the name of one of the major tributaries and of the main river farther downstream in Mozambique.

Termite hills feature among the scrubland of Kruger National Park

▶▶▶ Kruger National Park *174C3*

Having descended the precipitous heights of the ruggedly beautiful escarpment, the transition from the highveld to the subtropical lowveld, with its well-watered acacia and mopane woodland, is complete. The rolling plain seldom rises above 1,150 feet as it stretches eastward toward the Mozambique coast. It is a habitat perfectly designed for antelope and lion, elephant, giraffe and hippo; intensely hot and dry in summer, and a natural home to diseases such as malaria and sleeping sickness, it is less accessible for man. Ironically, the fever allowed a small corner of wild country to survive South Africa's farmers. Today, a substantial part of this area is the home of the Kruger National Park. Founded in 1903, the park is 217 miles long, up to 37 miles wide and covers an area of 4,815,008 acres—the size of Wales or Israel. Kruger has five major rivers, 300 types of tree, 114 types of reptile, 507 species of bird, and 147 species of mammal. At any given moment, there are thought to be around 8,000 elephant, 1,500 lion, 1,900 white rhino, 220 black rhino, 15,000 buffalo, and up to 900 leopard in the park.

With fences already down between the park and the surrounding private reserves, plans are afoot to double the core size of the park by creating another in Mozambique. This, eventually, would link with the new Dongola reserve (see page 177) and the parks of northern Natal, and reopen traditional elephant migration routes.

In general, the farther north you go, the drier and hotter the climate, the more desolate the vegetation, the fewer the tarred roads and the more sparse and rudimentary the camps. Most visitors huddle in the southern half of the park, within a day's drive of Skukuza, the main camp and park administration center, which has room for 3,000 visitors on any one night. Keep away from here if you want solitude.

Practicalities From north to south, the gates are: Pafuri, Punda Maria, Phalaborwa, and Orpen in the Northern Province; Paul Kruger, Numbi, Malelane, and Crocodile Bridge in Mpumalanga. The busiest is Paul Kruger, which is the nearest entry point for Skukuza Camp (310 miles from Johannesburg; reception tel: 013-735 5611. *Open* Nov–Feb 5:30–6:30; Mar, Oct 5:30–6; Apr 6–5:30; May–Aug 6:30–5:30; Sep 6–6. *Admission charge* expensive). There are scheduled air services to Skukuza within the park and to nearby Nelspruit and Phalaborwa. There are about 20 camps (reservations tel: 012-343 1991/021-222 810), ranging from small remote camping areas to the main camps which all have a shop, restaurant and cafeteria, picnic facilities, toilets, gas and diesel, telephones, first aid and accommodation. The Kruger is a malarial area, so take precautions. Do not leave your vehicle, drive off the road, or feed the animals. Speed limits are 30 mph on tarred roads, 25 mph on dirt roads.

Private game parks Along the western edge of the Kruger are a number of private game reserves, built up by rich ardent conservationists to contain luxury lodges and hunting grounds. The five major blocks, from south to north, are **Sabie Sand**, **Timbavati**, **Klaserie**, **Umbabat** and **Manyeleti**, of which the 148,266-acre Sabie Sand is by far the most important for tourism and home to a dozen different luxury game lodges such as Sabi Sabi and Inyati (see page 262). Here you can stay in quiet luxury, with the game coming to you at the water hole or river below the terrace. Most lodges are unfenced, and you could even find a buffalo or herd of kudu peering through your bedroom window. In 1993 all the fences between the private parks and the Kruger came down, and while your ranger may not be allowed to track an elephant onto someone else's land, the animals roam freely across all boundaries. You are probably more likely to see the "Big Five" at the lodges than in the main park, as you will be in an open Land Rover with qualified rangers and trackers, who are able to leave the road and take you out on night drives or on foot, activities strictly forbidden within the park itself.

Massive, graceful and spellbinding, elephants and giraffes are highlights of any visit to Kruger

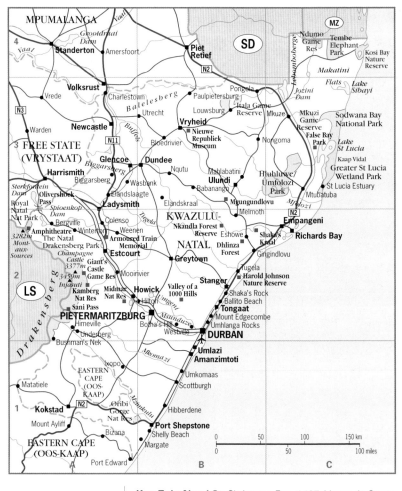

KwaZulu-Natal On Christmas Eve, 1497, Vasco da Gama dropped anchor off a lush green subtropical coast. In honor of the day, he christened it Natalia. Unaware of this fact, its inhabitants continued to raise and rustle cattle, the numerous small tribes squabbling constantly and violently. Nothing disturbed this existence until about 1809, when a formidable Mthethwa ruler, Dingiswayo, began to conquer and absorb many small groups and clans, a task continued by his successor, the great Shaka, from 1815 onwards. The Mfecane (see pages 30–1) marked the true birth of the Zulu nation.

At much the same time, the early Voortrekkers were beginning to look covetously at the fertile valleys, while the British were keeping a beady eye on any territory the Boers might open up. In 1838, the inevitable happened. The Zulus massacred a party of Boer settlers (see page 33) and the territorial disputes dissolved into bitter bloodshed. The Boers annexed much of the Zulu territory and broke away from the Cape Colony, creating the Republic of Natalia. The British took it all back in 1843, naming the new colony Natal. In 1877 the British tried and failed to

KWAZULU-NATAL

Indian Durban
With a huge Indian population to add to the architectural whimsy of the Raj, parts of Durban seem a continent apart. Start at the Victoria Street Market (corner of Queen and Russell streets, tel: 031-306 4021. *Open* Mon–Fri 6–6; Sat 6–2; Sun 10–2) and surrounding Grey Street trading area, a district clouded with spices and billowing gilt-embroidered silk. Other stops should include the beautiful Muslim Juma Mosque (155 Queen Street, tel: 031-306 1724); the Hindu Ganesha Temple (Mount Edgecombe, tel: 031-593 409) and the Shree Ambalvanar Alayam Second River Temple (Bellair Road, tel: 031-593 409) .

annex the Boer territory in northern Natal, and then focused on the Zulu heartland, deposing King Cetshwayo and absorbing his kingdom into the Empire. By 1902, with the final defeat of the Boers, the British had conquered the whole area.

Indian immigrants Natal was immensely fertile, with sugarcane and cotton in abundance, but there was a severe shortage of labor to work the fields. Slavery had been abolished in 1834 and the Zulus showed no interest in working for the white farmers. On November 16, 1860, a paddle steamer from Madras, the *S.S. Truro*, docked in Durban. On board were 342 indentured Indian workers (including 75 women, and 83 children under the age of 14): it was the first of many shipments. Thousands of poverty-stricken Indians were persuaded to sign five-year contracts which forced them to work under appalling conditions. They included Hindus, Muslims, and a few Christians, and came from all areas of the Indian subcontinent, although most were from the south and west. Other wealthier, free Indians also arrived to set up as traders. In 1913, the Natal government, alarmed by the competition from these hardworking merchants, banned general Indian immigration, and in 1920 the system of indentured labor was finally ended, under pressure from Mahatma Gandhi. Today, South Africa has an Indian population of about 1.25 million, 928,000 of them living in and around Durban. The community is renowned for its success in business, while a number of Indians hold high office in government. About 70 per cent are Hindu, 20 per cent Muslim, and the remainder Christian. There are several fine temples and mosques across the province, fascinating Indian markets, and some of the best curries in the world. The remains of Gandhi's first *ashram* still stand at Durban's Phoenix Settlement.

Durban's Golden Mile, natural habitat of Factor 15 sunblock

Sri Ambika — Ambalavanar

A modern kingdom Modern KwaZulu-Natal covers 35,321 square miles on South Africa's eastern seaboard. It is administered jointly from the old white capital, Pietermaritzburg, and Ulundi, the traditional royal seat of the Zulu kings. The monarchy was restored in 1951, although it has no actual power. Nevertheless, the current king, Goodwill Zwelithini, is revered by his people and is a significant force in national affairs.

Of all nine provinces in South Africa, KwaZulu-Natal is the only one that has not submitted happily and peaceably to the new constitution. Sadly, there is still some violence here, with the Inkatha Freedom Party—led by the prime minister of KwaZulu, Mangosotho Buthelezi (himself the grandson of King Dinizulu)—agitating for further autonomy or complete independence.

Both central government and non-Zulus in the province are reluctant for this to happen, but there is no practical reason why KwaZulu-Natal could not survive alone. It has the largest population (about 8.6 million) of any state in South Africa, with rich resources, including plentiful water, coal, minerals and agriculture (Natal produces 75 per cent of South Africa's sugar, along with timber, beef, dairy products, maize, poultry, and fruit). Durban is the largest port in Africa (and ninth largest in the world), while the bulk export harbor at Richards Bay is one of the world's largest coal export terminals. The province also has the most comprehensive tourist infrastructure in the country (with around 3.2 million visitors every year), even though only about 10 per cent of foreign visitors come here. The rest are missing a treat.

Natal has truly magnificent scenery, from the soaring peaks of the Drakensberg to the forest-covered dunes and lagoons of St. Lucia. It has superb Indian Ocean beaches and remote, dramatic game parks that equal or are even better than the Kruger, but with a fraction of the number of visitors. And it has history. It is a land for storytellers, with tales of confrontation and conflict, bloody treachery and glorious heroism. It is indeed a land fit for kings.

The Hindu Shree Ambalavanar Temple in Bellair Road

Natal parks
Most reserves in KwaZulu-Natal come under the jurisdiction of the Natal Parks Board (PO Box 1750, Pietermaritzburg 3200, enquiries tel: 0331-471 961, fax: 0331-471 037; reservations tel: 0331-471 981, fax: 0331-471 980. *Open* Oct–Mar 5AM–7PM; Apr–Sep 6–6. *Admission charge* expensive). A Golden Rhino Passport offers free entry to all Board properties except for taking vehicles onto the beaches, which requires a special permit. Most Zululand reserves are malarial. Accommodations range from self-catering A-frame chalets to three-bedroom cottages. Some provide a cook, but only Itala and Hluhluwe have fully catered lodges.

The marina and docks show that Durban is still a thriving port

Durban

This thriving metropolis is known as Durban to the British, eThegwini to the Zulus, Banana City to the irreverent, and the "city where the fun never sets" to its marketing department. Its population is approaching 4 million and it is growing faster than any other city in the world except Mexico City. It also has a multiple personality, with the normal sprawl of poverty-stricken townships around the edge, tight enclaves of white suburbia, and a decidedly Asian flavor in the middle. Indians make up nearly one-third of the city's population, and many, particularly the more confident and better educated

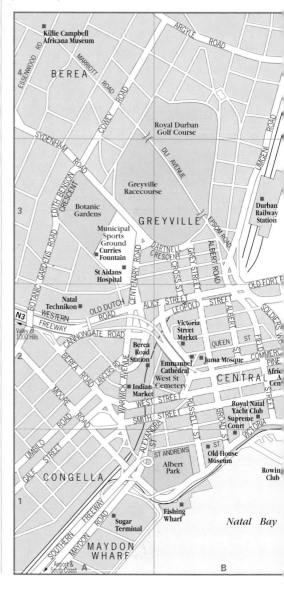

ones, have moved out of the shadows of apartheid and into the city center.

Durban is really about water, with a port so busy that ships sometimes have to line up for weeks before berthing, and a long fringe of sand so perfect that it could have been custom-crafted for the tourist trade. Although it can be very humid in summer, when the tip of the southwest monsoon brushes the coast, the normally pleasant subtropical climate provides 320 days of sunshine a year, and promotes a laid-back outdoor lifestyle with year-round bathing and water sports. Europe's mass-market tour operators are rubbing their hands in anticipation.

The Victorian City Hall is nearly dwarfed by towering office buildings today

Dick King, one of Durban's local heroes

DICK KING
SAVED NATAL MAY 1842

Heroes parade
Victoria Embankment is a gallery of memorial to local heroes: the Da Gama Clock (corner of Aliwal Street), donated by the Portuguese community in 1897, commemorates Vasco da Gama's first visit on Christmas Eve, 1497: the statue of Dick King (corner Gardiner Street) honors a man and his horse, Somerset, who rode 596 miles to Grahamstown in 10 days to raise the alarm and bring relief to besieged British troops in Durban's Old Fort; 14-year-old John Ross made an epic journey to the coast on foot to obtain medical supplies for the Durban settlers.

▶ **African Arts Centre** *193C2*
8 Guildhall Arcade, 35 Gardiner Street (tel: 031-304 7915)
Open: Mon–Thu 8:30–5; Fri 8:30–4; Sat 8:30–12:30
This non-profit gallery is one of South Africa's finest platforms for traditional African art. Browse among the best of the best, from imaginative township crafts to traditional Hlabisa baskets, Rorke's Drift weaving, Tugela River beadwork, and wood carvings from Empangeni. You should even find plenty of affordable souvenirs.

▶ **Botanic Gardens and Orchid House** *192A3*
Sydenham Road, Berea (tel: 031-211 303)
Open: daily Oct–Mar 7:30–5:15; Apr–Sep 7:30–5:45. Admission free
These botanic gardens are the oldest and most beautiful in Durban, with delightful woodlands, ancient cycads, a sunken garden, a scented garden for the blind, and a superb **Orchid House** (*Open* daily 9:30–12:30, 2–5) with over 3,000 specimens.

▶ **City Hall and Museums** *193C2*
City Hall, Smith Street (tel: 031-300 6200)
Francis Farewell Square has hosted the local market since Durban's first European settlers, Henry Fynn and Francis Farewell, set up a trading post here in 1824. It is now dwarfed by Durban's overblown City Hall (1910), a copy of the one in Belfast, Northern Ireland. Inside, the **Natural Science Museum** (tel: 031–300 6248; *Open* Mon–Sat 8:30–5; Sun 11–5. *Admission charge* inexpensive) has hundreds of stuffed animals, birds, reptiles and fish, a life-size model dinosaur, a virtually complete dodo skeleton, and South Africa's only Egyptian mummy. The Insect Arcade includes some truly mammoth cockroaches.

On the second floor, **Durban Art Gallery** (tel: 031–300 6237/8. *Open* Mon–Sat 8:30–5; Sun 11–5. *Admission charge* inexpensive) has fine collections of Victorian paintings, Chinese ceramics and French Lalique glass, as well as a powerful range of contemporary South African art, including magnificent Hlabisa basketware.

▶▶ **Golden Mile** *193D3*
Durban's Golden Mile now stretches 4 miles from Addington Beach, along snazzy, fun-filled Marine Parade to Blue Lagoon Beach. Its sand gleams silver and gold, the water is clearest sapphire, and the foam-topped waves were designed by surfers. As one would expect on a beach with such seductive appeal, it is usually teeming with hot, happy, bodies. For the more adventurous, there

are surfboards, bikes and paragliders (Addington Beach), and opportunities to sail, fish, snorkel and scuba-dive. Durban's beaches are a "Baywatch" special. Leave valuables at home; pickpockets do good business here.

The buzzing promenade is filled with souvenir sellers and ice-cream vendors. **Fitzsimon's Snake Park** (240A Lower Marine Parade, tel: 031-376 456. *Open* daily 9–4:30. *Admission charge* moderate) wriggles with snakes, crocodiles and iguanas. **Funworld** (Marine Parade, tel: 031-329 776. *Admission charge* moderate) has roller coasters, swings and bumper cars. **Mini Town** (Marine Parade, tel: 031-377 892. *Admission charge* moderate) displays scale replicas of Durban's best-known buildings. The **Amphitheatre** park has a busy Sunday flea market. Nearby is the rickshaw stand.

At **North Beach**, you can visit **Waterworld** (Snell Parade, tel: 031-376 336. Opening times vary according to the weather and the season. *Admission charge* expensive) for pulsating and looping water-propelled slides, and the **Umgeni River Bird Park** (Riverside Road, off the N2 , tel: 031-579 4600. *Open* daily 9–5. *Admission charge* moderate), where 100-foot cliffs with tumbling waterfalls provide the backdrop to a lush garden of palms and cycads, home to over 3,000 birds of 400 species.

Rickshaw runners
From 1893, public transportation in Durban included two-wheeled rickshaws. By 1904 there were over 2,000 clattering through the streets, laden with people and packages. The last commercial venture folded in the 1970s, but around 15 now offer rides for tourists. The runners wear colorful costume and, when posing for photographs, add towering headdresses. There are also a few auto-rickshaws (tuk-tuks), familiar to anyone who has been to India or the Far East.

The rickshaw runners are one of the city's most colorful sights

KWAZULU-NATAL

The Killie Campbell Museum houses a fascinating account of traditional ethnic dress in South Africa

▶▶ **Killie Campbell Museum**
192A4

Township tours
Like the other major cities, Durban now runs tours into its former townships. You can visit Newlands, KwaMashu, Richmond Farm, Lindelani, Ntuzuma and the Great Inanda Area, as well as Gandhi's first *ashram* at Phoenix. Not only will you get a whole new perspective on South Africa, but a bonus hangover if you choose a shebeen crawl. Contact Natal Sightseeing Tours (tel: 031-561 5322); Hamba Kahle Tours (tel: 031-305 5586).

Shopping
Durban may well be the country's finest source of souvenirs. There are several market areas, including the predominantly Indian Grey Street area; the Victoria Street Market, with an enticing mix of Asian and African goods, from witch doctors' potions to great heaps of spices; the Zulu Dalton Road Market; the huge Sunday flea market in the Amphitheatre; and the Church Street Arts and Crafts Market.

Add in several particularly good shopping malls, including the Wheel and the Workshop in the city center, and the Westville Pavillion and the Heritage Market on the road up to the Valley of a Thousand Hills.

Corner Marriott and Essenwood Roads, Berea (tel: 031-207 3711)
Open: Tue, Thu 8–1. Guided tours by appointment
Sugar baron Sir Marshall Campbell built himself a magnificent neo-Cape Dutch mansion, Muckleneuk, overlooking Durban. Now swallowed up by the suburbs, it is replete with suitably imposing furnishings collected by his son, William Campbell. His daughter, Dr. Margaret Roach Campbell, was a keen anthropologist and created one of South Africa's finest private libraries of Africana. She also collected a superb array of examples of African material culture, including musical instruments, beadwork, pottery, weapons and costume. A set of 250 meticulous paintings of tribal dress by local artist Barbara Tyrell complete the **Mashu Museum of Ethnology**.

▶ **KwaMuhle Museum**
193C3

132 Ordnance Road (tel: 031-300 6313)
Open: Mon–Sat 8:30–5; Sun 11–5. Admission charge: inexpensive
KwaMuhle means the "place of the good one." This exciting museum, housed in the 1930s offices of the Bantu Administration Board, honors J.S. Marwick, a civil servant during the Anglo-Boer War, who—together with his *iduna* Prince Pika Zulu—helped 7,000 migrant workers to escape from the Transvaal to Natal and Zululand. The museum covers the history of urban South Africa in the 20th century, seen through the eyes of the black community.

► **Local History Museum** 193C2

Aliwal Street (tel: 031-300 6241)
Open: Mon–Sat 8:30–5; Sun 11–5. Admission free
The Old Court House (1863) was Durban's first public building. It now houses a fascinating museum of local history, covering an eclectic mix of architecture and fashion, sugar to shipping, stamps, maps, documents and fine art relating to the city's history. It also runs a wide range of constantly changing and always interesting special exhibitions.

► **Natal Maritime Museum** 193C2

Victoria Embankment (tel: 031-306 6324)
Open: Mon–Sat 8:30–4:30; Sun 11–4:30.
Admission charge: inexpensive
Durban is all about boats, as proved by this harbor-front museum, its many smaller maritime exhibits collected around three old workhorses: the 1927 coal-fired steam tug, the *Ulundi*; the 1961 diesel steam tug, the *J R More*; and the SAS *Durban*, a World War II minesweeper. Sea View Cottage is a recreated early settler's home. There are excellent views of the docks from the deck of the **Harbour Terminal** (Stanger Street).

Old Fort and Warrior's Gate 193C3

Original home of the British garrison, the solidly built **Old Fort** (Old Fort Road, tel: 031-307 1776. *Open* Mon–Fri 10–5) came under attack by the Boer commandos in 1842. Nearby **Warrior's Gate** (NMR Avenue/Old Fort Road, tel: 031-307 3337. *Open* Tue–Sat 8:30–5; Sun 11–5) contains a fascinating collection of battlefield relics, medals, badges, and other military items belonging to the Memorable Order of Tin Hats (MOTHS), an association for former soldiers.

Old House Museum 192B1

31 St Andrews Street (tel: 031-300 6250)
Open: Mon–Sat 8:30–5; Sun 11–5.
Admission charge: inexpensive
This is an exact replica of a settler homestead, built by John Goodricke in 1894, and fully furnished and equipped with domestic items dating from 1850 to 1900.

►► **Seaworld** 193D2

2 West Street (tel: 031-373 536)
Open: daily 9–9. Admission charge:
moderate
Aquaria are always delightful, and this is one of the best: with cruising sharks (fed on Tue, Thu and Sat at 12:30), turtles, reef fish, dolphins, seals and penguins.

Whysalls Camera Museum
193D2

33 Brickhill Road (tel: 031-371 431)
Open: daily 8:30–12:30. Admission free
A surprising find, this little museum above a camera shop is a treasure trove of photographic memorabilia, from 1841 to the present day.

On the water
There are plenty of opportunities for spending a day out in a boat, from harbor tours to deep-sea fishing charters. Regular Deep Sea and Harbour Cruises (tel: 031-377 751) leave from Dick King Jetty, Victoria Embankment. Meridian Adventures (tel: 031-304 1500) run sailing trips on a 40-foot catamaran from the Royal Natal Yacht Club. For other options, contact the Durban Charter Boat Association (tel: 031-301 1115).

Hand-feeding the sharks in Durban Seaworld

Since 1994, South Africa has leapt back into the international arena with impressive prowess. In 1995, Nelson Mandela wore a rugby jersey to watch the Springboks win the Rugby World Cup on home ground. Even more recently, South Africa has taken on the cricketing fraternity with formidable results, and hosted—and won—soccer's 1996 African Nations Cup. The country already has some of the finest golf courses in the world. A new racing circuit is being planned near the coast in an attempt to put the country back on the Formula 1 tour. And Cape Town is bidding strongly to host the 2004 Olympic Games.

Nevertheless, sports except for soccer, still represent primarily a white man's world. The winning rugby team had only one black player, and few black townships or schools have the money for more than a dusty square of open ground where children can kick a ball around. For those with the money, anything you care to mention is on offer, from a full range of competitive sports to riding, hiking, climbing, water sports, ballooning and hanggliding, canoeing, fishing, tennis and golf. Facilities are universally excellent.

Triumph for South Africa in the 1995 Rugby World Cup

Spectator sports Cricket, rugby and soccer are the three top spectator sports, with keenly contested local and national leagues as well as the revitalized, headline-grabbing international competitions. **South African Cricket Union** (tel: 011-880 2810); **South African Rugby Board** (tel: 021-685 3038); **National Soccer League** (tel: 011-494 4520).

Golf Golf is immensely popular in South Africa, with multiple courses in major cities and tourist areas such as the Garden Route, Mpumalanga, and Sun City (home of the Million Dollar Golf Challenge, the biggest

cash prize on the international circuit). Up in the Northern Cape, there is even an all-sand desert course close to Upington. Visitors are welcome at most clubs during the week by prior arrangement (South African Golf Union, tel: 021-467 585). Equipment is available to rent at hotels with their own courses. Costs (inclusive of green fees, caddy fees and tips) vary, but are rarely too expensive.

Fishing There are excellent opportunities for deep-sea and coastal fishing, spear fishing and freshwater trout and coarse fishing. The deep-sea fishing season is November–April (marlin and sailfish) in the north, and September–April (longfin and yellowfin tuna) in

the south. Boat charters include equipment, bait and rods. Permission is not needed to fish in public freshwater, but you may need a license (see panel for contact addresses). They are compulsory for fishing in proclaimed trout angling waters.

Water sports Surfing conditions are among the best in the world, with the Gunston 500 International Surfing Championship in July (South African Surfriders Association, tel: 0391-21150). **Waterskiing** can be arranged on both inland lakes and offshore (South African Waterski Association, tel: 011-440 6421). There is **windsurfing** all year round on inland lakes and seaside lagoons, but most offshore locations are too rough (South African Windsurfer Class Association, tel: 011-726 7076). Equipment can be rented (Windsurfing Africa, 33 Stanley Avenue, Milner Park, Johannesburg 2000, tel: 011-726 7076). **Boats** available for hire range all the way from rowing boats and dinghies to powerboats, racing yachts and motor cruisers (South African Yacht Racing Association, tel: 011-783 4443).

Casting from the beach, East London

Fishing Associations
Contact addresses include: South African Game Fishing Association, PO Box 723, Bedfordview 2008 (tel: 011-53 1847); South African Ski-boat, Light Tackle Game Fishing Association, PO Box 4191, Cape Town 8000 (tel: 021-21 3611); South African Anglers Union, 26 Douglas Street, Horizon View, Roodepoort 1725 (tel: 011-726 5000); South African Freshwater Angling Association, PO Box 700, Vereeniging 1930 (tel: 016-22 1552).

200

Durban Environs

▮ North Coast 188B2

This is an attractive, although increasingly built-up area, with an abundance of places to visit of historical or natural interest.

At **Umhlanga Rocks** (11 miles north of Durban, tel: 031-561 4257), the **Natal Sharks Board** (off the M12, tel: 031-561 1001) offers audiovisual presentations, and dissections of sharks (Tue, Thu 9; Wed 9, 11, 2:30; 1st Sun every month at 2. *Admission charge* moderate). From **Ballito Beach** (Tourist Information, Ballito Road, tel: 0322-61997) onward, the area is tagged the "Dolphin Coast" after the bottlenose dolphins which ride the local surf.

At **Shaka's Rock**, Zulu warriors proved their manhood by leaping into the sea, while the women collected salt from tidal pools at **Salt Rock**. **Tongaat**, in the heart of the cane fields, is the oldest Indian community in South Africa, and features the **Vishwaroop Temple** and the **Juggernath Puri Temple** (1901), and a crocodile farm at **Crocodile Creek** (tel: 0322-23845. *Open* daily 10–4:30; closed Thu in low season. Feeding times: Wed 2; Sat–Sun 11, 3. *Admission charge* moderate). **Hulett's Maidstone Mill** (tel: 0322-24551. *Open* Tue–Thu 9, 11, 2) offers an audiovisual presentation on sugar production and tours during the crushing season.

The **North Coast Museum** (Stanger, tel: 0324-25500. *Open* Mon 12 noon–4:30; Tue 8AM–10:30AM; Wed 12 noon–4; Thu 8AM–1PM; Fri 12 noon–4) includes a sugar mill, household and farming implements, Zulu art and weapons. At the Tugela River mouth, the **Harold Johnson Nature Reserve** (tel: 0324-61574) surrounds **Fort Pearson** (1878) and the **Ultimatum Tree**, where, in 1878, the British demanded that Cetshwayo yield his sovereignty and army to imperial rule.

▮ South Coast 188B1

Central South Coast Publicity, 130 Scott Street, Scottburgh (tel: 0323-21364); South Coast Publicity, Main Beach, Margate (tel: 03931-22322)

The "Hibiscus Coast," as it is known, should be a paradise of golden sand, limpid waters, and tangled coastal forests. Unfortunately, its popularity has engendered a continuous strip of small resorts, making this the Miami Beach of South Africa.

Amanzimtoti (Tourist Information, Beach Road, tel:

Even crocodiles have charm in the baby stage

031-903 7498), known affectionately as "Toti," is a booming family resort with great beaches and endless
entertainments from beauty contests to lifesaving
competitions. **Scottburgh** has a miniature railroad and
Croc World (Old South Coast Road, tel: 0323-21103.
Open daily 9–5. Feeding times 11, 3), with over 10,000
crocs, an aquarium, audiovisual presentations and Zulu
dancing. **Port Shepstone** is home to the narrow-gauge
Banana Express railroad (see page 235), and has a small
Museum (near the beach, tel: 0391-21507. *Open* Wed,
Thu 12–4) covering local history, coastal shipping and
early trade and industry. Nearby is the spectacular **Oribi
Gorge** (15 miles long, 3 miles wide and 1,200 feet deep),
carved out by the Umzimkulwana River.

Shelly Beach, appropriately, has a fine **Shell Museum**
(995 Marine Drive, tel: 03931-75723. *Open* daily 9–5 in
high season; Wed–Sun 10–4 in low season. *Admission
charge* inexpensive). **Margate** is immensely popular with
the young and very young, and has a variety of freshwater
and tidal pools, beach entertainments, an amusement
park and a small **Art Museum** (Viking Street, tel: 03931-
22525. *Open* Tue–Fri 9–11, 11:30–5; Sat 10–1).

Valley of a Thousand Hills 188B2

The uplands surrounding the immense Umgeni River
valley have quintessentially English villages, cool breezes
and dramatic panoramic views. **Bergtheil Museum**
(Queens Avenue, Westville, tel: 031-861 331, ext 235.
Open Mon–Fri 8–1, 2–5. *Admission free*) is an 1850s
settler cottage, with displays about the German community. The **Paradise Valley Nature Reserve** (*Open* daily
7–5. *Admission charge* inexpensive) has 124 acres of
coastal bush with waterfalls and walking trails. **Phezulu**
(Botha's Hill, Durban, tel: 031-777 1405. *Open* 10, 11:30,
1:30, 3:30PM for dance displays. *Admission charge*
expensive) is a slightly commercial Zulu village. The
ticket also allows entry to the **Assagay Safari Park**
(Botha's Hill, tel: 031-777 1208), home to crocodiles,
snakes, and a children's animal farm.

*The extravagantly
named Valley of a
Thousand Hills*

Regal fratricide
In 1825, Shaka built a royal
kraal of some 2,000
beehive huts at Stanger,
known as KwaDukuza
("place of the lost person")
because of its labyrinthine
layout. He conducted
meetings under an old
mkuhla (Natal mahogany)
tree, which still survives in
Roodt Street. On
September 22, 1828, he
was murdered by his half
brothers, Dingane and
Mhlangane, who then
burned the entire town.
A memorial in Stanger
marks Shaka's grave.

Sardine run
In July each year, vast
schools of pilchards
(*Sardinops ocellata*)
migrate north from the
Cape coast, coming
inshore to avoid the fast-
flowing Mozambique
current. Driven ashore by
rampaging predators, they
beach themselves in great
flopping heaps. Locals
pour down to the beach
and simply pick them up.

Battlefields

Colenso 188A2

Tourist Information (tel: 03622-2113)

Colenso, on the Tugela River, was founded in 1855 and named after the controversial John Colenso, Bishop of Natal (from 1853 to 1883). It has several notable historic buildings, including the **R. E. Stevenson Museum** (*Open* Mon–Fri 8–6; keys available from the police station next door) in the Old Toll House (1879) next to Bulwer Bridge, which houses relics of the Anglo-Boer War's Battle of Colenso. On December 15 1899, Sir Redvers Buller made his first serious attempt to relieve the siege of Ladysmith (see pages 206–7). Fought along the river to the east and west of Colenso, the battle was a triumph for the Boer commander, General Louis Botha, and resulted in the deaths of 1,500 British and only eight Boers. Many of the dead are buried in the nearby **Ambleside Military Cemetery, Chieveley Military Cemetery** and **Clouston Field of Remembrance**.

Nearby, the **Armoured Train Memorial** (between Frere and Chievely on the R103) marks the spot where Winston Churchill, then war correspondent of the *Morning Post*, was captured by the Boers in 1899.

►► Dundee 188B3

200 miles from Durban.

Tourist Information, Victoria Street (tel: 0341-22121)

Founded by Peter Smith from Dundee in Scotland, this quiet town in the foothills of the Biggarsberg Mountains saw the first true battle of the Anglo-Boer War (see page 206). The **Talana Museum►►** (Vryheid Road, tel: 0341-22654. *Open* Mon–Fri 8–4; Sat 10–4; Sun 12–4. *Admission charge* inexpensive. The museum arranges tours of all the battlefields) is one of the most impressive local museums in South Africa, built around Peter Smith's cottage (used as a dressing station during the battle) and many of the battle's gun emplacements and forts. Displays include the development of Dundee, the local Stone Age site of Nkupe Cave, Zulu history, glass, blacksmithing and carpentry, and early mining. The coach-house features wagons, farming and transportation. Best of all are some stunningly graphic exhibitions on the Zulu and Anglo-Boer Wars.

The small **MOTHS Museum** (corner Beaconsfield and Wilson Streets, tel: 0341-21250. Open on request, ask at the cottage) has a fascinating collection of military memorabilia from 1879 onwards. About 12 miles from Dundee, the **Maria Ratschitz Mission** was built at the base of Hlatikulu Mountain in 1886 by Trappist monks. Although now abandoned, it is a delightful building with some fine paintings and stained glass.

►► Itala Game Reserve 188B3

Louwsburg, about 40 miles east of Vryheid (tel: 0388-75105)

For opening times see panel page 191

Most of this beautiful 73,276 acres park, in the Pongola River valley, is made up of rocky kopjes, deep valleys and bushy thickets, but about a quarter of the area is rolling golden grassland. It is well stocked with all the major

---

Shopping stops
Elandskraal, near Dundee, is a country town so in touch with its German roots that it still has an "oompah" band. The very cheap and very basic local Trading Store is used as a supply base by the local tribespeople, who wander the aisles dressed in traditional beads and blankets. At Wasbank, Tactile Handcrafts (tel: 034-651 1678) is very exclusive, each carpet or tapestry individually designed and created.

Dressing for war
During the Anglo-Zulu Wars, the British wore single-breasted red tunics, blue trouser and pith helmets. They carried .45 Martini Henry rifles, capable of firing 55 rounds every three minutes, with a range of 984 yards. Zulu warriors went into battle wearing a loincloth, and small headdress (to distinguish regiments). They carried a shield, a short stabbing assegai (spear), knobkerrie (heavy wooden battle hammer) and throwing spears. By the outbreak of war, they also had an estimated 10,000 obsolete rifles. They picked up 800 modern Martini Henry rifles, with ammunition, after the Battle of Isandlwana.

animals except lion, and includes a healthy rhino population. There are guided drives, night drives, and game walks. Those who want a real experience of the bushveld should join one of the three-day hiking trails.

Ladysmith see pages 206–7

▶   **Vryheid**   *188B3*
214 miles northeast of Durban
Tourist Information, Municipality, Hoog Street
(tel: 0381-812 133)
In 1884, the Boers in northern Natal helped Dinizulu, son of Cetshwayo, dispatch his rivals and take the throne. In recognition, he granted them land to establish a Boer republic. The pristine market town remains heavily Afrikaner.

There are a number of interesting museums (*Open* Mon–Fri 7:30–4. *Admission charge* inexpensive). The 1884 Cape Dutch revival **Lukas Meijer House** was the home of the president and is now the main cultural museum, with period furnishings and exhibits on banking, printing, mining, and Zulu crafts. The **Nieuwe Republiek Museum** was built in 1885 as the council chambers and government offices of the Volksraad, and tells the story of the short-lived republic; the fort and prison cells were added in 1887. The **Old Carnegie Library** (1906) houses the local history collection.

Three of the major battles of the Anglo-Zulu War were fought not far from Vryheid; one at **Ntombe Drift** (March 12, 1879); closely followed by those at **Hlobane** (March 28, 1879); and **Kambula** (March 29, 1879).

203

Red wool and brass buttons—a hot and visible uniform for an African war

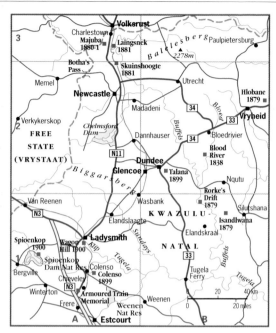

Tour The Disputed Territory

For over 50 years, the grasslands of northern Natal saw bitter conflict as a result of the territorial ambitions of the Zulus, Boers, and British. The area has South Africa's largest concentration of battlesites: most remain untouched and are intensely evocative of the action and the tragedies that once drenched them in blood.

The official Battlefields Route covers 11 towns, over 50 battlefields, and museums, war graves and memorials. Maps, guides, tapes and tours are all available. Many sites are reached only via minor roads and it is impossible to create a continuous route between them. Instead, they are arranged chronologically (see also **South Africa Was**, pages 30–9, **Battlefields**, pages 202–3, and **Zululand**, pages 212–13).

Boer-Zulu War (1838)
Blood River (30 miles east of Dundee *Open* daily 8–5). Following the massacre of Piet Retief (see page 33), a Boer commando of 464 men and 64 wagons, led by Andries Pretorius, took a solemn vow of retribution (see page

167). On December 15, they circled the wagons into a D-shaped formation at the confluence of the Ncome River and a *donga* (large ditch). Next morning, they woke to find themselves surrounded by over 10,000 Zulus. Three times the Zulus were driven off by fierce rifle fire, then Pretorius led a mounted charge: the Zulus fled, trapping their own reserve in the river. In all, 3,000 Zulus died, with only three Boers wounded. The river was renamed after the slaughter and December 16 remains a national holiday. Today, 64 bronze wagons mark the battlefield; there is a small interpretation center and a monument nearby.

Anglo-Zulu War (1879)
Isandlwana (50 miles southeast of Dundee, off the R68. *Open* daily 8–5. *Admission charge* inexpensive) was a tragic mistake. Neither side intended to fight, but at about 11:30 on the morning of January 22, 1879, a British patrol stumbled over the Zulu army of 20,000 warriors, who were forced into attacking the main British column of

Left: Rorke's Drift battlefield, from the Zulu perspective. Above: memorial wagons at Blood River

1,774 men. Within two hours, 1,329 British and over 1,000 Zulu soldiers lay dead. Survivors fled across **Fugitive's Drift,** where most were killed.

Rorke's Drift (26 miles from Dundee, off the R68, tel: 03425-627. *Open* daily 8–5. Craft Centre open Mon–Fri 8–4; Sat 10–3) is named after James Rorke, a British soldier who set up a trading post here in 1849. In 1878, the farm became a Swedish mission and a British military base. At 3:15 on January 22, 1879, two survivors of the battle at

Isandlwana raised the alarm at Rorke's Drift, 9 miles from Fugitive's Drift. The tiny garrison of 139 soldiers, 35 of them hospital patients, began to fortify the base using everything from maize sacks to cookie boxes. The attack, by four Zulu regiments (4,000 men) under the command of King Cetshwayo's brother, Dabulamanzi, began at 4:30. Twelve hours later the Zulus finally withdrew, leaving behind nearly 600 dead. Only 17 British soldiers were killed. Eleven Victoria Crosses were awarded to the defenders—more than any other single engagement in history. The rebuilt hospital now houses an interpretation center. Next door, the **ELC Crafts Centre** (tel: 03525-627) produces textiles, carpets, tapestries, and pottery.

First Anglo-Boer War (1880-81)
Majuba (on the N11 between Volksrust and Newcastle. *Admission charge* inexpensive). On April 12 1877, the British annexed the South African Republic; on December 13 1880, guerrilla resistance blossomed into full-scale war. The Governor of Natal, Sir George Colley, marched north, only to lose 150 men at Laingsnek (January 28) and a further 150 at Skhuinshoogte (February 8). On 27 February, Sir George camped on the Hill of Doves, Majuba, along

19th-century engraving of the battle at Rorke's Drift

with a force of 579 men. A commando of 150 Boer volunteers scaled the mountain and surprised the British, who panicked and fled. Colley himself was killed. It was the deciding point in the war. The British signed an armistice on March 6, returning the ZAR to the Boers.

Second Anglo-Boer War (1899–1902)

Talana (Dundee, see also page 202). By the time war was declared on October 9, 1899, there were 4,000 British troops stationed in Dundee, ready to protect the local coalfields. On October 20, **Talana Hill** (hiking trail from the Talana Museum) became the scene of the first battle of the Anglo-Boer War when a 14,000-strong Boer army attacked the British camp. In a hard-fought struggle, the British eventually repelled their attackers, leaving 51 British and 145 Boers dead. Two days later, the British retreated. (This was the first time the British abandoned their red coats in favor of practical khaki.)

Ladysmith►► (144 miles from Durban. Tourist Information, Town Hall, Murrchison Street, tel: 0361 22992) became a focal point for the Anglo-Boer war, following the British rout at Nicholson's Nek on October 30, 1899. From November 2, the little town on the Klip River was besieged by the Boers for 118 days, while 53,000 troops fought a series of bitter and bloody encounters nearby. The siege was eventually lifted by Sir Redvers Buller on February 28, 1900. Like Mafeking, it captured the public imagination, and Ladysmith became a household name across the Empire. It finally proved disastrous for the Boers, who had pinned down too many

> ❑ **Life under seige**
> At the start of the siege, there were nearly 20,000 people crowded inside the 17-mile perimeter of Ladysmith, 12,500 of them fighting men, many others battle-weary refugees from northern Natal. There were also 4,000 cattle and a good supply of rations. Although regularly shelled by the Boers, surprisingly little damage was done to people or property. As time wore on, however, the effects of poor sanitation and inadequate fresh food meant that almost 30 people were dying from disease every day. When Sir Redvers Buller finally arrived, he found 2,800 people sick and wounded, and 3,037 soldiers and 54 civilians dead. ❑

troops in an area with no lasting strategic value.

The **Siege Museum** (Murchison Street, tel: 0361-22231. *Open* Mon–Fri 8–4:20; Sat 8–12. *Admission charge* inexpensive) has vivid displays and graphic descriptions of events, and will provide a detailed guide to local sites, best appreciated from the high ground on one of the encircling hills. The museum building, originally the local market hall, was used as a rations store during the siege. Next door, the **Town Hall** (built 1893) acted as a hospital, but was still shelled by the Boers, who did not believe that the Red Cross flag was genuine. You can see the scars on the clock tower. In front stand two British 6.3inch Howitzer RML guns, Castor and Pollux, and a replica Boer Long Tom.

British Howitzer gun outside the Town Hall in Ladysmith

Spioenkop, an ignominious and unnecessary British defeat

Inside **All Saints Anglican church** (1882), memorial tablets list those who died in the Siege and the Relief, alongside stained-glass windows and the Regimental Standard, presented to the Natal Carbineers by the Prince of Wales in 1925. In the gardens of the Hindu **Vishnu Temple** is a statue of Mahatma Gandhi, who was a stretcher bearer with the relief column. The Muslim **Soofi Mosque** is considered one of the most beautiful in South Africa. The **Blockhouse Museum** (4 miles from Ladysmith, off the Harrismith road, tel: 0361-24091. *Open* by appointment) is a replica of a British blockhouse, with a collection of Zulu and Boer War artifacts.

Wagon Hill (Platrand, 3 miles south of Ladysmith) was a key British defensive position during the Siege of Ladysmith. On January 6, 1900, Boer commandos stormed the hill, but had to retire after a fierce battle. Various fortifications are visible and there are several memorials. The modern **Burgher Memorial**, with its seven stylized stone hands, commemorates the 781 Natal Boers who died during the war, 310 of whom are buried here.

Spioenkop (off the R600, west of Ladysmith. *Admission charge* inexpensive)

❏ **Long Tom**
The Boers had only four of these famous field guns. Made in France, the 155mm Creusot weapons fired 97-pound shells over a distance of about half a mile. Each gun weighed 7 tons and was pulled by 16 oxen. They were capable of doing an extraordinary amount of damage, and have achieved immortality in place-names such as Long Tom Pass, in the Mpumalanga Drakensberg. All four guns were destroyed by the Boers toward the end of the war, to stop them from falling into British hands. ❏

On January 23, 1900 this small, rocky hill was attacked by 1,700 British troops. The 15 Boers fled, leaving it deserted. The delighted British cheers reached the main Boer camp, and the next morning 3,600 Boers attacked in earnest. Although the battle lasted all day, the kopje was never reinforced from the 25,000 British troops below. By the evening, with 800 British and 200 Boers dead, both sides believed they had lost, and withdrew. Several hours later, the astonished Boers found the hill deserted and moved in. The battlefield is now part of the **Spioenkop Dam Nature Reserve**.

The Drakensberg

The high Drakensberg, which run for 125 miles along the western border of KwaZulu-Natal, are part of a much longer chain of basalt stretching from the Cape to the Limpopo. They were known to the Zulus as *uKhahlamba* (Barrier of Spears); the Afrikaners named them Dragon Mountains.

There are few set attractions here. With jagged 9,840-foot peaks, flowing fields of red-gold grass, meadows as rich in flowers as a medieval tapestry, San rock paintings, raptors soaring on the thermals, and gushing waterfalls, they would seem superfluous. The mountains are preserved as a recreational wilderness, with unsurpassed walking, hiking and climbing. Detailed maps are available at trailheads; permits are needed for most longer hikes. For the less energetic, there are numerous small resorts, cottages and campsites, with gentle strolls through the lower-lying hills. Activities include superb trout fishing, climbing, bird-watching, riding and hot-air ballooning. The best months to visit are probably April and May. The frosty winters are too cold, while midsummer mist and rain may obscure the view.

▶▶▶ **Central Drakensberg** 188A2

The central section of the Drakensberg has the highest mountains in the country, crowned by Injasuti (11,346 feet). Close behind are Champagne Castle (11,097 feet), Giant's Castle (10,870 feet), and Cathkin Peak (10,329 feet). Cathedral Peak (9,853 feet) is the easiest climb in the Natal range. Below them, the 85,253-acre **Giant's Castle Game Reserve** has splendid herds of eland while its birds include black eagle and lammergeier. Carcasses are laid out at the **Lammergeier Hide** (May–Sep, Sat–Sun; tel: 0363-24616; reservations essential, arrive before 8AM) to attract the huge, rare, bearded vultures. The area is also one of the world's richest stores of San art: the **Main Caves** (1¼ miles south of Main Camp. *Open* Mon–Fri, tours at 9 and 2; Sat–Sun 9–3; ask here for information on other caves in the area. *Admission charge* moderate) have over 500 paintings in a single large shelter. The **Kamberg Nature Reserve** has excellent trout fishing (season Sep 1–Apr 30; permits obtainable from the office), while the 2½-mile **Mooi River Trail** is specifically designed for the physically disabled. The **Ardmore Studio** (D275, off Champagne Castle Road, tel: 036-468 1314. *Open* daily 9–4:30) is a collective of over 40 superb Zulu and Sotho artists.

▶▶▶ **Northern Drakensberg** 188A2

The north is dominated by the **Amphitheatre**, a 5-mile crescent flanked by two peaks—the Sentinel (10,381 feet) and the Eastern Buttress (9,994 feet). Between them, the skinny **Tugela Falls** skip over several cascades before plummeting 2,014 feet. With a combined drop of 3,110 feet, these are the second highest falls in the world (the highest are the Angel Falls, Venezuela). Drive to the base of Sentinel Peak, and walk to the waterfall along the rim of the Amphitheatre on reasonably flat ground, or climb the summit of the Sentinel via a hiking trail and chain ladders. The Tugela River is only one of five major

---

Drakensberg museums
In Estcourt, Fort Durnford (Tourist Information and museum, tel: 0363-23000. *Open* Mon–Thu 9–12, 1–4:30; Fri 8–12, 1–3:45; weekends by appointment), the largest fort in Natal (1847), is now a military and social museum. Winterton Museum (Kerk Street, tel: 036-488 1620. *Open* Wed, Fri 1–4; Sat 9–12) covers local geology, flora, fauna, and history. In Himeville, a loop-holed fort, is now a museum of rural life (tel: 033-702 1184. *Open* Wed, Fri 10–12;, Sat–Sun 9:30–12. Admission free).

Guided hikes
The Mountain and Backpackers' Club (tel: 031-863 970) runs regular guided hikes through the Drakensberg and can provide information for those wishing to set out on their own. For other information, contact Natal Parks Board (see page 256).

rivers, which include the Orange, born on **Mont-aux-Sources** (10,765 feet). Much of this area comes within the 19,769-acre **Royal Natal National Park**, which has over 200 species of bird and several sites with San rock paintings. The road from **Bergville** (Tourist Information, tel: 036-448 1557) to Harrismith leads over the breathtaking 6,872-foot **Olivershoek Pass**.

▶▶▶ Southern Drakensberg   188A2

Tourist Information, Main Street, Underberg
(tel: 033-701 1096)
Although close to the coast and major cities, this is the most rugged of the three areas, with several small nature reserves and some heavy-duty hiking for those who want a challenge. The **Giant's Cup Trail** (37 miles, five days) runs south from Sani Pass to Bushman's Nek, and is part of the National Hiking Way.

The remote, tortuous, rugged and spectacularly beautiful **Sani Pass** is the highest in South Africa, climbing from 3,936 to 9,427 feet as it crests the jagged dragon's back. It follows the upper valley of the Mkomazana River and was always the traditional crossing between the Drakensberg and Lesotho. Much of the road runs through protected wilderness areas (four-wheel drive and passport required).

The sound of music
The Drakensberg Boys Choir is magnificent, equal to the best in the world. The school near Winterton educates boys from 9 to 15 years old. The choir has toured in the United States, Europe, Israel, and the Far East. When at home, it holds regular concerts on Wednesdays and Saturdays in the school auditorium (tel: 036-468 1012).

The Amphitheatre is the most dramatic and instantly recognizable rock formation in the Natal Drakensberg

The Colonial Buildings in Pietermaritzburg

Marathon
In May each year, South Africa's masochists have their day, with the running of the Comrades Marathon. It is a staggering 51 miles in length, between Durban and Pietermaritzburg, uphill and downhill in alternate years.

Pietermaritzburg and the Natal Midlands

▶ ▶ ▶ Pietermaritzburg   188A2

Founded by the Voortrekkers in 1838, and set in the fertile Msunduze Valley, Pietermaritzburg (Pietermaritzburg Publicity Association, 177 Commercial Road, tel: 0331-451 348) was named after two Boer trek leaders killed by the Zulus, Piet Retief and Gerrit Maritz. Since 1845 it has been capital of Natal (currently sharing the honor with Ulundi).

The streets around **Church Street** reveal a feast of magnificent Victorian and Edwardian architecture, in particular the towering redbrick **City Hall** (1900). Other buildings of note are the 1889 **Old Natal Parliament** (tel: 0331-458 233. *Open* Mon–Fri 8–4, by prior arrangement only); **Old**

Government House (home of the governors until 1910); and Philip Dudgeon's fine **Standard Bank** (1882). A statue of Mahatma Gandhi by Phil Kolbe stands in front of the old **Colonial Buildings**. John William Colenso, the bishop who established the Church of England in Natal is buried in the **Cathedral of St. Peter** (1872). **St. George's Garrison Church** (1898) is part of **Fort Napier** (1843). There is also a fine Hindu temple, the **Sri Siva Soobramoniar and Marriamen Temple** (Lower Longmarket Street. *Open* Mon–Sat 7–6; Sun 8–6).

Museums The **Natal Museum** (237 Loop Street, tel: 0331-451 404. *Open* Mon–Sat 9–4:30; Sun 2–5. *Admission charge* inexpensive) covers dinosaurs, birds and marine life, pan-African art, shipwrecks, and settler history. The **Macrorie House Museum** (11 Loop Street, tel: 0331-942 161. *Open* Tue–Thu 9–1; Sun 11–4. *Admission charge* inexpensive), the Victorian home of Bishop Macrorie, is now restored to former glories with beautiful antiques and costumes. The **Tatham Art Gallery** (corner Church Street and Commercial Road, tel: 0331-421 804. *Open* Tue–Sun 10–6. *Admission free*) is housed in the **Old Supreme Court** (1871) and contains late 19th- and early 20th-century paintings as well as porcelain and glass, and a collection of contemporary South African art. The annex is a living museum, showing ethnic arts in creation. The **Voortrekker Museum** (340 Church Street, tel: 0331-946 834. *Open* Mon–Fri 9–4; Sat 8–12. *Admission free*) is in the gabled **Church of the Vow**, built in 1841 in repayment of the Covenant (see page 167). Next door, **Welverdient House** was the home of Andries Pretorius (see page 162). The oldest two-story house in the city, **333 Boom Street**, has been refurbished as a Boer home.

Parks and Gardens The **Garden of Remembrance** contains a memorial to 13,000 South Africans who died at the Battle of Dellville Wood in World War I, with a Weeping Cross that oozes sap on its anniversary. The beautiful **Natal National Botanic Gardens** (2 Zwartkop Road, Prestbury, tel: 0331-443 585. *Open* Oct–Mar, Mon–Fri 7:30–6; Sat–Sun 8–6; Apr–Sep closes 5:30. *Admission charge* inexpensive at weekends, free midweek) contain plants indigenous to Natal.

The Natal Midlands   188A2

Between the Drakensberg and the coastal belt, the **Midlands Meander** (brochures available) leads through hills and country towns with stops at artists' studios, and antiques shops. In Howick (Tourist Information, tel: 0332-305 305), visit the 312-foot **Howick Falls** on the Mgeni River, and **Howick Museum** (Fallsview, tel: 0332-306 124. *Open* Tue–Fri 9–12, 2–3:30; Sun 10–1. *Admission charge* inexpensive; free on Wed) with local history and military memorabilia. The **Midmar Public Resort and Nature Reserve** offers game viewing and water sports, and the **Midmar Historical Village** (tel: 0332-305 351. *Open* daily 9–4. *Admission charge* moderate) is a multi-ethnic museum. The **Natal Railway Museum** at Hilton (Hilton Avenue and Quarry Road, tel: 0331-431 857. *Admission charge* inexpensive) has a collection of steam locomotives used on the **Umgeni Steam Railway** (see page 234).

Gandhi in Africa
On June 7, 1893 at Pietermaritzburg station, a young high-caste Indian lawyer, Mohandas Karamchand Gandhi, was ejected from first class and told to sit in the luggage wagon. When he protested, he was thrown off the train. The incident was a turning point in his life. For the next 20 years, he fought for the rights of Indians, developing his theories of *satyagraha* (passive resistance) and influencing the course of South African nationalism. He returned to India in 1914, was given the honorific "Mahatma" (Great Soul), and went on to change the course of world history and philosophy.

211

Emblems
Pietermaritzburg's coat of arms, supported by wildebeest, had to be altered in 1908 as the original version showed the animals running in the wrong direction —a symbol of cowardice. The elephant is a Zulu symbol for a great ruler's place, Umgungundhlovu.

The elephant marks Pietermaritzburg's status as a capital

Zululand

▶ **Eshowe and Environs** *188B2*

Tourist Information, Osborne Road (tel: 0354-74079)
Eshowe ("the sound of wind in the trees") is a lovely little
hill town near the last remnants of the indigenous **Dhlinza
Forest** ("a gravelike place of meditation"). Massive, brick-
built **Fort Nongqai** (1883) garrisoned the Natal Native
Police. It now houses the **Zululand Historical Museum**
(Nongqai Road, tel: 0354-42419. *Open* daily 9–4.
Admission charge inexpensive) with fine collections of
furniture, royal *ingxothas*, Zulu household items, St. Lucia
ammonite fossils, and a silver beer mug given to King
Cetshwayo by Queen Victoria in 1882.

Shaka built a kraal overlooking the Nkwalini Valley (about
16 miles from Eshowe on the P230). Here he executed all
those who had tormented his beloved mother during their
years of struggle, naming the place **KwaBulawayo** ("the
place of killing"). Warriors who returned without their
spears would be punished at the **Coward's Bush**.

Cetshwayo's first kraal (1860) was at **Gingindlovu**. The
name ("swallower of the elephant") commemorates his
victory over his brother, Mbulazi, for the Zulu throne. The
king died in 1884 and is buried in the aptly named
Nkandla Forest ("place of exhaustion"), 4,003 acres of
unspoiled indigenous forest.

Shakaland (9 miles from Eshowe on the R68, tel:
0354-600912. *Open* daily, tours at 11, 12:30, or stay
overnight) was created as a set for the TV series
Shaka Zulu in 1985, as the kraal of Shaka's father,
Zenzangakhona. It is popular with tourist groups from
Durban and does put on a good show with excellent
insights into Zulu culture. On the same farm, the
Simunye Pioneer Settlement combines the Zulu

The bloodstained king
In 1828, Dingane
(*c.*1795–*c.*1843)
assassinated his half-
brother, Shaka, and
became king of the Zulus.
In 1838, he met with Piet
Retief and a party of 101
Boers to negotiate a treaty.
He supposedly signed a
land deal, but then massacred the entire Boer party
before attacking Boer
camps at Bloukrans River
and Boesmans River.
Afrikaner retribution at
Blood River (see page 204)
led to his eventual down-
fall. In 1840 he was over-
thrown by his half-brother,
Mpande, and fled to
Swaziland.

*Men build the frame
of the house, but
women do the
thatching in Zulu
communities*

heritage with a Voortrekker experience, including ox-wagon rides.

Nearby, **KwaBhekithunga** (Stewart's Farm, off the R34 between Empangeni and Melmoth, tel: 0354-600644. *Open* for tours by appointment. *Admission charge* expensive) is a Zulu cultural village, with dancing, dinner, and an excellent craft center.

▶▶ Hluhluwe-Umfolozi National Park   *188C3*

Established in 1897, this is a 237,226-acre complex of two parks linked by a corridor of land 5 miles wide, with habitats ranging from woodland and forest to savannah

and grassland. It shares with St. Lucia the distinction of being the oldest wildlife sanctuary in Africa. In the 1960s, it was the home of Operation Rhino, a conservation program to ensure global survival of the white rhino, and the park still has the world's largest concentration of black and white rhino. It also has all the other major species, a wide selection of birds, and a small museum of Zulu culture and history.

Nearby **Dumazulu** (near Empangeni, tel: 035-562 0144/ 562 0343. *Open* 8:15, 11, 3:15 for tours and dance displays; and at 6PM including dinner—minimum 20 people. *Admission charge* expensive) is probably the best of the many Zulu villages in the country. The name means "thundering Zulu" and the whole complex was built by Zulus who also act as guides, under the close supervision of a cultural expert. Situated right out in the bush, it has an authentic feeling of old Africa which is entirely lacking at many of the more polished attractions. The 42,009-acre **Phinda Resource Reserve** includes sand forest, mountain, wetlands, and river valleys. The whole area has been restocked with a wide range of game, including the "Big Five", and has several luxury lodges which offer their guests excellent game watching, bushwalks, canoe safaris, and river cruises.

Impala at a water hole in Hluhluwe-Umfolozi National Park

▬ Mgungundlovu   *188B3*

In 1828, Dingane moved the Zulu capital to Mgungundlovu ("the place of the great elephant") in the Mfolosi valley. It was here, in 1838, that he murdered Piet Retief and his followers. The city was torched when Dingane abandoned it in 1839, but its core has been accurately rebuilt. It also has a small **museum** (tel: 03545-2254. *Open* daily 8–5) and an obelisk **memorial** to Piet Retief and his followers. Most of the ancestors of the Zulu royal lineage, including Dinizulu (1884-1913) and Senzangakhona (father of three kings: Shaka, Dingane, and Mpande), are buried near by at **eMakhosini** ("the place of kings").

213

Northern KwaZulu

Traditional homeland of the Tonga and Mabudu peoples, this remote Maputaland region of KwaZulu-Natal, near the Mozambique border, is 3,475 square miles of hot, flat, sandy, tree-covered terrain, crisscrossed by rivers, with heavy summer rains, dense populations of hippo and crocodile and a staggering array of birds. Much of the area is now carved up into magnificent remote game parks, rich in game and empty of people, such as the 85,609-acre **Mkuze Game Reserve** (about 208 miles northeast of Durban), an area of fever trees and fossils in the foothills of the Lebombo Mountains, and **Sodwana Bay National Park** (about 248 miles from Durban via the Lower Mkuze road), with lakes, coastal dune forest, and both tidal and coral reefs.

In the far north, the large inland **Ndumu-Tembe National Park** comprises the 24,711-acre **Ndumu Game Reserve**, often described as a miniature Okavango, teeming with wildlife, fish and over 400 species of bird, and the smaller **Tembe Reserve** set up to provide a safe haven for Mozambique's elephants. On the coast, **Kosi Bay Nature Reserve** (accessible only by four-wheel-drive vehicles) envelopes the magnificent forests around **Lake Sibaya** (South Africa's largest freshwater lake) with mangrove swamps, and golden sand beaches where leatherback and loggerhead turtles waddle ashore to lay their eggs.

▶▶▶ St Lucia   188C3

Tourist Information, corner Katonkel and McKenzie streets (tel: 035-590 1143)

The unique 95,587-acre **Greater St Lucia Wetland Park**, one of the three most important wetlands in Africa, surrounds an ancient 25-square-mile lake, with several distinct ecosystems including coastal dune, wetland, estuarine, bushveld, coastal forest, mangrove swamp, lily pan, and grassland. It is a magnificent bird-watching area, with 450 species including large colonies of pelicans and flamingos, Goliath and other herons, fish eagles and three species of kingfisher. **False Bay Park** on the northwestern shore of Lake St. Lucia comprises 5,553 acres of dry forest and coral ridges. Hundreds of rare pink-backed pelicans congregate in the trees on the banks of the Hluhluwe River from December to April.

The **Crocodile Centre** (*Open* daily 7–5:30; feeding time Sat 3. *Admission charge* moderate) has a small ecology museum and live crocodiles of every species in Africa. An 80-seat launch, the *Santa Lucia* (tel: 035-590 1340. *Tours,* taking two hours, daily at 8:30, 10:30, 2. *Admission charge* expensive) runs regular trips around the lake. It is also possible to rent private boats from Charters Creek and Fanies Island. There is good fishing (except in the Marine Reserve), but swimming and water sports are not a good idea, with about 2,000 crocodiles, 800 hippos, black-fin, and Zambezi River sharks. Deep-sea fishing is available from St. Lucia town. The **Marine Reserve** stretches along the coastline from Sodwana Bay in the north to Cape Vidal in the south and 2 miles out to sea. It contains the southernmost coral reefs in the world.

Animal traffic
Increasing numbers of South Africa's farmers and game reserves hold regular auctions at which anything from a cheetah to a dung beetle may be sold. The inclusion of species such as rhino is part of a serious drive to save them from extinction; gentler animals, such as antelope and zebra, may be bought purely for entertainment. There are many new hunting or game reserves opening for tourists, and there is also a move to farm game for the table.

Northern Natal, with its tropical waters, offers excellent fishing in the lagoons, lakes and open sea

Ulundi   188B3

Tourist Information (tel: 0358-21602)
Every Zulu king founded his own new capital abandoning that of his predecessor, and in 1873 Cetshwayo built Ulundi. On July 4, 1879, British troops, led by Lord Chelmsford, defeated 20,000 Zulus at Mahlanathini Flats. The military power of the Zulus was finally broken: King Cetshwayo was soon captured and his kingdom annexed to the British Empire. Ulundi is now joint capital of KwaZulu-Natal and seat of the **Legislative Assembly**, where amazing tapestries depict the history of KwaZulu (viewing by appointment only, tel: 0358-20211).

Ulundi was succeeded by a new capital at **Ondini** (meaning "the heights"), which was, in turn, destroyed by Swazi invaders. Archaeologists have uncovered the foundations, and the royal kraal has been completely rebuilt in the traditional style with dome-shaped woven grass dwellings *(uhlongwa)*. The kraal forms part of the **KwaZulu Cultural Museum** which is on the road now called King Cetshwayo Highway (tel: 0358-791 854. *Open* Mon–Fri 9:30–5).

BEYOND SOUTH AFRICA

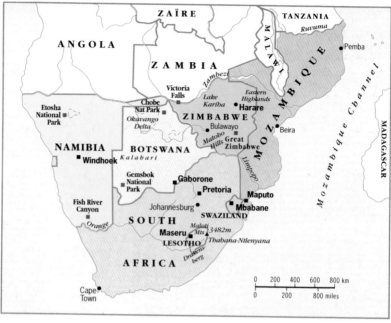

Practicalities

Check before leaving whether you need a visa to enter any of these other countries and, if you need one for South Africa, make sure it is multi-entry: a quick trip across the border, or even the short-cut through Swaziland, will cancel your initial entry. Namibia, Botswana, Zimbabwe, and Mozambique all have cere-bral malaria and you must take prophylactics. Few car rental companies will allow you to take a vehicle over the border, so shop around or arrange for a new vehicle to meet you at the border. The water should be safe in all coun-tries except Mozambique.

Right: Namibia's sand dunes are the highest in the world

South Africa has six neighbors—tiny mountainous **Lesotho**, tucked into the Drakensberg in the middle of South Africa; the gentle kingdom of **Swaziland** which tumbles off the escarpment between the Kruger National Park, Mozambique, and KwaZulu-Natal; trou-bled, poverty-stricken **Mozambique**, only now emerging tentatively from the devastation of war; the vast desert expanse of **Namibia**, famous for its diamonds and the shipwrecks of the Skeleton Coast; triumphant **Botswana**, which has quietly proved a stable democracy in the whirlwind of African politics; and **Zimbabwe**, home to the Victoria Falls, one of the seven natural wonders of the world, and to the Karanga-Rozwi, builders of the magnificent stone city of Great Zimbabwe, center of a mighty kingdom from the 13th century.

South Africa is at present remarkably orderly, organized and—by African standards—sophisticated, its population is largely urban and increasingly distanced from its heritage and traditions. By contrast, its neighbors were colonized for far shorter periods, with foreigners only taking full possession in the late 19th century, and hand-ing back the reins of power far earlier. With extraordinary luck and political cunning, Lesotho and Swaziland managed to remain independent protectorates through-out the colonial period. The result is that all have the distinct, flamboyant black cultures that are hard to find in South Africa itself. There can also be a greater degree of what may seem like chaos to outsiders, but it is all part of the diverse, exciting experience that is Africa.

Because these countries have far smaller populations than that of South Africa, most have managed to set aside much larger areas as national parks and reserves. You have a chance to experience nature in the raw from

the many small camps dotted across the wide open landscapes. Namibia, Botswana and Zimbabwe all have world-class game parks, with few of the crowds that gather at the Kruger. And then there are the spectacles—the biggest waterfalls, highest sand dunes and second largest canyon in the world; and the great rivers—the Zambezi, Limpopo, Orange (Gariep) and Okavango.

All distance is relative, and in Africa people happily travel hundreds of miles for a weekend. It may seem a long way to visit one of South Africa's neighbors, but it is easy to hop on a plane for a long weekend and sample an excitingly different view of Africa.

Lesotho

Practicalities
There are regular flights from Johannesburg to Maseru, and good connections by car (four-wheel drive recommended for some roads). The currency is the *loti* (plural *maloti*). Most E.U. and Commonwealth citizens can enter without a visa; other nationalities should check. For further information, contact the Lesotho Tourist Board, PO Box 1378, Maseru 100 (tel: 09266-312 896, fax: 09266-323 638). In South Africa tel: 012-322 6090; in the U.K. tel: 0171-373 8581; in the U.S.A. tel: 202-797 5533.

Lesotho, made up almost entirely of rugged mountains and totally surrounded by South Africa, calls itself the "Kingdom in the Sky". Its history began in the 1820s when a Sotho chief, who became known as Moshoeshoe the Great, fled to the mountains from the Mfecane wars raging across the highveld. Eventually he settled in a natural fortress, Thaba Bosiu (the "Mountain of the Night"), near modern Maseru, where he and some 40,000 followers formed the BaSotho nation. For almost a century, the tiny kingdom battled to survive, against other refugees, trekboers and the British. The king made alliances and skillfully steered a middle course, maintaining his kingdom's independence until his death in 1870. Basutoland eventually became a British colony in 1884 and voted to remain one in 1910 during the Union of South Africa, thus escaping apartheid. In 1966 it became an independent constitutional monarchy.

Above all, Lesotho caters for lovers of the great outdoors. It has only one museum, at the **Morija** mission station, while the capital, **Maseru** (meaning "red sandstone"), is a quiet place with pleasant but undistinguished architecture.

But the scenery is stunning, with vast mountain vistas including Thaba-Ntlenyana, the highest peak in southern Africa (11,421 feet). Walkers can ramble on moorland, by rocky streams, and through woodland. Pony trekking is a specialty; another is fishing. You can find fossil-laden cliffs and faint, ancient San paintings in the caves and under overhangs. Villages dot the hills and a thriving craft industry makes fine wool and mohair tapestries, basketry, leather, jewelry and pottery. And the huge Katse Dam water development project will provide Lesotho with a base for watersports.

The Sotho are great horsemen

National hats
The national dress of Lesotho is a colorful blanket and a conical straw hat, the *mokorotlo*, a word denoting disagreement. The hat is said to take its shape from the mountain of Qiloane, parting sight of Moshoeshoe's son who left court because he disagreed with dealings with the British. It became a symbol of nationalism.

Swaziland

Swaziland tumbles off the African plateau between South Africa and Mozambique, with high montane forest in the west and burning savannah lowveld in the east. Founded by King Sobhuza I during the upheavals of the Mfecane in the early 19th century, the country narrowly escaped absorption into South Africa. In the early 20th century, a fund was established to buy back land from the Boers, ensuring legal title for the Swazi people. The country was a British Protectorate for 66 years, gained independence in 1968, and is an absolute monarchy under the benign rule of King Mswati III. It is a peaceful, largely agricultural country with a population of about 800,000, and survives on the sugar crop and income from immigrant workers to the South African mines. South African tourists come here for the outdoor activities, but most visitors are passing through *en route* to Durban or the Kruger National Park.

The capital, **Mbabane**, is a pleasant, small, low-rise city. From here, a road leads southeast to Manzini through the **Ezulwini Valley**, the "heavenly place," heart of royal Swaziland. **Lobamba**, in the center, contains the Houses of Parliament, the National Museum, a traditional Swazi village and several fine crafts workshops. Nearby are the **Mlilwane Wildlife Sanctuary** and **Mantenga Falls**. **Piggs Peak**, in the mountainous northwest, offers spectacular views, walking and other outdoor activities. There are two further game parks in the eastern section, **Hlane Royal National Park** and **Mkhaya Game Reserve**.

The country blends ancient traditions and Western culture. You will see traditional villages and people wearing national dress, and twice a year there are major festivals. In the male **Ncwala**, or First Fruit Ceremony (Dec/Jan), the young men bring ocean foam and *lusekwane* (acacia) branches to the king, who dances with his warriors. The female **Umhlanga** (reed) dance (Aug/Sept), is in honor of the Queen Mother.

Royal succession

The new king is never the eldest son of the old king but is chosen from the royal clan, the Dlamini. The Queen Mother, who will automatically become regent, must be from a different clan. The new king is chosen when young and unsullied. He must be a single son, unmarried and have no child of his own at the time of his coronation, in order to secure the throne against family feuds. He may marry many times and have many children afterwards.

Practicalities

There are excellent road connections and regular flights from South Africa. The currency is the *elilangeni*, linked to the SA Rand. Department of Tourism, PO Box 338, Mbabane (tel: 268-44556, fax: 268-42774). In South Africa tel: 011-788 0742; U.K. tel: 0171-581 4976; U.S.A. tel: 202-362 6683.

The Organ Pipe Donga, in the Mkhondvo Valley

Zimbabwe

Due north of South Africa, across Kipling's famous "great, grey, green, greasy Limpopo River, all set about with fever trees," is Zimbabwe, a landlocked country with a turbulent history as the renegade colony of Southern Rhodesia. There are only two cities of any real size: **Harare**, the capital, in the northeast and **Bulawayo** in the southwest. The Nyanga, Vumba, and Chimanimani mountain ranges together form the lush, green **Eastern Highlands**, whose pine forests, coffee farms and mountain lakes are popular with locals escaping the searing summer heat. There are plenty of activities on offer including golf, riding, trout fishing and hill walking. In the far southwest, the outer fringes of the Kalahari Desert creep across the border to the magnificent rocky **Matobo Hills**. Most of the country is a high plateau (at around 3,280–4,920 feet), perfect for farming and wildlife.

There are two main tribes, the majority Shona and the Ndebele, an offshoot of the Zulus, whose first leader, Mzilikaze, fled north to escape the wrath of Shaka (see pages 30–1). Shona art has become world famous in recent years and the Zimbabweans are also brilliant musicians, with groups such as the Bundu Boys achieving international fame. Many people are immensely hospitable and charming with an infectious sense of humor.

Victoria Falls One of the wonders of the natural world, known locally as Mosi Oa Tunya ("the smoke that thunders"), these waterfalls on the massive Zambezi River are the largest on earth. They are 200–345 feet high, 5,537 feet wide, and in full flood some 120 million gallons of water cascade over the brim every minute, sending a jet of rainbow-sparkling spray 1,640 feet into the air. The town has a small game park, craft village and crocodile and snake farms, but the most popular activities involve the river. Leisurely cruises run upstream from the Falls while downstream, rafts tumble through 5 miles of twisting gorges tossed in some of the wildest white water anywhere.

Zimbabwe, ruinous capital of great priest-emperors, has handed its name onto a new country

Lake Kariba The Kariba Dam across the Zambezi is 413 feet high, contains 1,372,350 cubic yards of concrete and 12,125 tons of steel. The lake behind it is the fifth-largest man-made lake in the world, 180 miles long, up to 20 miles wide and up to 394 feet deep. On its shores and waters a booming vacation business has grown, with numerous water sports, sailing, houseboats, angling and game fishing, and beaches and beer for sunseekers.

Away from Kariba town, there are several small, remote reserves offering excellent game viewing.

Hwange National Park This vast game park, covering 5,656 square miles in the northwest corner of Zimbabwe, is one of the finest in Africa. It has 107 mammal and 410 bird species, but is renowned above all for its herds of elephant and for the stately sable antelope, national emblem of Zimbabwe. There are several rudimentary but comfortable camps within the park, while its borders are fringed by an increasing army of private game lodges offering luxury accommodations, guided drives by day and night, and even bush walking and riding.

Great Zimbabwe From the 13th to the mid-16th century Great Zimbabwe was the capital of a huge empire that stretched halfway across southern Africa and traded for gold and ivory with the Arabs and Portuguese. In its latter years it was ruled by the Mwene Mutapa (a title meaning "Great Plunderer"), an autocratic semi-divine priest-king. The city, the most magnificent of a number of virtually unknown stone-built towns in the region, is thought to have had a population of some 50,000 in its heyday. It gave its name to a nation, but is today abandoned to the baboons and is an atmospheric ruin, the largest stone structure in Africa after the pyramids. Off the beaten track for Zambezi tourists, it is only a short detour from the main Jo'burg–Harare road near Masvingo.

Victoria Falls, the largest and one of the most beautiful waterfalls in the world

Practicalities
There are good roads and train services and regular flights from South Africa to Gaborone and Maun. Nationals of most Commonwealth and E.U. nations and the U.S. may enter without a visa. The currency is the *pula*. Botswana Tourist Board, P Bag 0047, Gaborone (tel: 267-353 024, fax: 267-308 675). In South Africa tel: 012-234 24760; in the U.K. tel: 0171-499 0031; in the U.S. tel: 202-244 4990 and 212-889 0277.

Canals and reeds in the Okavango Delta

Botswana

Once the British colony of Bechuanaland, Botswana is as large as France or Texas but with a population of only about 1.5 million, mostly of the SeTswana tribal group. With nearly three-quarters of the country covered by uninhabitable Kalahari sand, almost the entire population is clustered in the lush green hills of the southeast corner, around the purpose-built capital, **Gaborone**.

At independence in 1966, Botswana was one of the 10 poorest countries in the world; today, it is one of the wealthiest in Africa, thanks to the discovery of massive diamond fields and the successful development of the beef cattle industry. It is peaceful, stable and democratic.

Nearly 20 per cent of the country is national park. In the far south, the huge arid **Gemsbok National Park** joins on to the South African **Kalahari Gemsbok National Park** and the smaller **Mabuasehube Game Reserve**. Together the three make up a desert reserve far larger than the Kruger, although the scarcity of water and the scrubby vegetation do not allow the same density of wildlife to survive. There are few roads and facilities in the Botswana section.

In the center of the country is the even larger and more remote **Central Kalahari Game Reserve**, set up originally as a home for the San people. In the far north, near the Zimbabwe border, the **Chobe National Park** is the richest in game and facilities of all Botswana's parks, offering game viewing equal to the great parks of Kenya and Tanzania, and particularly famous for its massive herds of elephant.

Pride of place, however, goes to the **Okavango River** which heads south and west from Angola toward the sea, but never makes it, fanning out instead into a magnificent, 5,019-square-mile inland delta, with over 350 species of bird. It is a fantastic wilderness of reeds and water lilies, much of it only negotiable by canoe. The neighboring **Moremi Game Reserve** offers excellent game viewing.

Namibia

Namibia is four times the size of Germany, with a population of a little over 1 million. A German colony (South West Africa) from 1890, it was handed over to South Africa at the start of World War I and remained part of that country until independence in 1990. There is a distinctly Germanic air to the architecture, especially in the little coastal towns of **Luderitz** and **Swakopmund** and in the hilly capital, **Windhoek**. German cakes, sausages, beer and oompah bands add a slightly surreal quality to local festivals, and there is still one tribe, the Herero, whose married women wear the full heavy skirts and cloth headdresses of 19th-century German missionaries.

Most of Namibia is desert, with the Kalahari merging into the even more forbidding **Namib Desert**. Even the coast is desolate. A huge area in the far south is forbidden territory, left to the diamond diggers, while the northern section is known as the **Skeleton Coast** after the many who died in shipwrecks on its terrifying rocks. Between them is the **Namib Naukluft Park**, an enormous reserve of red-gold sand dunes, including the 984-foot-high **Sossusvlei Dunes**, the highest in the world.

Inland is another geological marvel, the **Fish River Canyon**. This massive ravine, second in size only to the Grand Canyon, is 100 miles long, 17 miles wide and up to 1,804 feet deep. A 15-mile road leads to a number of viewing platforms and there is a rugged 56-mile, five-day hiking trail along the bottom.

In the north, where the desert gives way to acacia savannah, the 8,598-square-mile **Etosha National Park** is centered around a 1,930-square-mile pan. The name means "place of dry water" but there is still enough to support one of the largest concentrations of wildlife in Africa. Yet more excellent game viewing can be found in the **Caprivi Strip**, the neck of land which stretches out into the Zambezi Valley in the far north.

Practicalities
There is a good road north and regular flights to Windhoek from Johannesburg and Cape Town. Most E.U. and U.S. citizens can enter without a visa. The currency is the Namib dollar, which has the same value as the SA Rand. Namibia Tourist Board, PO Box 11534, Windhoek (tel: 061-391 2050, fax: 061-228 461). In South Africa, tel: 011-331 7055 or 021-419 3190; in the U.K., tel: 0171-636 2924.

223

The wind whips the Namib desert into towering pinnacles of red-gold sand

Mozambique land-scape

Mozambique

A long, skinny country running north for 1,217 miles up the Indian Ocean coastal plain, Mozambique began life as part of the Omani Sultanate, at the southernmost tip of the Arab gold, ivory and slave trade. It is hot and humid and the swamp fevers nearly defeated the earliest Portuguese traders, but the promised prizes inland were great and it became a Portuguese colony. Best known as a scruffy but charming Mediterranean-style playground for white Rhodesians and South Africans, it used to be a source of good food, wine and loose women, with some of the finest beaches in Africa.

Independence changed all that. In 1975, the Portuguese withdrew abruptly (some 80 per cent of whites departed), decimating the infrastructure. Frelimo, a hard-line Marxist organization, took power and instituted extreme Socialist government. Almost at once civil war broke out between Frelimo and the anarchic Renamo (Mozambique Resistance Movement), largely funded by Rhodesia and South Africa. When peace was restored after nearly 20 years, the country had become one of the poorest in the world.

Today, Mozambique has renounced its hard-line policies and is trying desperately to reconstruct some sort of life for its citizens. Roads are gradually being opened, power restored and the land cleared for agriculture so that the hundreds of thousands of refugees can return. The first glimmerings of renewed tourism are also in view. The capital, **Maputo**, has one luxury hotel, the Polana, run by the South African Karos group, and you can again stroll the boulevards and eat peri-peri prawns. The second city and largest port, **Beira**, is also making great efforts to re-create a holiday environment. However, most tourism is still concentrated on the islands of **Santa Carolina** and **Benguela** whose chic resorts fly their guests directly out from Johannesburg without setting foot on the mainland. For now, the rest of the country is suitable only for those with a good four-wheel drive and a strong sense of adventure.

Practicalities
All visitors must obtain a visa before arrival. The currency is the *metical*, but many places may ask for payment in US$ or SA Rand. Roads across Mozambique are gradually opening up but it may be safer to fly and you should always get local advice before traveling. Do not stray beyond clearly marked settlements: there are an estimated 2 million land mines still to be located and defused. For information, contact the Centro de Informacao e Turismo (CIT), Caixa Postal 2446, Maputo (tel: 0258-1-425 011/2). In South Africa, tel: 011-339 7275; in the U.K., tel: 0171-283 3800; in the U.S., tel: 202-293 7146.

PRACTICALITIES

Accommodations

White South Africans have an exceptionally high standard of living, and even higher expectations, so while the tourist industry murmurs self-deprecatingly about pulling standards up to the international norm, South Africa actually provides excellent accommodations, with service often surpassing European levels.

The Cellars-Hohenort Hotel, Cape Town

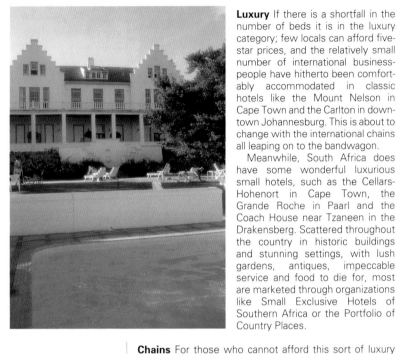

Luxury If there is a shortfall in the number of beds it is in the luxury category; few locals can afford five-star prices, and the relatively small number of international business-people have hitherto been comfortably accommodated in classic hotels like the Mount Nelson in Cape Town and the Carlton in downtown Johannesburg. This is about to change with the international chains all leaping on to the bandwagon.

Meanwhile, South Africa does have some wonderful luxurious small hotels, such as the Cellars-Hohenort in Cape Town, the Grande Roche in Paarl and the Coach House near Tzaneen in the Drakensberg. Scattered throughout the country in historic buildings and stunning settings, with lush gardens, antiques, impeccable service and food to die for, most are marketed through organizations like Small Exclusive Hotels of Southern Africa or the Portfolio of Country Places.

Chains For those who cannot afford this sort of luxury there are several chains with cross-country facilities, although here you pay for comfort and convenience, not atmosphere. Southern Sun operate all the local Holiday Inns, from the upmarket Crowne Plazas to the basic three-star and very affordable Garden Courts. Karos Hotels have 15 three- or four-star properties. Protea, the largest, have a huge network, but the star ratings, price and efficiency vary widely from property to property, so check before reserving blind.

Further information
For central booking numbers and hotel listings, see pages 258–263. Most guest houses have only two or three rooms available, so few are listed here. SATOUR and the South African AA both publish annual guides to recommended guest houses, farmhouses, bed-and-breakfast and self-catering establishments. Alternatively, ask at the local tourist office.

Game lodges A trip to Africa would not be complete without at least a couple of nights' game viewing. Those with the cash should head for one of the exclusive game lodges, such as Sabi Sabi and Inyati in Mpumalanga, Phinda and Bushlands in Natal, or Shamwari in the Eastern Cape. Not only are they totally charming, but the game viewing is superb and the knowledge of the wardens encyclopedic. You can also get off the roads, and do walks and night drives, activities still largely taboo in the National Parks.

The facilities offered within the National Parks are much cheaper. Most have at least one full-service lodge, they all have self-catering chalets, *rondavels* (small, simple circular rooms), camping and trailer facilities, a camp store with basic foods, and a gas station.

Traditional African architecture receives a starry gloss at many bush lodges

Self-catering If you want to travel cheaply, this is the way to do it. There is an extraordinarily wide choice of options available, with many establishments offering a range to satisfy all tastes and pockets. Timeshare is big along the Natal coast, but most timeshare buildings will also rent to casual visitors. Rural retreats offer full service or self-catering in furnished chalets, tents with fitted bathrooms, simple huts or real bush camping. In most small towns someone has a spare cottage, often charmingly furnished, at a ludicrously low price. The only drawback, from the international traveler's point of view, is that you will have to take cutlery and crockery for picnics and supply yourself with the basic foodstuffs—only feasible if you have your own transportation.

Guest houses The bed-and-breakfast business is booming right across the country, with more opening up every week. Usually tucked away in residential suburbs, many are delightful historic houses, such as Cape Dutch farms and rambling, old Victorian mansions, furnished with four-posters and Grandma's patchwork quilt. Prices are reasonable and you get a huge cooked breakfast and charming hospitality from a regiment of middle-aged Afrikaner ladies, all of whom want nothing more than to sell the delights of their country to you.

Official approval
The SATOUR approved accommodations scheme works on two levels. The number of stars depends purely on the facilities offered within the category, so you can have a three-star hotel or a three-star bed-and-breakfast. They are also rated for ambience and hospitality with bronze, silver, or gold categories. Gold has never yet been awarded.

BED & BREAKFAST
ROOSJE
VAN DE KAAP
← 80 m
☎ 0291-43001

Bed-and-breakfast South-African style is affordable and often delightful

Food and drink

South Africans like meat—lots of meat. It may be beef, lamb or pork, or a variety of more exotic options, from springbok or impala to crocodile and ostrich, but it must come in large quantities. They also have a very sweet tooth. If anything is a South African staple today, it is a vast slab of steak, smothered in barbecue or monkey-gland (chutneyish) sauce.

In the small towns, there is often little choice about where to eat, but the meal you get will be filling and wholesome, and you can request half portions, sauceless steaks and salads. Along the coast, in the main cities and in the top hotels, the story is very different, with South Africa offering the best of imaginative *haute cuisine*, often based on traditional recipes and using the finest of local ingredients.

Cape Dutch food The famous Cape Dutch cuisine grew from several intertwined influences. The newly arrived Dutch brought their traditional thick soups, stews, *frikkadels* (meatballs) and breads, adapting them to available ingredients. Many had Cape Malay servants and the spices and curries of the East Indies and South India soon crept into the diet. Later arrivals included German settlers who brought their sausage-making skills, and French Huguenots who brought *konfyt* (preserved fruits) and endowed the Cape winelands

Menus offer a wide choice in South Africa

Tomato bredie *(left) and* bobotie *(right) are two of the classic mainstays of Cape Dutch cuisine*

with a taste for fine dining that survives to this day.

The Voortrekkers had to survive away from civilization for years on end, in intense heat and very primitive conditions. *Biltong*, strips of meat salted, spiced and dried, was probably their best way of carrying protein. It can be eaten dry or reconstituted as part of a stew, can be made from beef or game shot *en route*, and can be easily cured in the sun on a drying rack. *Biltong* is still a universal food in South Africa and is now even creeping into high society, with fine shavings in soups and salads.

The *braaivleis* (literally "roasted meat") is a ritual as central to the white South African lifestyle as the "barbie" is to the Australians—and for much the same reason. It began with whatever could be shot being grilled over an open fire—tough food for tough men. Today, the central ingredient is still steak, and with it comes *boerewors* (literally "farm sausage"), highly spiced pork, mutton and beef sausage, flavored with coriander, ginger, mace, cloves, nutmeg, thyme, fennel, rosemary, mint, and red wine or vinegar. *Sosaties* are kebabs marinated for several days in sweet and sour sauces, based on Indonesian satay. On the side are the salads, roasted mealies (corn on the cob), pot bread (baked in a cast-iron pot) or *roosterkoek* (bread cooked on the coals or ashes)—and plenty of alcohol.

Healthy diet
Traditionally cooked over an open fire, the black African staple is a thick porridge (*pap*) of indigenous sorghum or maize, introduced to the continent by the 15th-century Portuguese sailors. Accompanying this come thin stews of spinach, beans, pumpkin, tomatoes, and onions with added chicken, mutton or beef on special occasions. Other protein comes from sour milk, mopani worms, grasshoppers, ants, and edible beetles. It is a remarkably healthy diet, with little fat, salt or excess sugar, but is being superseded by a dependency on sugary soft drinks, bottled beer, and white bread.

229

Stews, known as *bredies* in the Cape and *potjiekos* in the Transvaal, are traditionally fat-tailed mutton or venison cooked very slowly in a three-legged cast-iron cooking pot (a *potjie*—pronounced "poykey") over an open fire. Any available vegetable can be thrown in, but common additions are tomato, pumpkin, butternut squash, beans, onion, potato, and *waterblommetjie* (water lily). The savory stew is often served with something sweet, such as a compote of dried fruit, sweet potatoes glazed in orange caramel, or sugary pumpkin fritters.

Biltong is still a South African staple

Food and drink

Pancakes make a handy snack

Asian cuisine Alongside those dishes, which have been adopted and adapted into the white diet, there is still a strong tradition of "Malay" and Indian cuisine; this received a fresh injection of authenticity with the arrival of the Indian cane workers in Natal in the early 20th century. Here are the real curries and rice-based *breyanis* (similar to the Indian biriyani), served with *sambals* (chutneys) and *atjar* (pickles). Most famous of the Malay dishes is *bobotie*, a mild baked curry of minced lamb with dried fruit, topped with an egg custard, which has been designated the South African national dish.

Fish With two oceans and the inland fresh water to choose from, one of the greatest treats in the country is the extraordinary range of fish available. As well as oysters, mussels, limpets, crayfish and perlemoen (abalone), there are superb white fish such as kingclip, yellowtail, snoek, and kabeljou. The finest prawns are said to be from Mozambique, served Portuguese style in a marinade of olive oil, lemon juice, garlic, bay leaves, *peri-peri* (chili) and ground cloves. Alternatively, look for Cape-Malay pickled fish (Cape salmon, kingclip, yellowtail, or any other firm white fish), served traditionally at funeral feasts. Inland, try the smoked salmon trout or barbel.

Desserts To finish your typically South African meal, leave room for a calorie-laden dessert such as *melk-tart* (cinnamon-flavored milk tart of Dutch origin), Cape brandy pudding (a British-style steamed pudding laden with brandy) or *koeksisters* (small braided doughnuts soaked in honey or a thick syrup of concentrated fruit juices).

Alcohol
Maheu, a thick white beer made from sorghum, is the drink of choice for all social occasions in traditional black society. White South Africans wash down their *braai* with a lager (Castle, Lion, Ohlssons or Amstel) or some Cape wine (see pages 88–9). Finish your meal with a local liqueur, such as the *naartjie* (tangerine)-based Van der Hum. Beware local moonshine firewaters—*mampoer* or *witblitz*—unless you have a head like iron or a death wish.

Shopping

Souvenirs of South Africa are plentiful, some tacky, many expensive and some exquisitely beautiful. Unfortunately, many of the best—ostrich feathers, huge stone statues, fire-baked pots, helicopters made of wire, 7-foot-tall wooden giraffes—are extremely difficult to transport.

Animal products Ostrich farms offer expensive shoes or handbags, and cheap feather dusters or "blown" ostrich eggs (plain, filled with fruit, painted—usually badly—or carved). Antelope skins are legal if you can face the social comment, but do not buy ivory—you are not allowed to take it home.

Pots and baskets in Umgababa Market, near Durban

Few of the more spectacular shells and corals you see are actually South African, and most shells for sale are collected live. It may be illegal and it is certainly not eco-friendly. Collect your own abandoned shells on the beach; they come free and you will not harm the environment. The rich blue perlemoen shells or shell jewelry are fine, as the contents are harvested for food.

Baskets, bowls, and beads Many traditional crafts, such as stunningly patterned baskets made by the Sotho and Zulus and simple hardwood bowls and spoons, are still going strong. Intricate Zulu beadwork is magnificent at its best; look for traditional aprons and veils, or simpler (and cheaper) pen holders .

231

Jewelry and gemstones Gold and diamonds are both on offer in abundant quantities, as are many other gemstones, from emerald earrings to huge slabs of amethyst crystal. For an entertaining half hour, head for the gemstone scratchpatches, found in all the main cities. These contain huge cans filled with tumble-polished semi-precious stones. Select your favorites and buy by weight at unbelievably low prices.

Food, wine, and flowers Look for estate-bottled wines; dried or glacé fruit, *konfyt* or jams (try more unusual flavours such as prickly pear); *biltong* (vacuum-packed); dried flowers and proteas (but check import restrictions before buying any fresh produce).

Curios Finally, there are the almost obligatory soapstone heads, wooden hippos, copper ashtrays, and T-shirts, which range from the pleasant to the totally awful.

Entertainment

There is surprisingly little entertainment. Most socializing in South Africa is done at home, though people are beginning to eat out more, and most towns of any size have a movie theater with latest-release international films. But there are few lively bars and clubs: many people get up with the sun, so dining is early and most nightlife is over by 11PM.

Traditional music and dance These days tribal dance is almost exclusively a tourist attraction. Several "tribal villages," particularly in Natal, put on dance displays. Go to at least one, as the Zulu and Shangaan dancers are spectacular and it will probably be your only chance to see something of a fast-vanishing lifestyle. The quality of the performances and explanations varies enormously, so choose carefully. Some of the best are found in and around Durban in Natal, at Dumazulu, Shakaland, KwaBhekithunga, and Phezulu (see pages 201 and 212–13); and in Johannesburg, at Gold Reef City, and Phumangena (see pages 152 and 156).

Township jazz Headed by such luminaries as Miriam Makeba, Ladysmith Black Mambaza, and Hugh Masekela, South Africa's township musicians combined tribal rhythms with jazz and swing to create a unique, thriving heritage of music and dance, many of its themes, such as the *toyi-toyi* (struggle dance of the people), the *mapantsula* (township jive) and *isicatamiya* (a choir tradition from the mines and men's hostels) growing out of the struggle. Music was one of the few relatively safe ways in which to protest against apartheid.

It is only safe to visit most township *shebeens* (illegal pubs), in which the movement has its roots, on organized tours, but the musicians are beginning to move into mainstream venues.

CAPE TOWN
Manenberg's Jazz Café, Dumbarton House, corner Adderley and Church Streets (tel: 021-238 304). Lively central venue, with reasonable food and seemingly around-the-clock music. Cape Town tourist office produces a brochure of recommended jazz and live music venues, and several local tour operators offer jazz tours: **Heart-stoppers Jazz Tours** (tel: 021-761 0811) and **One City Tours** (tel: 021-387 5351).

DURBAN
Africafé, Smith Street Arcade (tel: 031-301 0890). Bright and snazzy ethnic venue.

JOHANNESBURG
Kippies at the Market, Market Precinct, Newtown (tel: 011-834 3741). Jazz, Afro-jazz, jazz fusion, blues.

The costumes of the Gold Reef City dancers are carefully designed not to offend family sensibilities

PRETORIA

House of Jazz, Host International Hotel, Church Street East, Arcadia (tel: 012-341 7455). Daily jazz by a wide range of performers.

The classics The cultural boycott isolated South Africa from the rest of the world, but it also forced the country to rely on its own resources, resulting in flourishing local culture. Johannesburg's Market Theatre was particularly dynamic, creating a theater of protest that drew rave reviews in London and New York. Today, however, classical music and theater are under siege, with government funds being diverted to lay drains and build houses, while the outbreak of peace has left many writers temporarily silent.

Each of the main cities has its own symphony orchestra, ballet corps, opera and theater. The focus is firmly European, but artists broke the race barrier long before most, and the townships are beginning to produce some stunningly talented, classically trained black actors, dancers, and singers.

Major Venues

CAPE TOWN

Nico Malan Opera House, D F Malan Street, Foreshore (tel: 021-21 5470). Concerts, theater, opera, and ballet.

DURBAN

Natal Playhouse, Smith Street (tel: 031-304 3631). Home of the opera and the Natal Philharmonic Orchestra, with various theaters—The Cellar, The Drama, The Loft and The Studio.

JOHANNESBURG

Civic Theatre, Loveday Street Extension, Braamfontein (tel: 011-403 3408).
Market Theatre, Wolhuter Street, Newtown (tel: 011-832 1641).

PRETORIA

State Theatre, Church Street (tel: 012-322 1665). Six auditoria in one complex offering ballet, opera and music, as well as some of the most dynamic theater being put on in the country.

Sun City is South Africa's answer to the glitter of Las Vegas

Entertainment info
To find out what's on, check the relevant section of local daily newspapers, the national *Weekly Mail & Guardian* (published Fridays), or the regional Metro sections of the *Sunday Times*. In Cape Town and Durban, a monthly *What's On* is available free from major hotels and tourist information offices. In Johannesburg, buy Blakes Guide to Johannesburg and its Environs; *Johannesburg Alive!*, published by *The Star.*

Tickets for major venues from Computicket: Cape Town (tel: 021-21 4715); Durban (tel: 031-304 4881); Johannesburg (tel: 011-331 9991); Pretoria (tel: 012-323 6607). *Open:* Mon–Fri 9–5 and Sat 9–4. Cash or credit card.

Intermittent service
Hobby steam services run by enthusiasts include the twice-monthly Magaliesburg Express (from Johannesburg Station, Gauteng; tel: 011-888 1154); the narrow-gauge Midmar Steam Railway, near Pietermaritzburg, Natal (see page 211) on the second Sunday of every month (tel: 0332-30 5933); the Karoo-based Ostrich Express, between Oudtshoorn and Calitzdorp, Western Cape on weekends (weekdays by arrangement; tel: 0443-23 2202); and the Umgeni Steam Railway (tel:013-72 6734), which operates on the second Sunday of every month, Oct–Jun, from the Natal Steam Railway Museum, Hilton.

South Africa has a magnificent network of railroad lines. Unfortunately, it has virtually no trains. Half the tracks are derelict, many run freight only, and even major intercity routes have only one scheduled passenger service a day. Cape Town is the only city in the country with an efficient suburban network, and while this is popular by day, it is not particularly safe after dark.

Main-line Racism and snobbery killed off the passenger services, which were seen as downmarket and dangerous. In fact, while second class is not that comfortable for long journeys, first class is cheap, safe, comfortable and spacious. Trains are slow, but you can stretch out between crisp white sheets for a leisurely night's sleep, after an old-fashioned dinner in the dining car. There are not enough services to make touring by train practicable, but they are excellent for cross-country journeys.

Reserve first- and second-class tickets at least 24 hours in advance either at the stations or by phone: Cape Town (tel: 021-405 2200, reservations 021-405 3871); Durban (tel: 031-361 7098, reservations 031-361 7621); Johannesburg (tel: 011-773 5878, reservations 011-773 2944). Order your bedding at the same time. For general information, contact Spoornet, Room 1724, 222 Smit Street, PO Box 2671, Joubert Park 2004, Johannesburg; tel: 011-773 8920 (Mainline trains), 011-774 4469 (The Blue Train), fax: 011-773 7478 (for all services).

The Blue Train, run by Spoornet (see above for contact details), is the successor to the original Union Limited, replacing the venerable steam service in 1939. It is now one of the most famous—and expensive—trains in the world, running regular scheduled services between Pretoria and Cape Town, a sybaritic 24-hour journey; from Gauteng to Nelspruit for the Kruger Park; and north to Zimbabwe's Victoria Falls.

The Pride of Africa, run by Rovos Rail, Victoria Hotel, PO Box 2837, Pretoria 0001 (tel: 012-323 6052, fax: 012-323 0843), is billed as

International commuters between Zimbabwe and South Africa at the taxi rank beside Messina station

the "world's most luxurious train." From its home base in Pretoria, the company offers services to Cape Town, along the Garden Route to Knysna, via the Kruger to Maputo in Mozambique, and via Victoria Falls to Dar es Salaam (Tanzania). With vintage locomotives and carefully refurbished original cars, the train is less a mode of transportation than a vacation in itself, with numerous stops and tours to places of interest *en route*.

For total historical accuracy try the **Union Limited**, 3 Adderley Street, PO Box 4325, Cape Town 8000 (tel: 021-405 4391, fax: 021-405 4395), whose locomotives and cars are all accurately restored originals. There are day trips from Cape Town to the winelands and other nearby areas, with infrequent 5-, 9- and 15-day safaris to the Garden Route, Mpumalanga, and the Zambezi. Profits go toward preservation work at the Transnet Museum.

The **Shongololo Express,** named after a shiny brown millipede, aims for a high standard of comfort but more affordable prices, doing a huge loop of South Africa, taking in most tourist highlights, from Kruger to the Cape. Contact 10 Amelia Street, Dunvegan, Edenvale 1610 (tel: 011-453 3821, fax: 011-454 1262).

The **Banana Express** (tel: 039-682 4821) is based at Port Shepstone on the Natal South Coast. There are two itineraries, a 90-minute journey through the banana and sugar plantations to Izotsha, and a twice-weekly day trip to Paddock and the Oribi Gorge (daily in season; four days a week out of season; reservations essential). In the Western Cape, the **Outeniqua Choo-Tjoe,** one of the most enjoyable and scenic services in the country, runs through the heart of the Garden Route between George and Knysna (Mon–Fri, and Sat in Dec, tel: 0441-738 202).

Opposite, top: the Blue Train. Below: luxurious living on the Pride of Africa

PRACTICALITIES *Hiking*

Top trails – 1
Boland Trail, Hottentots-Holland Reserve, Western Cape (25 miles, two- or three-day options; tel: 021-886 5858); Cederberg Mountains, Western Cape (one–seven day routes; tel: 022-921 2289); Drakensberg Mountains, Natal (one hour–10 days; tel: 0331-471 981); Blyderivierspoort Trail, Mpumalanga (40 miles, five days; tel: 01315-81216); Klipspringer Trail, Augrabies Falls National Park, Northern Cape (25 miles, three days; tel: 012-343 1991).

Up Table Mountain, the hard way

South Africa is a hiker's paradise, with superb hill walking in the Cederbergs, KwaZulu-Natal and Mpumalanga Drakensberg, coast and forest paths along the Garden Route, savannah, and even desert walking in the Northern Cape and Northern Province. There are over 200 designated long-distance trails and a multitude of other options, from short strolls to more arduous day trips. Most are accessible by anyone of reasonable fitness, and a few are even laid out for wheelchair access. Brochures and sketch maps of many walks are available, and most are clearly route-marked.

Selecting your trail Look out for local terminology. A **backpacking trail** is simply a designated area, usually fairly rugged, in which you select your own path and choose your own campsite. A **hiking trail** is a designated route, marked by painted footprints or stakes, and usually several days' in length. There are basic accommodations in huts or chalets, but you will be expected to pack all your own supplies. **Day walks** are precisely what they say, an energetic, self-guided day out. **Guided wilderness trails** are usually relatively easy day trips in the parks and reserves, led by a knowledgeable ranger. **Interpretive trails** are short, well-cleared and marked paths with regular explanatory displays.

Many trails limit the number of people in any party and on the route, so reserve a place in advance. You may also need a permit. The local tourist office will be able to give you details, but for longer-range planning, contact the **Hiking Federation of South Africa**, PO Box 1420, Randburg 2125 (tel: 011-886 6524, fax: 011-886 6013) and the **National Hiking Way Board**, tel: 012-299 3382. Alternatively, buy *Hiking Trails of Southern Africa* by Willie and Sandra Olivier (published by Southern Book Publishers), probably the best of the current crop of detailed hiking guides.

On the track Never underestimate the environment and do not hike on your own. Ideally, go in a group of at least three or four. Get a detailed route map and study it carefully, for gradient as well as distance. Always let someone know where and when you are going and when you expect to return, so they can raise the alarm should you fail to show. Keep a safe distance from all wildlife, big or small. For more on safety in the bush, see page 252.

Take the climate into consideration when deciding on the degree of difficulty you are prepared to tackle.

South Africa's mountains are not particularly high and you will not have to acclimatize to the altitude, but they do produce some treacherous and very fast-moving weather. Several people are killed each year in the Drakensberg and even on Table Mountain trying to escape from incoming fog. If the mist comes down, find shelter and sit it out. In winter the mountains can be cold, wet and slippery, while in bright sunshine the glaring heat and harsh light can damage tender foreign skins and eyes.

The problems of heat are greatly increased in the savannah of the Northern Province or the Kalahari scrub of the Northern Cape, where in midsummer it can be like hiking in the Sahara. Treat the sun with extreme respect, do not try to be too energetic during the blazing midday hours, and make sure you drink far more water than you think you need. Savage thunderstorms may whip across the country on summer afternoons. Keep well clear of trees or prominent rocks in case of lightning, and stay out of riverbeds, however dry they may seem, in case of flash floods. And never, never start an unprotected fire or throw away a match: the vegetation is often tinder dry and a bush fire can rampage for miles before it burns out or is brought under control.

The Drakensberg is relatively painless hiking territory

Top trails – 2
Magoebaskloof Trail, Northern Province (two sections – Dokolewa, 22 miles, three days; Grootbosch, 30 miles, three days; tel: 01315-41058); Otter Trail, Tsitsikamma Coastal National Park, Eastern Cape (25 miles, five days; tel: 012-343 1991); Swartberg Trail, between the Great and Little Karoos, Western Cape (40 miles, five–six days; tel: 0443-291 739).

Game walks offer a quieter and more intimate bush experience

Tours and safaris

GENERAL TOUR OPERATORS

Abercrombie & Kent Safaris, PO Box 782607, Sandton 2146 (tel: 011-884 8103, fax: 011-884 3845. In the U.S., tel: 800-323 7308 toll-free or 708-954 2944, in the U.K., tel: 0171-730 9600). Specialized worldwide tour operator, running organized tours and tailor-made itineraries in South Africa and surrounding countries.

Rennies Travel, Head Office, 7th Floor, Safren House, 19 Ameshoff Street, Braamfontein 2017 (tel: 011-407 3211, fax: 011-339 1247. In the U.S., tel: 805-855 1572; in the U.K., tel: 01733-330 111). One of the largest incoming tour operators in South Africa, with some 70 branches nationwide.

Springbok Atlas, PO Box 819, Cape Town 8000 (tel: 021-448 6545, fax: 021-47 3835). Tours of most major cities, day trips and safaris.

Tour d'Afrique, PO Box 957, White River 1240 (tel: 01311-32652/51552, fax: 01311-31228). Bus and minibus tours and self-drive packages.

Welcome Tours and Safaris, PO Box 2191, Illovo 2121 (tel: 011-268 1607, fax: 011-268 1622). Bus and minibus tours throughout the country.

SOUTH AFRICA BY AIR

Airtrack Adventures, PO Box 630, Muldersdrift 1747 (tel: 011-957 2322/3, fax: 011-957 2465). Hot-air balloons over Johannesburg and the Pilanesburg.

Bill Harrop's "Original" Balloon Safaris, PO Box 67, Randburg 2125 (tel: 011-705 3201/2, fax: 011-705 3103). Hot-air balloon rides over the Magalies River Valley, Gauteng.

Civair Helicopters, PO Box 120, Newlands, Cape Town 7725 (tel: 021-419 5182, fax: 021-419 5183). Tailor-made and charter helicopter tours of Cape Peninsula, winelands, and whale spotting.

Court Helicopters, PO Box 2546, Cape Town 8000 (tel: 021-934 0560, fax: 021-934 0568). Helicopter charters, tailor-made tours and regular sightseeing flights over the Cape Peninsula and winelands, Sun City, and the Natal coast.

Dragonfly Helicopter Adventures, PO Box 1042, White River 1240 (tel: 013-750 1060, fax: 013-750 1061 or 011-880 4232). Helicopter tours of Mpumalanga, Johannesburg, Sun City, Cape Town, and Durban. The group also offers a variety of safaris and day trips across the country.

SPECIALIST NATIONWIDE OPERATORS

Adventure Safaris & Sports Tours, PO Box 32176, Camps Bay, Cape Town 8040 (tel: 021-438 5201, fax: 021-438 4807). Short breaks, mini safaris, and special-interest tours including golf, cycling, diving, hiking, fishing, hunting, river rafting, game viewing, whale watching, wine tasting, and sailing.

African Routes, PO Box 201700, Durban North 4016 (tel: 031-304 6358). Safaris, hikes, balloon safaris, rafting, diving, adventure trails, houseboats, and trans-Africa routes for the 18–35s.

C. Africa Tours, PO Box 882, Benoni 1500 (tel: 011-421 6386, fax: 011-421 8550). Tailor-made and small group tours for those following Kosher or Halal customs.

Other useful addresses
Association of Southern African Travel Agents (ASATA), PO Box 5032, 2000 Johannesburg (tel: 011-403 2923).
  The Council of Adventure Travel Associations of Southern Africa (CATASA), PO Box 67, Randburg 2125 (tel: 011-705 3201/2). An organization representing specialist operators for some 40 different sports and outdoor activities from archaeology to ballooning, caving and white-water rafting. If you are looking for an adventure, start with the list of CATASA members.

Drifters Adventours, PO Box 48434, Roosevelt Park, Johannesburg 2129 (tel: 011-888 1160, fax: 011-888 1020). Adventure camping safaris throughout southern Africa.

Felix Unite River Adventures, 1 Greigmar House, Main Road (PO Box 96) Kenilworth 7745 (tel: 021-762 6935/6, fax: 021-761 9259). South Africa's leading river operator, with tours on the Orange (Gariep), Tugela, Doring, Cunene, and Breë Rivers.

Golf Line, PO Box 611, Alberton 1450 (tel: 011-907 1632/3, fax: 011-907 2246). Golf and more golf, mixed with game viewing for nongolfers.

River Runners, 31 De Korte Street (PO Box 31117) Braamfontein 2017 (tel: 011-403 2512/339 7183, fax: 011-339 4042). Canoeing and kayaking on the Orange River.

Southern Africa Adventure Tours, PO Box 4300, Kempton Park 1620 (tel: 011-396 1860/1/2, fax: 011-396 1937). Action and adventure vacations, from diving and canoeing to hiking and game-ranger training courses.

Specialized Tours, PO Box 14049, Green Point 8051 (tel: 021-253 259, fax: 021-253 329). Cycling, bridge, whale watching, gardens, Namaqualand flowers, botanical tours, rock paintings, wine, gourmet tours, cattle production, and tours for senior citizens.

Trout Adventures Africa, 9 Green Street, Cape Town 8001 (tel: 021-26 1057, fax: 021-24 7526). Fly-fishing vacations with a professional guide.

Which Way Adventures, 34 Van der Merwe Street, Somerset West 7130 (tel: 024-852 2364, fax: 024-852 1584). Four-wheel drive and camping safaris, whitewater rafting, canoeing and rappeling on the Doring, Breë, and Orange rivers.

239

Elephants keep a wary eye on passing safaris

REGIONAL SPECIALISTS

For day trips in and around the major cities, see the relevant A–Z listings.

Eastern Cape

Kei Leisure, PO Box 1410, East London (tel: 0431-95 43310, fax: 0431-43315). Custom-designed tours and scheduled departures in the "Footsteps of the President," tracing Nelson Mandela's life and South African history.

Western Cape

Eco Explorers, PO Box 21246, De Tyger, Cape Town 7502 (tel: 021-929 361, fax: 021-930 5166). Specializing in the west coast, Cederberg, and Namaqualand, with a particular emphasis on the flora and eco-tourism.

Cape Canoe Trails, PO Box 457, Noordhoek 7985 (tel: 021-789 2136). Day trips from Cape Town to canoe or kayak the relatively easy Berg or Klein Rivers. Hotel pickup included. Ideal for a newcomer or someone on a tight schedule.

Vineyard Ventures, 5 Hanover Road, Fresnaye, Cape Town 8001 (tel: 021-434 8888, fax: 021-434 9999). From a half day to a week touring the Cape winelands, with tastings and cellar tours.

Gauteng

Sunwa River Adventures, PO Box 313, Parys 9585 (tel: 0568-77107, fax: 0568-77362). Leisurely rafting in inflatables from a bush camp on the Vaal River.

Hikers by the Mac Mac pools

KwaZulu-Natal

Timeless Afrika, PO Box 2406, Durban 4000 (tel: 031-307 3800/1, fax: 031-307 3822). Official marketing organization for tourism in KwaZulu-Natal.

Zululand Tours and Safaris, PO Box 10305, Marine Parade, Durban 4056 (tel: 031-368 5399, fax: 031-37 4235). Bush lodges and camps, Zulu culture, game viewing and customized itineraries in northern Natal.

Mpumalanga

Lawson's Tours, PO Box 507, Nelspruit 1200 (tel: 013-755 2147, fax: 013-755 1793). Specialist bird-watching, wildlife, and photographic tours.

Safari Services, PO Box 1405, Nelspruit 1200 (tel: 013-752 6259, fax: 013-752 8146). Excellent custom-designed tours of the heart of big-game country.

Northern Province

Equus Trails, 36 12th Avenue, Parktown North, Johannesburg 2193 (tel: 011-788 3923, fax: 011-880 8401). Horseback riding and camping in the Waterberg Mountains.

TRAVEL FACTS

241

Arriving by air

Of the three major international airports, the most important is **Johannesburg International**, 15 miles east of Johannesburg, tel: 011-356 1111 (reservations); airport shuttle (tel: 011-884 3957).

Cape Town International is 14 miles east of Cape Town (tel: 021-934 0407); airport shuttle (tel: 021-794 2772).

Durban International is 12 miles southwest of Durban (tel: 031-42 6156); airport shuttle (tel: 031-203 5407). All have duty-free facilities, bus links with the major hotels, taxis, car rental offices, tourist information and hotel reservation desks.

There are scheduled flights from all over the world. Destinations of the state airline, **South African Airways (SAA)**, include New York, Miami, Hong Kong and Sydney, with regular services from London Heathrow to Johannesburg, Cape Town and Durban.

An arrival **tax** is included in the price of an international or domestic ticket. A special tax is collected on

Short-term parking at Cape Town International

arrival at Skukuza (Kruger National Park) airport. This is more if you are visiting a private game reserve than if you are staying in the Kruger.

SAA offices abroad:

Australia 9th Floor, 5 Elizabeth Street, Sydney NSW (tel: 02-223 4448)

U.K. St George's House, 61 Conduit Street, London W1R 0NE (tel: 0171-312 5005)

U.S.A. 9th Floor, 900 Third Avenue, New York 10022 (tel: 212-826 0995).

Airline offices in South Africa:

South African Airways (SAA) PO Box 7778, 39 Wolmarans Street, Braamfontein, Johannesburg 2000 (tel: 011-356 1111); Cape Town (tel: 021-403 1111)

Air France PO Box 41022, 196 Oxford Road, Craighall (tel: 011-880 8055)

Alitalia PO Box 937, Oxford Manor, Oxford Road (tel: 011-880 9254)

British Airways PO Box 535, Parklands, 158 Jan Smuts Avenue, Rosebank (tel: 011-441 8600)

KLM Royal Dutch Airlines PO Box 8624, Sable Place, 1a Stan Road, Morningside (tel: 011-881 9696)

Lufthansa PO Box 1083, 22 Girton Road, Parktown (tel: 011-484 4711) **Qantas** PO Box 651350, 2010 Benmore Village Walk, Maud Street, Sandton (tel: 011-884 5300).

Arriving by land
South Africa has borders with Namibia, Botswana, Zimbabwe, Mozambique, Swaziland and Lesotho. Most crossings are open at least 8AM–6PM daily. There are good roads into all neighboring countries, and bus and train links with Namibia, Botswana, Mozambique and Zimbabwe. Those requiring visas should remember that a shortcut across Lesotho or Swaziland will invalidate your reentry unless you have a multiple-entry visa.

Arriving by sea
Several cruise companies, including CTC Cruise Lines, P&O Cruises, Royal Viking Line and Starlauro, offer stops in South Africa on their routes. The *RMS St Helena* runs four scheduled services a year between the U.K. and Cape Town (tel: South Africa – 021-251 165; U.K. – 01326-563 434; U.S.A. – Traveltips 718-939 2400); several shipping companies provide passenger services on cargo freighters.

Customs regulations
Currency You may only import or export up to R500 in notes, but unlimited foreign currency and travelers' checks may be imported. You may need exchange control receipts to reconvert large quantities of leftover rand on departure.
Duty-free allowance For visitors over

The Romans would have been proud of the Free State roads

18 years old, the allowance is 400 cigarettes, 250 grams of tobacco and 50 cigars, 1 liter of spirits, 2 liters of wine, 50ml of perfume and 250ml of toilet water. You may take in gifts worth up to R500.
Drugs Narcotics and habit-forming drugs are prohibited. If you are carrying prescription drugs, carry a letter from your doctor.

Travel insurance
Take out travel insurance which covers medical treatment, air ambulance and repatriation (South Africa has no national health service and treatment can be expensive), as well as loss or theft of luggage, papers or money, and travel delays or cancellation. Those planning to take part in any adventure sports may have to pay an additional premium.

Documents
Visitors to South Africa need a full passport, valid for at least six months beyond the intended stay. Citizens of Australia, Canada, Ireland, New Zealand, United Kingdom and the United States do not need a visa.

You may need proof (such as a credit card) that you can support yourself and to show that you have a ticket home, or the means to buy one.

Your national driver's license is valid if it is written in English and includes your photograph. If not, apply for an international driver's license, valid for up to three years (depending on the type of permit) before leaving home.

Climate

As a whole, South Africa has an average annual rainfall of 18 inches a year and an average of 8.5 hours of sunshine a day. Average midwinter (June–July) temperatures range from ±32 degrees F at night to ±68 degrees F at midday. Average midsummer (December–January) temperatures are ±59 degrees F at night to ±95 degrees F at noon.

This means little, however, as there are several distinct climatic zones in the country dependent on longitude, latitude, vegetation, and altitude. It can be cool and gray in temperate Cape Town, hot and sticky in monsoon Durban, crisp and chilly in the high Drakensberg and hot and dry in the Kruger, all at the same time. It can also go from cool and overcast to blasting sun in the same place in the space of a few minutes. Always check local conditions, but always add sunblock, a hat, an umbrella and a sweater or jacket when packing.

National holidays

January 1	New Year's Day
March 21	Human Rights Day
March/April	Good Friday
March/April	Easter Sunday
March/April	Easter Monday
April 27	Freedom Day
May 1	Workers' Day
June 16	Youth Day
August 9	National Women's Day
September 24	Heritage Day
December 16	Day of Reconciliation
December 25	Christmas Day
December 26	Day of Goodwill

Time differences

South African Standard Time is two hours ahead of Greenwich Mean Time (Universal Standard Time), seven hours ahead of U.S. Eastern Standard Time and eight hours behind Australian Eastern Standard Time.

Opening times

Banks: Mon–Fri 9–3:30, Sat 8:30–11. Most have Automatic Teller Machines (ATMs) outside, operational 24 hours a day.
Businesses: Mon–Fri 8–5 , with an hour for lunch between 12 and 2. Some open limited hours on Saturday morning.
Petrol stations: most open 7AM–7PM daily; many are open 24 hours a day.

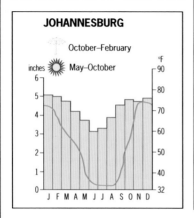

CAPE TOWN (KAAPSTAD)

May–August

October–March

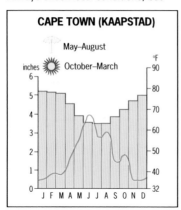

JOHANNESBURG

October–February

May–October

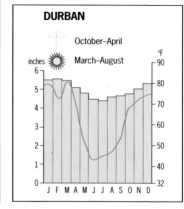

DURBAN

October–April

March–August

Shelves are piled high in the back street grocery stores

Post offices: Mon, Tue, Thu and Fri 8:30–4:30, Wed 9–4:30, Sat 8–12 noon.

Shops: Mon–Fri 8–5, Sat 8:30–12:30 – although hours are often longer in the main shopping areas.

Many small towns, still controlled by the Dutch Reformed Church, close down completely on Sunday, so make sure you stock up on gas, food, and other essentials on Saturday.

Money matters

Currency The South African currency is the Rand (R), divided into 100 cents. Bank bills are issued in denominations of R200, R100, R50, R20, and R10.

Exchange facilities Most banks have exchange facilities for major currencies, but it is advisable to carry U.S. dollars or U.K. sterling. The Standard Bank, with 900 branches across the country, is part of the worldwide Cirrus network and you can obtain money from its ATM machines if your national check card or credit card bears the Cirrus logo. Thomas Cook (Rennies) and American Express operate bureaux de change in all major cities. Banks require identification when changing money.

Checks and credit cards Many hotels, stores and restaurants in tourist and urban areas will accept travelers' checks in lieu of cash. Most businesses, tour operators, airlines, hotels and restaurants accept international credit cards including Visa, MasterCard, American Express and Diners Club. MasterCard holders may use any Thomas Cook Network location to report loss or theft of their card and obtain an emergency card replacement free.

Thomas Cook MasterCard Travellers Cheque Refund Centre (24-hour service – report loss or theft within 24 hours), tel: 0800-998175.

Prices Certain items, such as housing and fuel, are far cheaper than in Europe, and there is a secondary economy, based on the former townships, where prices are a fraction of those in the old white habitat. For most tourists, South Africa is affordable, but not particularly cheap. Hotel and restaurant prices are on a par with those in the U.S.; car rental is more expensive.

VAT Value Added Tax at 14 per cent is levied on most items and services, including hotel accommodation, goods, transportation and tours. Save receipts on anything over R250 and claim back the tax at the international departure point.

By car

Car rental Budget Rent-a-Car and Avis have offices throughout the country, including all main airports; you can rent from one office and return at another (for a premium). Local firms offer a cheaper, more limited service. Everything from an economy compact to four-wheel drive, chauffeur-driven limousine, Kombi (Volkswagen minibus) or motor home (RV) is available, all in excellent condition. However, car rental is expensive, with hefty base rates doubled by extras such as Collision Damage Waiver and insurance. Shop around for deals and, with huge distances to cover, always look for unlimited mileage. You should not need 4WD, even in the game parks, but check that your insurance covers you for dirt roads (some policies forbid them, which cuts out serious game viewing). Make sure you have a full set of spares and jack before setting out.

Car rental offices:
Budget PO Box 1777, Kempton Park 1620 (tel: 0800-016622 toll free)
Avis PO Box 221, Isando (tel: 0800-021111 toll free)
Dolphin PO Box 4613, Kempton Park 1620 (tel: 0800-011344 toll free)
Imperial PO Box 260177 Excom 2023I (tel: 0800-131000 toll free or 011-337 2300, fax: 011-336 8695)
Le Cap Motor Cycle Hire 45 Bloem Street, Cape Town 8001 (tel: 021-23 0823, fax: 021-23 5566).

Driving tips South Africa has excellent roads. Traffic is light, tempting drivers to go too fast, and the country has an appalling accident record. Concentrate every second—anything from a herd of goats to a child can appear from nowhere. There is a growing number of toll roads; keep some change handy for the tolls, which are reasonable.

Fuel is cheaper than in Europe. Gas stations are plentiful on major routes, infrequent elsewhere. Most service stations accept local garage cards, but not credit cards so carry enough cash. Windshield washing is standard. On long journeys, check the oil, water and brakes before setting out,

bring a can of fuel, together with a spare tire (and jack) and fan belt. Carry water, emergency food supplies and a blanket in case you get stuck overnight. The AA of South Africa (see below) recommends remaining on national routes where help can be summoned quite easily.

Regulations Driving is on the left. The speed limit is 37mph in built-up areas, 62mph on rural roads, and 74mph on freeways, unless otherwise indicated. You will be severely fined if caught exceeding the designated speed limit. Yield to the right at intersections and traffic circles. Seat belts are compulsory, always carry your driving license and do not drive under the influence of alcohol. Traffic laws are strictly enforced and penalties are harsh if they are ignored.

The **Automobile Association of South Africa** (tel: 011-407 1000) has reciprocal arrangements with many other national driving associations and will give advice and travel information as well as arrange emergency rescues.

By air

Several small airlines together create an excellent network of domestic flights, serving surprisingly small towns and some of the main tourist sights. Fares are not particularly cheap, but there are usually discounts for advance booking. Chartering a small plane may not prove outrageously expensive if several of you can share the cost, and you may even be able to rent your own light aircraft, so bring your pilot's license if you have one.
Nationwide Air tel: 011-975 5830
Comair tel: 011-921 0111
SA Express (the domestic wing of SAA) tel: 011-978 5577
SA Airlink tel: 011-973 2941
Sun Air tel: 011-397 2233/44.

By train see page 234

By bus

Long-distance buses are the most popular form of public transportation with services around the clock on all intercity routes. Always reserve in advance.

Greyhound Citiliner PO Box 11229, Johannesburg 2000 (information and reservations tel: 011-333 2130)
Intercape PO Box 618, Bellville 7535 (reservations and inquiries tel: 011-333 5231 or tel: 021-386 4444, fax: 021-386 4455)
Translux Express PO Box 2383, Johannesburg 2000 (tel: 011-774 3333, fax: 011-774 3318)

By taxi
The cheapest (but most uncomfortable) way of getting around is via the growing army of taxis: unlicensed minibuses which began as commuter transportation between the black townships and white cities. They are now fanning out to provide a countrywide network of routes. There is no advance booking and no schedule; they simply wait until full (and that can mean 22 people in an eight-seater). Standards of maintenance and driving are sometimes suspect, with a high accident rate, and the city depots are usually in the former townships. They are not usually recommended for tourists, though efforts are being made to upgrade the service, and some minibuses are now licensed.

Hitchhiking
Hitchhiking is not recommended anywhere in the country. Contact Backpackers in Cape Town (tel: 021-234 530) or consult the notice boards hanging up in some tourist information offices to arrange safe lifts in advance.

City transportation
There is little useful public transportation in South African cities. Durban has a reasonable local bus service, the **Mynah Shuttle** (tel: 031-307 3503), between the city and the surrounding suburbs. Cape Town and Johannesburg have infrequent and inefficient services, safe only in daylight hours.

Taxis are common, metered and expensive in major cities, almost nonexistent in smaller towns. You cannot hail them on the street and ranks are few and far between. Most shops and restaurants are happy to call one for you, even if you just walk in off the street.
Cape Town Marine Taxi (tel: 021-434 0434)
Durban Eagle Taxis (tel: 031-378 333/368 1706)
Johannesburg King Taxis (tel: 011-486 0042); Rose's Taxis (tel: 011-725 3333 or 1111)
Pretoria BTR (tel: 012-320 7513/4)

Durban is the only city in South Africa with a good local bus service

247

Student and youth travel

There is a growing range of good cut-price backpackers' accommodations, and student and youth discounts are available at some sights and museums. Take an International Student Identity Card (ISIC) and join Hostelling International (the Youth Hostel Association) before you leave home.

Hostelling International South Africa (HISA), 1st Floor, Room 101, Boston House, 46 Strand Street, Cape Town 8001 (tel: 021-419 1853). Youth hostel information and reservations and a budget travel and information service.

South African Student Travel Service (SASTS), University of the Witwatersrand, Student Union Building, Ground Floor, East Campus (tel: 011-716 3138). With offices in every university, SASTS handles all student and youth discount cards, and operates a full student travel agency.

Media

Television and radio The South African Broadcasting Corporation operates four television services in seven languages and 22 radio services in 11 languages. M-Net is a mainly English-language cable network. CNN and Sky TV are available outside SABC broadcasting hours (including the morning news); BBC World Service TV is available in a limited number of hotels; and satellite TV will be operational shortly. One of the best radio stations is the English-language SAFM.

The press There are five daily national and five Sunday national newspapers. The *Sowetan* has the highest circulation, followed by *The Star* and the *Sunday Times*. The *Weekly Mail & Guardian* has international news.

Post

There is a good postal service. For post office hours, see Opening times, page 244. *Poste restante* facilities are available in the main post office in each town; take identification to claim mail.

Cape Town GPO, corner Parliament and Darling Streets (tel: 021-461 5543)
Durban GPO, corner West and Gardiner Streets (tel: 031-305 7521)
Johannesburg GPO, corner Jeppe and Von Brandis Streets (tel: 011-222 9111).

Telephones

The telephone system is good, but public phones are thin on the ground. Phonecards for green public phone booths are available in pubs, newsagents, etc. Cash telephone kiosks operate on a minimum of 20 cents. There are three rate bands: expensive is Mon–Fri 7AM–6PM and Sat 7AM–1PM; medium is Mon–Fri 6PM –8PM; and cheap is Mon–Fri 8PM–7AM and Sat 1PM until Mon 7AM. Prices for overseas calls are high, with massive markups in hotels.
Vodacom have 24-hour desks at all major international airports offering rental of mobile phones.

- International dialing code for South Africa 27
- Domestic information 1023
- Domestic operator services 0020
- International information and other inquiries 0903
- International operator 0900
- International direct dial 09 + the country code

International codes include: Australia 61; Botswana 267; Canada 1; Lesotho 266; Namibia 264; New Zealand 64; Swaziland 268; U.K. 44; U.S. 1; Zimbabwe: 263.

South Africa is part of the Home Direct scheme and you can use most home telephone charge cards. Calling collect: Australia (tel: 0800-99 0061); Canada (tel: 0800-99 0014); U.K. (tel: 0800-9900 44); U.S. (AT&T) (tel: 0800-990 123).

Telex and fax
Most hotels and businesses have fax and telex facilities. Local stationers or "copy shops" often have public faxing machines. Fax numbers are listed alongside telephone numbers in the local telephone directory.

Language
There are 11 official languages—English, Afrikaans, Ndebele, Northern Sotho, Southern Sotho, Swazi, Tsonga, Tswana, Venda, Xhosa, and Zulu. The language of government and administration is English. Most people speak at least a smattering of English and Afrikaans.

Multilingual do's and dont's

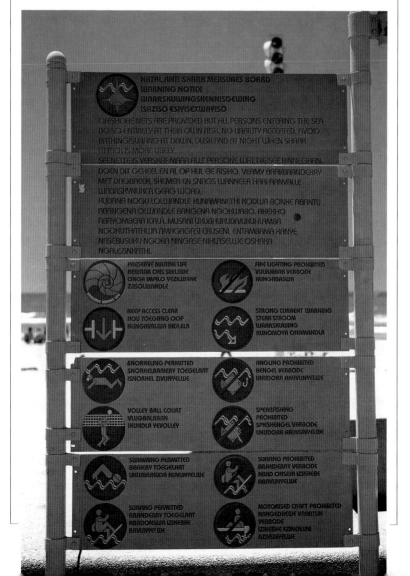

Police

To contact the South African Police (SAP), see listing SA Police Service under Government Departments in local telephone directories.

Emergency telephone numbers

Police Flying Squad: 10111
Emergency and Crisis Services (ambulance, fire, mountain rescue, etc): 1022 and ask for the relevant service
AA Breakdowns: tel: 0800-010101 toll free.

Embassies and consulates

South African embassies abroad
Australia Rhodes Place, State Circle, Yarralumla, Canberra, ACT 2600 (tel: 62-273 2424)
Canada 15 Sussex Drive, Ottawa, Ontario K1M 1M (tel: 613-744 0330)
United Kingdom Trafalgar Square, London, WC2N 5D (tel: 0171-930 4488)
United States 3051 Massachusetts Avenue, N.W., Washington D.C. 20008 (tel: 202-232 4400)

Foreign embassies in South Africa

Australia 292 Orient Street, Arcadia, Pretoria (tel: 012-342 3740)
Canada 1103 Arcadia Street, Hatfield (tel: 012-342 6923)
Ireland Tulbagh Park, 1234 Church Street, Colbyn, Pretoria (tel: 012-342 5062)
U.K. "Greystoke," 255 Hill Street, Arcadia (tel: 012-43 3121)
U.S.A. 877 Pretorius Street, Arcadia (tel: 012-342 1048).

Health

Inoculations For your own peace of mind, it is worth keeping up polio, typhoid and tetanus boosters and the 10-year hepatitis A vaccination.

Medical help Medical and hospital standards are excellent. Doctors are listed in local telephone directories under "Medical Practitioners." Pharmacies include:
Cape Town K's Pharmacy, 52 Regent Road, Sea Point (tel: 021-434 9331; *Open*: 9–9); Rustenberg Pharmacy, Fountain Shopping Centre, Main Road, Rondebosch (tel: 021- 685 5998; *Open*: 8:30AM–10PM)
Durban No 24-hour pharmacies, but Medicine Chest Chemist, 155 Berea Road, Berea (tel: 031-305 6151) and Daynite Pharmacy, 9a Nedband Circle, corner Point Road and West Street (tel: 031-368 3666) are open until 10:30PM.
Johannesburg
Link Pharmacy, Shop 6, Sandton Square, 5th Street, Sandton (tel:011-784 213. *Open*: Mon–Fri 8–6, Sat 9–2, Sun 10–4).

Hazards AIDS is endemic, with 8–10 per cent of the sexually active population estimated to be HIV positive: practice celibacy or safe sex. Condoms are freely available. Blood for medical use is carefully screened and treated.

Rabies is fatal if not caught in its early stages, so get treatment immediately if bitten by any animal. Check with a doctor if you are bitten by a snake, spider or scorpion, or if you stand on any creature in the ocean. Treat even minor grazes with caution as there are parasites and poisonous plants to which you will have no immunity. Clean, disinfect and cover any wound and see a doctor if it shows signs of going septic.

Malaria is found only in the Northern Province, Mpumalanga, and KwaZulu-Natal. You must take prophylactics if going into these areas or any of the surrounding countries. You must start taking the pills a week before you leave and continue to do so for four weeks after you return home. As the disease can take up to six months to develop, you should check with your doctor if you have flulike symptoms within this period.

Tap water is safe. In bush camps, check before drinking. Do not drink from rivers or lakes without purifying the water, and don't swim or paddle in natural water without checking. In certain areas, the water may be infected with bilharzia—and there is the possibility that crocodiles or hippos are lurking.

Skin cancer is on the rise in the white population and visitors should take precautions. Wear a hat, high-factor sunblock and stay in the shade during the intense midday heat. If you feel giddy in the sun, go indoors, drink large quantities of cool liquid and have a cool bath. If this does no good, call a doctor, as you may have heatstroke.

People hiking in the mountains or in the desert should beware of exposure and, in extreme cases, hypothermia. Take a foil space blanket, warm clothes and a good sleeping bag if planning to camp, and some means of providing high-energy food, preferably hot. In emergencies, the fastest way of warming someone up is with the heat of a human body.

Survival

The urban jungle Most South African cities have a bad security problem. Central Cape Town and Durban require normal vigilance and precautions in daylight hours, but large segments of Johannesburg are virtual no-go areas.

The first rule is to try not to look rich: don't walk the streets festooned in cameras or wearing jewelry. Use

Guard against pickpockets when in holiday mood

travelers' checks and credit cards wherever possible instead of carrying cash; take only what you need for the day, and always keep your money in several places. Never walk the streets after dark—take a taxi, however short the journey.

If you are mugged, hand over your valuables—do not resist. Wait until your assailant is out of sight before heading for the phone.

Try to make long-distance journeys in daylight hours and to reach your destination before dark. Keep car doors locked and wind up windows at traffic lights. Do not pick up hitch-hikers or stop to help people: if they seem to be in real trouble, telephone the nearest police station. Always park in well-lit and preferably busy places.

The former townships are generally unsafe for foreigners unless you go with an escorted tour.

Surviving in the wilds However cuddly they seem, many wild animals will happily take your hand off. Do not attempt to pet or feed animals, or even get out of the car for a better photo, without an experienced armed guard.

When bush walking, always tell somebody where you are going and when you plan to be back. Wear desert boots with good treads and ankle supports, thick socks and long trousers to protect your legs against thorns and wildlife. Take a hat, sunglasses, and high-factor sunblock, a long stick for dealing with unwanted wildlife, a water bottle and emergency high-energy rations (such as "trail mix"). A foil space blanket, some analgesic tablets, water purifiers, antihistamines for any allergic reaction (after a bite), insect repellent, and adhesive bandages are useful for emergencies. If you stumble on a snake, try not to provoke it. If bitten, stay calm, but get immediate help. Keep checking for spiders, scorpions and ticks; if you are bitten seek immediate medical advice.

Camping is popular and facilities are excellent

When camping, take warm clothes for the evening and wet- and cold-weather gear in the mountains. Shake out your sleeping bag before you get in and hang your shoes upside down to deter creepie-crawlies. Keep food well sealed and out of reach of ants and monkeys.

Be careful about swimming on empty beaches. The African seas are treacherous with dangerous currents, riptides and backwash. Never let children swim unattended or go into the surf on rafts. If the beach is packed but nobody is swimming, there is probably a good reason. Many beaches have lifeguards though they are not on duty around the clock.

Camping and caravanning

South Africa has a network of pleasant campsites, with shady pitches, good washing and cooking facilities (including your own *braai*/barbecue and a generous stack of wood). Larger sites may have self-catering cottages, a store, gas station, swimming pool and restaurant. Travelers with trailers or campers (RVs) are unlikely to find individual hookups for electricity, water, etc. The South

African Automobile Association publishes an annual guide to good campsites, available from them (tel: 011-407 1000) or local bookshops.

Camping rough is not a good idea for security reasons.

Camper rental:
Campers Corner Rental 357 Jan Smuts Avenue, Craighill, PO Box 48191, Roosevelt Park 2129 (tel: 011-789 2327, fax: 011-787 6900)
CI Leisure Rentals Tulbagh Road, PO Box 4300, Kempton Park 1620 (tel: 011-396 1860-2, fax: 011-396 1937)
Holiday Camper Hire Inchanga Ranch, Inchanga Road, Witkoppen, Johannesburg (tel: 011-708 2176, fax: 011-708 1464)
Knysna Camper Hire PO Box 1286, Knysna 6570 (tel: 0445-22444/82 5516, fax: 0445-82 5887).

Children
South Africa is probably the most child-friendly country in Africa, with a fine climate, glorious beaches, on-stream entertainment in major centers, good food and hygiene and excellent health care. There are plenty of family accommodation options, including self-catering and camping, and for fussy eaters pizzas and hamburgers are on tap. Shops are well stocked with all the essentials from diapers to formula baby food, and there is no problem finding reliable baby-sitters.

The only drawbacks are the various stinging and biting things which lurk in long grass and under water, the ferocity of the midday sun, and the enormous distances when touring. Take plenty of snacks and entertainments and make sure your children wear sunblock, hats and shoes when outside. Keep them in view and above all make sure they are properly supervised by a strong swimmer in the sea. There can be treacherous tides and waves as well as jellyfish, sea urchins, and even the occasional stray shark.

Only children over the age of 4 are permitted on game-viewing expeditions organized by private safari companies and lodges. If you have your own transportation, they can start younger, but remember that children have a limited attention span and are not disposed to sit quietly while watching the animals. Also, peak game-viewing times are early morning and late afternoon/early evening—which may disrupt schedules for young children.

Parent-free breaks
Several companies offer parent-free adventure breaks for older children (usually 7–9 years and up), with everything on offer from volleyball to abseiling, and canoeing to ecology classes:
The Wilderness Trust of South Africa PO Box 577 Bedfordview 2008 (tel: 011-453 7645)
National Environmental Adventure Trust PO Box 260, Gilletts 3603 (tel: 031-77 3334)
River Runners, see page 239.

For a list of other, similar organizations running such breaks for children and young people, contact the Department of Environmental Affairs and Tourism (Environmental Education)—tel: 012-310 3707, or the regional tourist information offices.

Visitors with disabilities
Many major sights and hotels

have wheelchair ramps and toilets for the disabled, but facilities vary enormously. Staff are usually willing to assist those with special requirements who telephone ahead. For information about specialist tours, services, etc:

National Council for Persons with Physical Disabilities in South Africa (tel: 011-726 8040)

Disabled People South Africa (tel: 0431-431 579)

South African National Council for the Blind (tel: 012-346 1171)

South African National Council for the Deaf (tel: 011-482 1610)

National Accessibility Scheme Satour (tel: 012-347 0600)

Wilderness Wheels Africa 117 St George's Road, Observatory, Johannesburg 2198 (tel: 011-648 5737). A tour operator specializing in bush adventures and game viewing for disabled travelers.

For information before you travel:

U.K.—RADAR (Royal Association for Disability and Rehabilitation), 12 City Forum, 250 City Road, London EC1V 8AF (tel: 0171-250 3222, fax: 0171-250 1212)

U.S.A.—SATH (Society for the Advancement of Travel for the Handicapped), 347 Fifth Ave, Suite 610, New York NY10016 (tel: 212-447-7284; fax: 212-725-8253).

Senior citizens

There are some facilities for senior citizens, but most are for South African nationals only. It never hurts to ask, however, so keep proof of your age handy and you may be able to get discounts on some national parks accommodations, movie and theater tickets, and even in some restaurants.

The Association for Retired Persons and Pensioners (ARP&P) (tel: 021-531 1758)

South African National Council for the Aged (tel: 021-246 270).

Maps

There is a wide range of free maps of

The Jama Madjid mosque, Durban

the country, regions and cities available from SATOUR and individual local publicity associations. Most are as good or better than anything on sale, other than the full A–Z city plans, which are far more comprehensive than most tourists need. CNA booksellers are probably the best places to buy commercial maps, while hiking trail maps are available from the National Parks shops.

Measurements
South Africa uses the metric system of measurement.

Places of worship
You will find Christian churches of every denomination, from Catholic, Anglican and Dutch Reformed to a variety of evangelical sects throughout the country. With large Jewish, Indian and Malay populations, there are plenty of synagogues, mosques and Hindu temples. Look in the local telephone directory.

Electricity
220–230 V A.C. 50 Hertz. Plugs have three round pins. Adaptors from three square pins are available, but may be in short supply. Power is reliable in cities, but you may experience some problems in remote areas, and bush camps may not be equipped with electricity. Take a flashlight for dark paths. Appliances may need a transformer.

Tipping
Tipping is common, but not obligatory. Give waiters and taxi drivers 10 per cent and porters R1–R2 per bag. Many hotels run a staff box at the front desk for one lump sum on checkout. Otherwise, give a few rand to the room staff and doorman. Expect to tip tour guides and game rangers at least R10–R20 a head per day.

Toilets
Most tourist venues, service stations and shopping centers have good public toilets. In nature reserves, parks and at the seaside they are sometimes more primitive but are usually spotlessly clean. Users may be charged a small fee.

CONVERSION CHARTS

FROM	TO	MULTIPLY BY
Inches	Centimetres	2.54
Centimetres	Inches	0.3937
Feet	Metres	0.3048
Metres	Feet	3.2810
Yards	Metres	0.9144
Metres	Yards	1.0940
Miles	Kilometres	1.6090
Kilometres	Miles	0.6214
Acres	Hectares	0.4047
Hectares	Acres	2.4710
Gallons	Litres	4.5460
Litres	Gallons	0.2200
Ounces	Grams	28.35
Grams	Ounces	0.0353
Pounds	Grams	453.6
Grams	Pounds	0.0022
Pounds	Kilograms	0.4536
Kilograms	Pounds	2.205
Tons	Tonnes	1.0160
Tonnes	Tons	0.9842

MEN'S SUITS							
UK	36	38	40	42	44	46	48
Rest of Europe	46	48	50	52	54	56	58
US	36	38	40	42	44	46	48

DRESS SIZES						
UK	8	10	12	14	16	18
France	36	38	40	42	44	46
Italy	38	40	42	44	46	48
Rest of Europe	34	36	38	40	42	44
US	6	8	10	12	14	16

MEN'S SHIRTS							
UK	14	14.5	15	15.5	16	16.5	17
Rest of Europe	36	37	38	39/40	41	42	43
US	14	14.5	15	15.5	16	16.5	17

MEN'S SHOES						
UK	7	7.5	8.5	9.5	10.5	11
Rest of Europe	41	42	43	44	45	46
US	8	8.5	9.5	10.5	11.5	12

WOMEN'S SHOES						
UK	4.5	5	5.5	6	6.5	7
Rest of Europe	38	38	39	39	40	41
US	6	6.5	7	7.5	8	8.5

255

South African Tourist Offices (SATOUR) abroad

Australia Level 6, 285 Clarence Street, Sydney, NSW 2000 (tel: 2-261 3424)
U.K. 5/6 Alt Grove, London, SW19 4DZ (tel: 0181-944 8080)
U.S.A. 500 Fifth Avenue, 20th Floor, New York, NY 10017 (tel: 212-730-2929).

SATOUR in South Africa

Cape Town Private Bag X9108, Cape Town 8000 (tel: 021-21 6274)
Durban PO Box 2516, Durban 4000 (tel: 031-304 7144)
Johannesburg PO Box 849, Parklands 2121 (tel: 011-447 6030). Local publicity association offices are all listed in the A–Z section of this guide, under the relevant town.

National parks

Most game parks provide rest-camp accommodations with basic *rondavels* and camping; larger ones have a lodge with hotel-standard accommodations. All have at least one restaurant, a provisions store and fuel, while some have their own post office, fax and laundry facilities. Opening hours for all parks are from sunrise to sunset (roughly 6AM– 6PM); you should reach the gate well

Self-drive tours are easy in the Kruger

before that to allow time to drive through to the camp. The self-catering camps are popular with South African tourists and it is worth booking in writing well in advance (up to 13 months), especially in local school and public holidays. For details of each individual park, see the relevant entry in the A–Z section. (See also Surviving in the wilds, page 252.)

National Parks Board PO Box 787, Pretoria 0001 (tel: 012-343 1991); National Parks Board Hotline (fax: 012-343 2006). Operates 11 of the major parks across the country, including the Kruger. Those planning to visit several should ask for a Golden Rhino pass, a single ticket offering access to all.

Natal Parks Board PO Box 662, Pietermaritzburg (tel: 0331-47 1981). Manages all parks in KwaZulu-Natal. Numerous smaller parks and reserves run by local conservation bodies (for scenery rather than wildlife) offer walking, hiking, and climbing.

For further information, contact the regional offices:

Cape Nature Conservation PO Box X9086, Cape Town (tel: 021-483 4083)

Department of Nature Conservation PO Box 517, Bloemfontein, Free State (tel: 051-405 5263)

Transvaal Nature Conservation Private Bag X209, Pretoria 0001 (tel: 012-323 3403).

HOTELS AND RESTAURANTS

HOTELS AND RESTAURANTS

ACCOMMODATIONS

Central Booking

Bed 'n' Breakfast, PO Box 91309, Auckland Park 2006 (tel: 011-482 2206/7, fax: 011-726 6915). In the U.K. tel: 01787-228 494. Central H.Q. for a wide range of small guest houses, bed-and-breakfast and self-catering establishments throughout South Africa.

The Conservation Corporation, 4 Naivasha Road, Sunninghill, Sandton (tel: 011-803 8421). Small and very exclusive chain of private game parks with luxury bush lodges.

Holiday Inn bookings, in the U.K. tel: 0800-897 121 (toll-free); in the U.S.A. (toll-free) tel: 800-421 8905. Large chain of large hotels, from 2- to 5-star, including the local Holiday Inns in their many incarnations.

Hostelling International South Africa, 101 Boston House, 46 Strand Street, Cape Town 8001 (PO Box 4402, Cape Town 8000; tel: 021-419 1853, fax: 021-216 937). The local youth hostel affiliate.

Jacana Country Homes and Trails, PO Box 95212, Waterkloof 0145 (tel: 012-346 3550/1/2, fax: 012-346 2499). Central marketing for a wide range of farm stays and country cottages.

Karos Hotels, PO Box 87534, 2198 Houghton (tel: 011-484 1641, fax: 011-484 6206). In the U.K. tel: 0181-875 1404. Chain of large international 3- to 5-star hotels, popular with businesspeople.

Leading Hotels of South Africa, PO Box 78291, 2146 Sandton (tel: 011-884 3583, fax: 011-884 0676). Lavish hospitality and luxury at high prices.

National Parks Board, 643 Leyds Street, Muckleneuk, Pretoria (PO Box 787, Pretoria 0001; tel: 012-343 1991, fax: 012-343 0905) and 44 Long Street, Cape Town (PO Box 7400, Rogge Bay 8012; tel: 021-222 810, fax: 021-246 211). All accommodations within the national parks, from campsites to lodges.

Portfolio Town and Country Retreats, Shop 5E, Mutual Square, Oxford Road, Rosebank, 2196 Johannesburg (tel: 011-880 3414, fax: 011-788 4802). Central marketing for a wide range of guest houses and small hotels, throughout South Africa, from the most basic to the most luxurious.

Protea Hotels, 5th Floor, Nedbank Foreshore Building, Heerengracht, Cape Town 8000 (tel: 021-419 5320, fax: 021-252 956). In the U.K., tel: 01789-204 269. The largest of the South African chains; most hotels are comfortable, reasonably priced, if lacking in atmosphere.

Small Exclusive Hotels of Southern Africa, 62 Pall Mall, London SW1Y 5HZ, UK (tel: 0171-930 1717, fax: 0171-930 1515). Atmosphere by the cartload, along with antiques and excellent meals. The name says it all.

Southern Sun Hotels, PO Box 782553, 2146

Sandton (tel: 011-482 3500 or toll-free: 0800-117 711, fax: 011-726 3019). For **Sun International**, PO Box 784487, 2146 Sandton (tel: 011-780 7800, fax: 011-780 7457). In the U.K. tel: 01491-411 222; in the U.S.A. tel: 00-1-954-713 2501. A range of hotels from the very comfortable to the totally luxurious, including Sun City. Most with casinos. Existing properties are in the former homelands; more promised.

Much of the best cheap accommodations are in small bed-and-breakfasts which have only a couple of rooms and have not been listed here. Ask the agencies or local tourist offices for recommendations.
The following recommended hotels have been divided into three price categories:
- budget ($)
- moderate ($$)
- expensive ($$$)

WESTERN CAPE

Cape Town and the Cape Peninsula

The Back Pack ($) 74 New Church Street, Cape Town (tel: 021-234 530, fax: 021-230 065). A self-catering hostel, close to the center of town. Swimming pool.

The Bay ($$$) Camps Bay (tel: 021-438 4444, fax 021-438 4455). 5-star, the only beach hotel in Cape Town, with superior service and accommodations. The Restaurant at The Bay, with stunning views, has a superb menu. Swimming pool.

The Breakwater Lodge ($$) Seapoint (tel: 021 406 1911, fax: 021 406 1070). A converted 19th-century prison on the Waterfront, with easy access to many shops, bars, and restaurants.

Cellars-Hohenort ($$$) Alphen Road, Constantia (tel: 021-794 2137, fax: 021-794 2149). Magnificent (5-star) small Cape Dutch hotel with extensive gardens, fine views of Table Mountain and a delectable restaurant. Swimming pool, riding.

Greenmarket Square Holiday Inn Garden Court ($$) Greenmarket Square, Cape Town (tel: 021-232 040, fax: 021-233 664). A no-frills 3-star hotel beside the famous flea market, ideally located for exploring the city on foot.

Mijlof Manor ($$) 5 Military Road, Cape Town (tel: 021-261 476, fax: 021-222 046). A comfortable private hotel (3-star), with a relaxed atmosphere. The bar and bistro are popular with the locals. The fare is basic, but tasty and good value.

Mount Nelson ($$) 76 Orange Street, Cape Town (tel: 021-231 000, fax: 021-247 472; in U.K. tel: 0171-620 0003). 5-star. An elegant, startlingly pink hotel in the heart of the city, the "Nellie" is up there with Raffles or the Plaza as one of the world's great historic hotels. It also boasts three of Cape Town's finest restaurants, serving *alfresco* Mediterranean-style buffets, Italian, Californian, and haute cuisine. Swimming pool.

Victoria and Alfred Hotel ($$) V&A Waterfront, Cape Town (tel: 021-419 6677, fax 021-419 8955). 4-star. This restored and tastefully decorated Victorian building is an integral part of the Waterfront development. The Waterfront Café is an excellent place to meet, with an affordable and innovative menu.

Vineyard Hotel ($$) Protea Road, Newlands (tel: 021-683 3044, fax 021-683 3365). Built in 1799 and surrounded by beautiful gardens, this historic 4-star hotel has been restored and furnished with period antiques. Swimming pool.

The Winelands, Breë Valley and West Coast

L'Auberge du Quartier Français ($$/$$$) Huguenot Street, Franschhoek (tel: 021-876 2151). Small elegant country house hotel, with two superb restaurants, Le Quartier, serving formal French cuisine, and the outdoor Café Français, with Cape Provincial cuisine. Reservations advised.

De Ouwe Werf ($$) 30 Church Street, Stellenbosch (tel: 021-887 4608, fax: 021-887 4626). B&B in a central historic house built in1803. Swimming pool. Delicious light lunches, traditional Cape and continental dining and a coffee shop with homemade cakes.

Diemersfontein Country House ($$) R303 between Paarl and Wellington (tel: 021-873 2671, fax: 021-864 2095). Located in the Wellington wine region, this private, friendly hotel offers traditional Cape hospitality. Swimming pool. Riding.

The Farmhouse ($$) Langebaan (tel: 02287-22062, fax: 02287-21980). Country house overlooking the Langebaan lagoon. Home-cooked meals. Swimming pool.

Grande Roche ($$$) 5 Plantasie Road, Paarl (tel: 021-632 727, fax: 021-863 2200). A sumptuous 5-star hotel in the heart of the famous Paarl vineyards. The restaurant has been awarded "Restaurant of the Year"— and deserves it. The wine list runs to 58 pages. Swimming pool.

Kagga Kamma ($$$) 60 miles north of Ceres (tel: 0233-70888, fax: 0233-70870). "The Place of the Bushmen" is a private game reserve, with resident San population, in the Cederberg. Accommodations consist of a rest camp with chalets and the Bushmen Lodge. Very expensive, but price includes all meals and excursions.

Lanzerac Hotel ($$$) Jonkershoek Road, Stellenbosch (tel: 021-887 1132, fax: 021-887 2310). 3-star hotel in 150-year-old Cape Dutch homestead on the outskirts of Stellenbosch. The restaurant offers traditional Malay fare.

Marine Protea Hotel ($$) Voortrekker Street, Lamberts Bay (tel: 027-432 1126, fax: 027-432 1036). This historic 3-star hotel is situated in a part of the Cape famous for its crayfish; the restaurant is renowned for its superb seafood.

Mooikelder Manor House ($$) Agter–Paarl Road, North Paarl (tel: 021-863 8491, fax: 021-863 8361). Located close to Paarl, this lovely Cape Dutch homestead was built in 1835, and includes Cecil John Rhodes among its past owners. Friendly, enthusiastic hospitality and antique furnishings. Normally bed-and-breakfast, but other meals available on request. Swimming pool.

Strassberger's Hotel ($/$$) Clanwilliam (tel: 027-482 1101, fax: 027-482 2678). Relaxing, historic 2-star hotel. Swimming pool.

The South Coast, Garden Route and Karoo

Arniston Hotel ($$) Arniston (tel: 02847-59000, fax: 02847-59633). A comfortable 3-star hotel in a charming 200-year-old fishing village. Good seafood restaurant. Swimming pool. Water sports. Alternatively, book a self-catering cottage ($) from Arniston Seaside Cottages (tel: 02847-59772).

Belvidere Manor ($$) Knysna (tel: 0445-871 055, fax: 0445-871 059). 27 Victorian-style cottages, each with its own fireplace, around an historic house beside Knysna lagoon. Excellent restaurant. Swimming pool. Boating.

Eight Bells Mountain Inn ($$/$$$) 22 miles from Mossel Bay on the Oudtshoorn road (tel/fax: 0444-951 544). 3-star. Superbly situated for the coast and the Karoo, this is a luxurious little resort with *rondawels*, Swiss-style chalets, and an excellent country restaurant.

Hunter's Country House ($$/$$$) 6 miles from Plettenberg Bay on the N2 to Knysna (tel: 04457-7818, fax: 04457-7878). A delightful, exclusive country hotel, with cozy thatched cottages scattered across manicured gardens on the edge of the last remaining indigenous forests. Superb set dinner. Swimming pool. Riding.

Klippe Rivier Homestead ($$) 6 miles west of Swellendam (tel: 0291-43341, fax: 0291-43337). A delightful Cape Dutch homestead with antique furnishings, situated close to historic Swellendam.

Lake Pleasant Hotel ($$) Groenvlei, off National Road, Sedgefield (tel: 04455-31313, fax: 04455-32040). A quiet country inn (3-star) with friendly, helpful staff, on the shores of a beautiful lagoon.

Lord Milner Hotel ($/$$) Logan Road Matjiesfontein 6901 (tel: 023-551 3011, fax: 023-551 3020). The tiny village of Matjiesfontein is a national monument. This 2-star hotel harks back to the days when the British aristocracy came to take the clean Karoo air. There is a variety of restaurants (some requiring jacket and tie) as well as a Victorian country pub.

Old Post Office Tree Guest House ($$) Market Street, Mossel Bay (tel: 0444-913 738, fax: 0444-913 104). Comfortable central guest house with antique furnishings, in the third-oldest building in town.

The Plettenberg ($$$) Plettenberg Bay (tel: 04457-32030, fax: 04457-32074). Highly comfortable, modern 4-star hotel on a rocky headland, with magnificent views and a fine restaurant. Swimming pool.

Rosenhof Country Lodge ($$) 264 Baron van Rheede Street, Oudtshoorn (tel: 0443-222 232, fax: 0443-223 021). Delightful small Victorian hotel with antique furnishings and a fine country restaurant.

Swartberg Hotel ($/$$) Main Street, Prince Albert (tel: 04436-332). Delightful old Victorian hotel (2-star) offering history, a friendly laid-back atmosphere, and good, plain country cooking.

Windsor Hotel ($$) Marine Drive, Hermanus (tel: 0283-23727, fax: 0283-22181). Comfortable, large holiday hotel (2-star) in town center, with ocean and mountain views.

EASTERN CAPE

Cathcart Arms Hotel ($$) 5 West Street, Grahamstown (tel/fax: 0461-27111). Charming, country-style 2-star hotel. 14 bedrooms with early Cape country furniture.

The Cock House ($/$$) 10 Market Street, Grahamstown 6140 (tel: 0461-311 295, fax: 0461-311 287). A delightful small guest house, built in 1830 and now a National Monument. The food is highly recommended.

Die Tuishuise ($$) Cradock (tel: 0481-711 322). A wonderful hotel with 11 lovingly restored houses, all filled with antiques and each distinctively different. The price of a room gets you a whole house.

Drostdy Hotel ($$/$$$) 30 Church Street, Graaff-Reinet (tel: 0491-22161, fax: 0491-24582). Charming 3-star hotel designed in 1806 by the noted Cape Dutch architect Louis Michel Thibault, and carefully restored to its original glory. The rooms are in 1855 slave cabins. Swimming pool.

The Halyards Resort Hotel ($$/$$$) Port Alfred 6170 (tel: 0464-42410, fax: 0464-42466). Resort hotel (4-star) at the mouth of the Kowie River. Rooms have private balconies overlooking the marina. Water sports, riding.

King's Lodge Hotel ($$) Alice Road, Hogsback (tel: 045-962 1024, fax: 045-962 1058). Basic but atmospheric and friendly mountain hideaway surrounded by forest.

Port Elizabeth Hostel ($) 7 Prospect Hill, Port Elizabeth 6065 (tel: 041-560 697). Guests have a choice of dormitories, double or family rooms.

Shamwari Game Reserves ($$$) 45 miles from Port Elizabeth on the banks of the Bushmans River (tel: 042-831 1135). Luxury private game reserve, with accommodations in a lovingly restored manor house and Settler homes. Swimming pools. Game viewing. Expensive, but including all meals and game drives.

Trennery's Qolora River Mouth, Wild Coast (tel: 0474-3293). Charming colonial hotel with lush gardens, ocean views and excellent seafood (especially Sat). Other delightful small getaway resorts along this stretch of coast include **Seagulls** (tel: 0474-3287); **Wavecrest** (tel: 0474-3273); and **The Kob Inn** (tel: 0474-4421).

Walmer Gardens Hotel ($$) 10th Avenue, Walmer, Port Elizabeth 6065 (tel/fax: 041-514322). Comfortable, centrally located 2-star hotel. Swimming pool.

THE FREE STATE, NORTHERN CAPE AND NORTHWEST PROVINCE
The Free State

De Oude Kraal ($$) 22 miles south of Bloemfontein (tel: 05215-636, fax: 05215-635). Historic country house with pleasant rooms and excellent traditional restaurant.

Franshoek Mountain Lodge ($) 2 miles east of S384/S385 junction, Ficksburg, Eastern Highlands (tel/fax: 05192-3938). Small, intimate sandstone and thatch lodge (2-star) in a valley at the foot of the Witteberg. Good country cooking. Swimming pool. Hiking, fishing, climbing, polo.

Holiday Inn Garden Court ($$) Zastron Road, Brandhof, Bloemfontein (tel: 051-447 0310, fax: 051-430 5678). 3-star. Basic, but comfortable and only a few miles from the city center. Swimming pool.

Mount Everest Game Lodge ($) off the Verkykerskop road, 13 miles north of Harrismith, Eastern Highlands (tel: 05861-21816, fax: 05861-23493). Swiss cottages and thatched *rondawels* among the rhinos in a private game park. Swimming pool. Riding, hiking, fishing.

Oaklands Country Manor ($$) Van Reenen, Eastern Highlands (tel: 05867-883, fax: 05867-921). On the Free State-KwaZulu-Natal border, at the top of the Van Reenen's Pass. Quiet, owner-managed manor with facilities for children. Swimming pool. Riding and trout fishing.

Northern Cape

Chateau Guesthouse ($) 9 Coetzee Street, Upington (tel: 054-27504, fax: 054-27064). Comfortable, art deco-style bed-and-breakfast near the town center.

Gariep Lodge ($$) 24 miles east of Upington, on the Olifantshoek road (tel: 054902 ask for 919 812). A real Kalahari getaway with small cabins and tented accommodations scattered across the dunes in a small private game reserve on the banks of the Orange River. All meals under the stars.

Kimberley Holiday Inn Garden Court ($) Du Toitspan Road, Kimberley (tel: 0531-31751, fax: 0531-21814). A no frills, centrally located 3-star hotel.

Korannaberg Estate ($$$) near Kuruman (tel: 05375-215, fax: 05375-234). Two comfortable lodges (5-star and 3-star) provide accommodations in this 62,000-acre private game park. Very expensive, but rates

include all meals and game drives.
Pembury Lodge ($$) 11 Currey Street,
Kimberley (tel: 0531-824317). Centrally locat-
ed Edwardian guest house, with excellent
food. Dining room open to nonresidents.
Sydney-on-Vaal ($$) 40 miles northwest of
Kimberley (tel/fax: 011-706 0348). This
exclusive country retreat is set in a 9,885-
acre estate amid a vast conservation area
full of game and bird life. Swimming pool.

Northwest Province
Lindbergh Lodge ($$) Wolmaransstad
(tel/fax: 01811 22041). Luxury lodge in
25,000-acre game reserve, close to a water
hole. Self-catering cottages and blind avail-
able. Swimming pool. Golf.
Madikwe River Lodge ($$) Derdepoort (tel:
014778-891, fax: 014778-893). Big 5 game
viewing at this exclusive game lodge close
to the Botswana border, with luxury chalet
overlooking the Marico River. Swimming
pool. Price includes everything.
Sun City ($$/$$$) 46 miles from Rustenburg.
The ultimate resort, with accommodations
ranging from simple family self-catering
units at the **Cabanas**, the plusher **Cascades**
and the comfortable but ordinary **Sun City**
itself (tel: 01465-21000, fax: 01465-74210),
and the ultra-luxurious **Palace at the Lost
City** (tel: 01465-73000, fax 01465-73111).
Swimming pools and other sporting facilities. Casino. See also page 145.

GAUTENG
Johannesburg
The Carlton ($$$) Marshall Street, City
Centre (tel: 011-331 8911, fax: 011-331 3555;
for U.K. bookings tel: 0171-225 0164). If you
wish to spoil yourself, stay at this large,
luxurious (5-star) downtown hotel.
Swimming pool.
The Cullinan ($) 115 Katherine Street,
Sandton (tel: 011-884 8544, fax: 011-884
8545). Charming, small(ish), definitely
exclusive city hotel (4-star) with excellent
nouvelle cuisine style restaurant.
The Explorers Club ($) 9 Innes Street,
Observatory (tel: 011-648 7138, fax: 011-648
4673). Basic, safe and clean backpackers'
hostel, happy to store luggage and give
expert travel advice.
Holiday Inn Garden Court ($$) 84 Smal
Street, City Centre (tel: 011-336 7011, fax:
011-336 0515). Modern, central 3-star hotel
with large, comfortable rooms and three
restaurants (one Chinese). The hotel is
linked to the major shopping centers.
Swimming pool.
**Holiday Inn Garden Court Johannesburg
Airport ($$)** 6 Hulley Road, Isando,
Kempton Park (tel: 011-975 1121, fax: 011-
975 5846). 3-star. Less than a mile from the
airport, this is ideal if you have a plane to
catch. Swimming pool.
Karos Johannesburger Hotel ($$) 60 Twist
Street, Hillbrow (tel: 011-725 3753, fax: 011-
725 6309). 3-star. Convenient for both

shopping and the many restaurants nearby, although Hillbrow is rough on security.
Good value for money and standards are
high. Swimming pool.
Sandton Sun ($$$) Fifth Street, Sandton
(tel: 011-780 5000, fax: 011-780 5002). Large
and luxurious 5-star city hotel, beloved of
visiting businessmen and dignitaries.
Traveller & Backpacker's Retreat ($) 55 First
Street, Bez Valley (tel: 011-614 4640, fax:
011-614 2497). Cheap, cheerful and secure
International Traveller's Hostel which acts
as headquarters for others around southern
Africa.

Pretoria
Best Western Pretoria Hotel ($$) 230
Hamilton Street, Arcadia (tel: 0800-12 0886,
fax: 012-44 2258). A 3-star hotel which
offers value-for-money accommodations, a
high standard of service and very friendly,
helpful staff.
The Farm Inn ($$) Lynnwood Road, Pretoria
(tel: 012-809 0266, fax: 012-809 0146).
Situated next to the Silverlakes Golf Estate,
this stone and thatch palace (3-star) offers
outdoor activities and a private game sanc-
tuary. Swimming pool.
Marvol Guest House ($$$) 358 Aries Street,
Waterkloof Ridge (tel: 012-346 1774, fax:
012-346 1776). Stately Cape Dutch style
house with 11 well-equipped rooms.
Facilities include chauffeur-driven
transportation, secretarial service, a gym,
sauna and two swimming pools.
Oxnead ($$) Moreleta Park, Pretoria (tel:
012-984 515, fax: 012-998 9168). A charming
Cape Georgian style guest house offers
excellent food and vintage wines in a luxu-
ry setting. Swimming pool.
Victoria Hotel ($) Corner Scheiding and
Paul Kruger Streets (tel: 012-323 6052, fax:
012-323 0843). 5-star. This is the original
19th-century hotel, a recently restored,
colonial building furnished with antiques.
The hotel and restaurant are excellent but
the surrounding area, opposite the train
station, can be dangerous at night.

NORTHERN PROVINCE
The Coach House ($$/$$$) Agatha, 9 miles
from Tzaneen, in the Magoebaskloof
Mountains (tel: 0152-307 3641, fax: 0152-
307 1466). This 19th-century coaching inn
(5-star) has delightfully comfortable rooms,
panoramic views and some of the finest
food in South Africa. Swimming pool. The
same management also runs two other
excellent properties locally, the 3-star
Magoebaskloof Hotel ($$) tel: 015 276-4276,
and the 2-star **Troutwaters Inn** and
Lakeside Chalets ($) tel: 015-276 4245.
Lalapanzi ($$) Bandelierkop, 17 miles south
of Louis Trichardt on the N1 (tel: 015-516
1362, fax: 015-516-1363). Cottage-style
hotel in the bush, with good food and wine.
The Mountain View Hotel ($$) on the N1
5 miles north of Louis Trichardt (tel/fax:

261

HOTELS AND RESTAURANTS

015-517 7031). Small family-run hotel, convenient for exploring the Soutpansberg and Venda.

MPUMALANGA
Luxury Lodges at Kruger
Most of the lodges scattered through Sabie Sand and Timbavati (see pages 186–7) are similar in style, with a large private game park, and small camps with thatched cottages scattered round a central block. The complex is usually open to the bush with animals, from monkeys to elephant, wandering through at will. All meals are outdoors in good weather, with breakfast and lunch on the terrace, overlooking a water hole or river. Dinner is around the bonfire in a *boma* (open-air enclosure, with fencing against animals and the wind). All those listed offer the highest quality service, accommodations, food, atmosphere and game viewing. All have swimming pools. Prices are high, but are usually fully inclusive (check before booking). You are paying not only for world-class luxury accommodations, but for the upkeep of an expensive private game reserve. If only for a couple of nights, it is worth splashing out ($$$$ means *very* expensive). Telephone and, fax numbers are for reservations.

Idube ($$$) Sabie Sand (tel: 011-888 3713, fax: 011-888 2181). Luxury chalets and a rustic tented bush camp.

Inyati ($$$) Sabie Sand (tel: 011-493 0755, fax: 011-493 0837). Charming small, friendly lodge, with luxuriously appointed thatched chalets, on the Sand River.

Londolozi ($$$$) Sabie Sand (tel: 011-803 8421, fax: 011-803 1810).Three swanky camps along the Sand River.The Conservation Corporation also operate tiny **Singita** nearby, and **Ngala**, the only private lodge within the boundaries of the park itself.

Mala Mala ($$$$) Sabie Sand (tel: 011-789 2677, fax: 011-886 4382). One of the best known exclusive resorts in South Africa, patronized by the international jet set.

Motswari and M'Bali ($$$) Timbavati (tel: 011-463 1990, fax: 011 463 1992) Motswari has thatched bungalows; M'Bali offers more rustic "Habi-tents."

Sabi Sabi ($$$$) Sabie Sand (tel: 011-483 3939, fax: 011-483 3799; in the U.K. tel: 0181-875 1404). 6 miles of river frontage, and three luxurious lodges, including tree and tented camps. The emphasis here is on expert, personalized service. Game-ranger training courses on offer.

Hotels outside Kruger Park
Casa do Sol ($$/$$$) near Hazyview, on the R536 to Sabie (tel: 013-737 8111, fax: 013-737 8166). Designed like a Spanish village, in the heart of little Ilanga Nature Reserve, with African waiters in French berets and smocks, this hotel appeals strongly to those with a sense of the absurd. It is great fun, very comfortable and the food is excellent.

Swimming pool. Riding. Walking trails. Tennis. Golf. Fishing.

Cybele Forest Lodge ($$$) 14 miles from Hazyview, off the R40 to White River (tel: 013-750 0511, fax: 013-751 2839). An exclusive, country cottage-style mountain retreat (4-star), ideal for rest and relaxation, with beautiful grounds and wonderful meals. Easy access to Kruger Park. Swimming pool. Trout fishing. Riding.

Farmhouse Country Lodge ($$) 25 miles north of Nelspruit on the Hazyview road (tel: 013-737 8780, fax: 013-737 8783). 4-star country house hotel with fine gardens on a working farm, tucked into the valley bottom. Swimming pool. Riding. Walking. Easy access to Kruger Park.

GwalaGwala Country Lodge ($) White River, on the R40 to Nelspruit (tel: 013-750 1723, fax: 013-750 1999). Small, informal, family-run country hotel within easy reach of Kruger and the escarpment area. Swimming pool. Mountain bikes, riding.

Hotel Bundu ($) White River (tel/fax: 013-758 1221). 2-star. Good location for exploring the Kruger. Relaxed atmosphere, and kind to the budget. Swimming pool. Riding.

Mount Sheba Hotel ($$) Pilgrim's Rest (tel: 011-788 1258, fax: 011-788 0739; also 080 111 4448 toll free). 3-star hotel situated on the summit of the escarpment, in a private nature reserve and indigenous forest. The restaurant serves delicious country food. Swimming pool.

The Royal Hotel ($$) Main Street, Pilgrim's Rest (tel: 013-768 1100, fax: 013-768 1188). Beautifully restored and atmospheric Victorian hotel at the center of this little mining town.

KWAZULU-NATAL
Durban and Environs
Brackenmoor ($$$) Skyline Road, Uvongo, near Margate, South Coast (tel: 03931-75165, fax: 03931-75109). Elegant country house hotel in formal gardens, with an excellent restaurant.

Cabana Beach ($$) 10 Lagoon Drive, Umhlanga Rocks, North Coast (tel: 031-561 2371, fax: 031-561 3522). Huge beachfront 3-star hotel with family suites, complete with kitchenette. Swimming pools.

The Country Lodge ($$) Southbroom, South Coast (tel: 03931-78380, fax: 03931-78557). Charming, friendly African-style lodge tucked into a cycad forest near the beach. Excellent restaurant.

The Edward ($$$) Marine Parade, Durban (tel: 031-373 681, fax: 031-321 692). Large, newly and beautifully refurbished art deco seafront hotel (5-star), complete with five excellent restaurants.

Holiday Inn Garden Court – South Beach ($$) 73 Marine Parade, Durban (tel: 031-372 231, fax: 031-374 640). Relaxed 3-star family hotel with comfortable rooms. Good selection of restaurants, and right on the beach front. Swimming pool.

Oyster Box Hotel ($$) Umhlanga Rocks, North Coast (tel: 031-561 2233, fax: 031-561 4072). 3-star. The hotel takes its name from the first cottage built in the area in 1869. Enjoy the gardens and beachfront location in colonial comfort. Swimming pool.

The Royal Hotel ($$$) 267 Smith Street, Durban (tel: 031-304 0331, fax: 031-307 6884; for U.K. bookings tel: 0171-225 0164). 5-star. The Royal has been collecting awards as the city's best hotel and best restaurant for years. Central location, ideal for exploring and shopping. Swimming pool.

Selborne Country Lodge and Golf Resort ($$) Pennington, South Coast (tel: 0323-975 1133, fax: 0323-975 1811). This elegant country lodge and golf club is situated on a superb 200-acre estate on Natal's south coast, just 40 minutes' drive from Durban. Swimming pool.

Tekweni Backpackers' Hostel ($) 169 Ninth Avenue, Morningside, Durban (tel: 031-303 1433). Budget accommodations in an old colonial house, offering twin rooms or dormitories, close to the beachfront. Swimming pool.

Battlefields and Zululand

Balbrogie Country House ($) Under a mile from the N11 between Ladysmith and Dundee, Wasbank (tel/fax: 034-651 1352). Live graciously in this lovingly restored family-run Victorian farmhouse.

Bonamanzi ($/$$) 6 miles north of Hluhluwe village (tel: 035-562 0181, fax: 035-562 0143). Private 10,380-acre game park near Hluhluwe/Umfolozi, with a range of accommodations from basic self-catering tree houses to luxury lodges with a private cook.

Bushlands Game Lodge ($$/$$$) Hluhluwe (tel: 035-562 2071, fax: 035-562 2070). A unique lodge with rooms connected by elevated wooden platforms and walkways. Situated near the national parks of Hluhluwe/Umfolozi, St Lucia, Mkuzi and Sodwana Bay. Swimming pool. Meals and game drives cost extra.

Fugitive's Drift ($$) 9 miles from Rorke's Drift, near Dundee (tel: 03425-843, fax: 0341-23319). Comfortable lodge on a 5,100-acre natural heritage site beside the Buffalo River, overlooking Isandlwana. Extensive library of Africana and the owner is a registered battlefield tour guide and one of the best raconteurs in the region.

Isibindi Eco-Reserve ($$) 6 miles from Rorke's Drift; 33 miles from Dundee off the R33 to Greytown (tel/fax: 03425-620). Rustic clifftop cabins, surrounding a central stone-built lodge. Right in the bush on a small private game reserve, with a traditional Zulu village. River trips.

Kamnandi Guest House ($) 91 Victoria Street, Dundee 3000 (tel: 0341-21419/21423). Comfortable bed-and-breakfast in a charming old town house.

Ndumo Wilderness Camp ($$$) Ndumo Game Park (reservations tel: 011-884 1458, fax: 011-883 6255). Tiny tented camp next to Banzi Pan, amid South Africa's best bird-watching country.

Ntshondwe Camp ($$) Itala Game Reserve, Louwsburg 3150 (tel: 0388-75105, fax: 0388-75190). Delightful hillside game lodge tucked between a rocky *kopje*, a water hole and the open grasslands, inside the national park. Self-catering cabins and full restaurant facilities.

Phinda Resource Reserve ($$$) about 18 miles north of Hluhluwe village (reservations tel: 011-803 8421, fax: 011-803 1810). Pristine, private, big-five game reserve between Mkuzi and St. Lucia. Forest Lodge has elegant Japanese-style glass cabins scattered through the woods, Nyala Lodge has more traditional chalets.

Rocktail Bay Lodge ($$$) Maputaland Coastal Forest Reserve, south of Kosi Bay (reservations tel: 011-884 1458, fax: 011-883 6255). Small, remote lodge with wood and thatch tree houses, next to a deserted turtle beach.

Drakensberg and Midlands

Cathedral Peak ($$) 19 miles from Winterton (tel/fax: 036-488 1888); **Champagne Castle** ($$) 20 miles from Winterton (tel: 036-468 1063, fax: 036-468 1306); **Royal Natal National Park Hotel** ($$) Mont-aux-Sources (tel: 036-438 6200, fax: 036-438 6101). All comfortable, popular, well-run mountain hotels with spectacular scenery and hiking. Swimming pools.

Granny Mouse Country House ($$/$$$) Balgowan, off N3 between Howick and Mooi River (tel: 033-234 4071, fax: 033-234 4229). Africa meets Beatrix Potter in this apogee of chintz, thatch and chocolate cake in the heart of the Natal Midlands.

Imperial Hotel ($$$) 224 Loop Street, Pietermaritzburg (tel: 0331-426 551, fax: 0331-429 796). 3-star. A hotel since 1878, it was named after the Prince Imperial, one of its first patrons. It has been the premier hotel in the city ever since and still exudes an air of slightly faded colonial grandeur.

Old Halliwell Country Inn ($$) Howick tel: 0332-302 602, fax: 0332-303 430). A welcoming inn, dating from the 1830s, near the historic hamlet of Curry's Post.

Rawdons ($$) Nottingham Road (tel: 0333-36044). Low, thatched "little England" country house hotel with charm and elegance.

Reheboth ($) 276 Murray Road, Lincoln Meade, Pietermaritzburg (tel: 0331-962 312, fax: 0331-964 008). Self-catering Victorian-style apartments in landscaped gardens, About 4 miles from the center of town.

Sandford Park Lodge ($$) Bergville (tel: 036-448 1001, fax: 036-448 1047). Delightful 2-star country house hotel first opened as a coaching inn in 1850. Good food, lush gardens and a roaring log fire in winter. Within easy reach of the central Drakensberg area.

RESTAURANTS

Outside the major cities, restaurant hours are short in the evening, with serving between about 7.30 and 9PM. Many restaurants do not have a liquor license although you can bring your own drinks; others restrict diners to wine and beer. Check before you go.

In many instances, particularly outside the major cities, the finest restaurants are attached to the good hotels. To save space they are not listed again here, so try consulting the hotel list when choosing where to eat.

Visitors from Europe and North America will find food reasonably priced. The following recommended restaurants have been divided into three price categories (see page 258).

WESTERN CAPE *MAMA AFRICA*

Cape Town and Environs

Africa Café ($$) 213 Lower Main Road, Observatory (tel: 021-47 9553). Small, snazzy, friendly back-street restaurant serving traditional pan-African food. Open for dinner Mon–Sat. Reservations advised.

Arlindo's ($$/$$$) Shop 155, Victoria Wharf, V&A Waterfront (tel: 021-216 888). One of several very good restaurants in the Waterfront development featuring seafood and game, pasta, salads and poultry. Most locals have their favorite; take a walk and study the menus. Reservations advised.

The Brass Bell ($$) Kalk Bay Railway Station (tel: 021-788 5455). Upstairs seafood restaurant and downstairs pub overlooking Kalk Bay.

Buitenverwachting ($$$) Klein Constantia Road, Constantia (tel: 021-794 3522). Magnificent food at one of South Africa's finest wineries.

Floris Smit Huijs ($$) 55 Church Street, Cape Town (tel: 021/23 3414). Delectable continental and South African food in a cozy setting. Lunch Mon–Fri, dinner Mon–Sat. Reservations essential.

Gaylords ($$) 65 Main Road, Muizenberg (tel: 021-788 5470). Small, cozy north Indian restaurant.

Jonkershuis ($$) Groot Constantia (tel: 021-794 6255). Friendly country-style restaurant at the winery and stately home. Traditional Cape Dutch food with sampler plates.

Noon Gun Tearoom ($) Signal Hill, Bo-Kaap (tel: 021-240 529). Coffee and Malay sticky buns on the terrace of a private home with a spectacular view. Full meals available only if you reserve ahead, but this is about the only place in Cape Town to get really good, truly authentic Cape Malay food.

The Winelands, Breë Valley and West Coast

Bosduifklip ($$) 2½ miles from Lambert's Bay

on the Clanwilliam road (tel: 027-432 2735). Popular open-air restaurant, serving grills, seafood and salads. Reservations.

De Akker ($) 90 Dorp Street, Stellenbosch (tel: 021-833512). Old-fashioned country pub with wood paneling, blazing fires and simple, wholesome food.

De Volkskombuis ($$$) Aan de Wagenweg, Stellenbosch (tel: 021-887 2121). Name and address translating as "the people's kitchen on the wagon road," this fine restaurant on the banks of the Eerste River is housed in a Herbert Baker building. The spectacular menu includes many traditional Cape recipes.

La Petite Ferme ($$) Pass Road, Franschhoek (tel: 021-876 3016). Simply prepared and utterly delicious farm-fresh food, with rainbow trout a specialty. Wonderful views across the Franschhoek Valley. Open daily for lunch and tea. Reservations essential.

Paddagang ($$$) 23 Church Street, Tulbagh (tel: 0236-300242). Traditional Cape specialties, including smoked snoek pâté, *waterblommetjie bredie* and *bobotie*, on a delightful terrace in the historic heart of Tulbagh. Open daily, breakfast, tea, lunch and wine tastings. Reservations.

Rhebokskloof ($$$) Agter–Paarl Road, Paarl (tel: 021-863 8606). Haute cuisine and Cape Dutch food at a charming winery. Try the 7-course, 7-wine *dégustation* menu.

Rheinholds ($) Main Street, Clanwilliam (tel: 027-482 1101). Traditional South African food, accompanied by delicious home-baked bread.

The South Coast, Garden Route and Karoo

Bientang se Grot ($$) Marine Drive, Hermanus (tel: 0283-23651). A highly rated buffet-style seafood restaurant in a cave overlooking the sea.

Copper Pot ($$$) Multi Centre, Meade Street, George (tel: 0441-743 191). Haute cuisine, seafood and impeccable silver service in one of the best restaurants on the Garden Route.

The Islander ($$) 5 miles from Plettenberg Bay on the N2 to Knysna (tel: 04457-7776). Casual, buffet-style seafood restaurant. Always heaving with people.

Jetty Tapas ($$) Thesens Wharf, Knysna (tel: 0445-21927). Casual seafront restaurant with a great view and nonstop supply of fresh Knysna oysters.

Tom's Tavern ($) Wilderness Shopping Centre, Wilderness (tel: 0441-877 0353). Fresh fish and Indonesian specialties add welcome relief to the usual steak house menu. The setting and décor are not wonderful, but you can sit outdoors and the food is good, cheap and simple.

Zindago's Restaurant ($$) Cango Crocodile Farm, Cango Caves Road, Oudtshoorn (tel: 0443-292656). About 6 miles north of the town, this large, cheerful restaurant stands beside the deerpark water hole on the crocodile farm. The set menus include crocodile and ostrich fillets and a tour of the park. Open 9AM until late.

EASTERN CAPE

Sir Rufane Donkin Rooms ($$/$$$) 5 George Street, Upper Hill, City Centre, Port Elizabeth (tel: 041-555 534). One of the best restaurants in the region, in a building dating back to 1850. The menu changes every two months, and is full of mouthwatering surprises. Reservations essential.

Up the Khyber ($) cnr Western Road and Belmont Terrace, Port Elizabeth (tel: 041-522 200). Friendly licensed Indian restaurant, with excellent curries and nonspicy options available.

THE FREE STATE, NORTHERN CAPE AND NORTH-WEST PROVINCE

Le Must ($$) 11 Schröder Street, Upington (tel: 054-24971). A popular, pretty restaurant, serving tasty local dishes.

Onze Rust ($$) just outside Bloemfontein (tel: 051-441 8717). South African traditional food, at "Boerekos," former residence of President M. J. Steyn of the Boer Republic. Reservations essential.

Schillaci's ($$) 115 Zastron Street, Bloemfontein (tel: 051-448 2835). Atmospheric Italian trattoria and pizzeria with garden dining. Reservations a must.

Star of the West ($$) corner North Circular and Barkly Roads, Kimberley (tel: 051-82 6463). The food is ordinary, but the atmosphere is great in this authentic 19th-century miners' pub.

GAUTENG

Johannesburg

Anton van Wouw ($$) 111 Sivewright Avenue, Doornfontein (tel: 011-402 7916). A full menu of game, *boboties*, *bredies*, and South African desserts. Closed Sunday. Reservations advised.

Carnivore ($$) Muldersdrift Estate, off D F Malan Drive (tel: 011-957 2099). Little brother to the famous Nairobi venue, this large, cheerful restaurant cooks all sorts of meat, including game, over an open fire. Also soups, salads and vegetarian options.

Fisherman's Grotto ($$$) at Cento, 100 Langerman Drive, Kensington (tel: 011-622 7272). Famous for both the seafood, and cellar, boasting over 20,000 bottles.

Gramadoelas at the Market ($/$$) Market Theatre Precinct, corner Breë and Wolhuter Streets (tel: 011-838 6960). A must for all visitors, this is one of the great exponents of African food, from Cape Malay dishes to ostrich omelets and mopani worms. Closed Sunday.

The Hut (La Palhota) ($$) 59b Troye and Pritchard Street, City Centre (tel: 011-337 6377). Authentic Angolan/Portuguese country cooking. Reservations.

Ile de France ($$$) Cramerview Centre, 277 Main Road Bryanston (tel: 011-706 2837). One of the finest dining establishments in town, serving French provincial cuisine. Lunch Sun–Fri, dinner daily. Reservations essential.

Linger Longer ($$$) Wierda Road (off Johan), Wierda Valley, Sandton (tel: 011-884 0465). Multi-award winning and elegant restaurant offering fine dining with full silver service and innovative French cuisine.

Randburg Waterfront ($/$$) (tel: 011-789 5052). For a wide variety of restaurants, from pizzerias to steak houses and hamburgers, try this popular development which has 66 eateries around a small lake with a 1,000-nozzle, 164-foot high musical fountain. It also has a large number of shops and a flea market.

Pretoria

Chagall's ($$$) Fountains Valley, Pretoria (tel: 012-341 7511). An elegant restaurant serving fine French food.

Georgina's ($$) Corner Dumbarton and Nassau Roads, Bryntirion (tel: 012-342 4407). The menu is short, and changes weekly, depending on availability of fresh ingredients.

Gerard Moerdyk ($$$) Park Street, Arcadia (tel: 012-344 4856). Named after the man who designed the Voortrekker Monument, this is a traditional South African restaurant in a charming 1920s neo-Cape Dutch house.

La Madeleine ($$$) Esselen Street, Sunnyside (tel: 012-44 6076). This Belgian-run restaurant, serving classic French cuisine, is one of the finest in South Africa.

KWAZULU-NATAL

Battlefields

Edwards Restaurant ($$) The Mews, Dundee (tel: 0341-22585). A popular local restaurant, with pleasant surroundings, good food, a cheerful buzz and candlelight.

Durban and Environs

Adega ($$) Parry Road (tel: 031-304 6476). The best of the many Portuguese restaurants in Durban. Closed Sun.

Chatters ($$$) 32 Hermitage Lane, Durban (tel: 031-306 1896). An award-winning and very popular Durban restaurant which specializes in seafood and duck. Reservations advised.

Langoustine-by-the-Sea ($$) Old Millway, Durban North (tel: 031-83 7324). As the name suggests, excellent seafood with a wave view.

Pakistani ($$) 92 West Street (tel: 031-326883). Curry is almost obligatory in Natal. Come here for Pakistani specialties. No alcohol allowed. Closed Mon. Reservations advised.

1

2

3

Teeming with life

South Africa has over 130 bird and game sanctuaries, covering nearly 20 million acres. It hosts a staggering 870 bird species; about 160 species of mammal; 115 species of snake, approximately a quarter of which are poisonous; some 5,000 spider and scorpion species; and a vast multitude of other reptiles and insects.

Up before dawn

To see the best of the game, go out between dawn and 10AM, and from 4PM to dusk. Most animals simply melt into the shade to sit out the heat of day. Wear neutral colors and ideally use a vehicle that gets you above the line of the bushes. In the game parks, animals are used to vehicles and will not be startled as long as there are no loud noises or strange shapes. Talk quietly, don't stand up or wave your arms out of the window, and above all stay in your vehicle.

Watch the birdie!

South Africa has six broad bird habitats: fynbos (heathland) in the Cape; desert and semidesert in the northwest; thornveld and broad-leaved woodland in the northeast; grasslands in the center; tropical forest along the Natal coast; and the coastal strip itself. Probably the single most satisfying area for bird-watching is northern Natal, where Hluhluwe, Nduma and St. Lucia together offer almost the whole range of options.

BIRD LIFE

Out of southern Africa's 870 species of bird, about 500 are either local in distribution, retiring or classed as vagrants. Consequently, only about 300 can be seen regularly and identified by the nonspecialist, and of these, some—including many of the females—are small, drab "LBJs" (little brown jobs). Keen bird-watchers need a good guide, binoculars and a great deal of time. Heretical as it may seem to say so, most ordinary tourists simply want to identify those birds which are large or flashy—ideally both.

Savannah dwellers The largest of all, and instantly identifiable, is the huge, flightless **ostrich** (8) which, in the wild, wanders the *vlei* (open savannah grasslands) in company with zebra, antelope and wildebeest. In practice, you get a far better view of them on farms, in and around Oudtshoorn (see page 80). There are plenty of other options in the grasslands however. Pride of place goes to the gawky **secretary bird** (7), whose gray wings, black legs and crest resemble a clerk's jacket, trousers and quill pen. The **kori bustard** (13), the heaviest bird in the world still capable of sustained flight, strides the veld on long legs, with a tawny back, white underparts, black-spotted upper wings, black and white feathering on the neck and a black crest.

The pure white **cattle egret** (11) follows the herds, whether cattle or rhino, picking up the insects dislodged by their feet, while the little brown **red-billed oxpecker** actually catches a ride on their backs, feeding off their ticks and fleas.

Ungainly **hornbills** are unbalanced by their huge, heavy beaks. The **ground hornbill** (10) is as big as a turkey, black all over except for bald red eyes and throat, and flies clumsily only when pushed; the smaller and more agile **yellow-billed hornbill** has a black-and-white patterned back, white front and yellow beak. Less commonly seen are **trumpeter**, **grey** and **red-billed** (9) species.

The **red-eyed dove** (15), **ring-necked Cape turtle dove**, black-faced **Namaqua dove** and gentle little **laughing dove** (16) in its pastel coat of pinks and blues coo in the dawn from the acacia trees. Game birds scuttle underfoot: the white-spotted **helmeted guinea fowl** (20) with its blue and red head; and the round, sandy **crested francolin** (19). Seen frequently in similar habitats is the pout-chested, pointy-tailed **Namaqua sandgrouse** (17).

Storks are sociable birds, building large, scruffy nests in tenement trees and often forsaking the bush for the rich pickings of the agricultural lands. The **white stork** has a white upper body, black wing tips and tail, and a red bill and legs. **Abdim's stork** (18) is shorter, squatter and largely black with white underwings. Also found in the region are **saddle-billed**, **African open-billed** (29) and **yellow-billed storks**. With them you will often find the very noisy, curious and gregarious **Hadada ibis** (12), grayish-brown with a wickedly curved beak.

As dusk draws in, the **nightjars** flutter down to take dust baths and the eyes of the owls blink open. There are numerous species of **owl**, big and small—**African Scops**, **white-faced Scops** (14), **barn**, **spotted eagle**, **pearl-spotted eagle**, and **Verreaux's eagle owls**.

Raptors The great raptors wheel over the veld on the morning thermals. Largest of all is the majestic **lammergeier** (21). The **bataleur** (25) has a dark body, pale underwings and scarlet beak and claws, and there are two species of **fork-tailed kites**—the dusty brown black and the black-shoudered, whose markings are similar to those of a gull. The large black-breasted **snake eagle** has a dark brown back and head, white belly and white underwings, banded with black, while the **long-crested eagle** (24) is smaller, dark brown with a distinctive crest, white-feathered legs and white patches on the wings. Other hunters roaming the skies include several species of **buzzard**, **falcon**, **kestrel**, and **goshawk**, of which the most interesting are probably the **jackal**

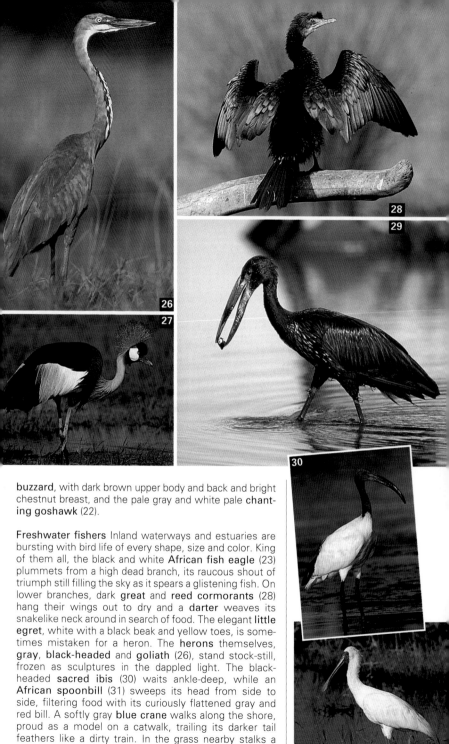

buzzard, with dark brown upper body and back and bright chestnut breast, and the pale gray and white pale **chanting goshawk** (22).

Freshwater fishers Inland waterways and estuaries are bursting with bird life of every shape, size and color. King of them all, the black and white **African fish eagle** (23) plummets from a high dead branch, its raucous shout of triumph still filling the sky as it spears a glistening fish. On lower branches, dark **great** and **reed cormorants** (28) hang their wings out to dry and a **darter** weaves its snakelike neck around in search of food. The elegant **little egret**, white with a black beak and yellow toes, is sometimes mistaken for a heron. The **herons** themselves, **gray**, **black-headed** and **goliath** (26), stand stock-still, frozen as sculptures in the dappled light. The black-headed **sacred ibis** (30) waits ankle-deep, while an **African spoonbill** (31) sweeps its head from side to side, filtering food with its curiously flattened gray and red bill. A softly gray **blue crane** walks along the shore, proud as a model on a catwalk, trailing its darker tail feathers like a dirty train. In the grass nearby stalks a magnificent **crowned crane** (27), with a charcoal-gray body, gold wingtips, black-and-white face, red chin and proud crown of golden bristles.

32
33
34
35
36

Tawny **hamerkops**, **blacksmith** and **crowned plovers** and **black-winged stilts** wade the shallows in search of frogs and insects, **spur-winged** and **Egyptian geese** gather in noisy crowds, stately parties of **white-faced and yellow-billed ducks**, Cape (32) and **red-billed teals** float gently by, the **moorhens** scrabbling furiously through the water in an effort to keep up. There is a flash of color in the reeds from a lurking **purple gallinule**, and another from the overhanging branches as a shining turquoise and orange **malachite kingfisher** streaks past, far outstripping even its own pretty cousins, the **woodland, brown-hooded** (38), **giant, pied,** and **striped kingfishers**.

By the sea To the north, in the Natal dunes, salmon-pink **greater** (3) and **lesser flamingos** stroll the shallow lagoons as heavy flights of **white and pink-backed pelicans** (36) zoom overhead. Down on the far south of the Cape coast, colonies of **jackass penguins** (33) strut the rocks with self-importance. From the skies above, **Cape cormorants** dive-bomb a shoal of sardines. The inshore waters are patrolled by raucous flocks of **terns, grey-headed gulls** and **Cape gannets** (35), with yellowy heads and black-tipped wings. Far out to sea, swooping over the ocean are the massive **black-browed albatross** (34) and smaller **yellow-billed albatross**, the geometrically painted black and white **pintado petrel**, the **white-chinned petrel** and the **sooty shearwater**, the birds of legend and storm.

Great little show-offs What they lack in size, many of South Africa's smaller birds make up for in vivid color. The chestnut head, black-and-white back and distinctive crest of the **hoopoe** and the orange breast and punk-like crest of the **purple-crested lourie** positively pale beside the chesnut back, turquoise, lilac and black of the **lilac-breasted roller** (40) or the green, yellow, black and chestnut of various **bee-eaters**. Some starlings are drab, but the incandescent **glossy** and **plum-coloured starlings** (43) with their petroleum sheen more than make up for it. Bright yellow **weaver birds** drip-hang neat round nests from the trees and fluffy little **yellow**, **blue** (37) and **violet** (41) **waxbills** descend in flocks on new-mown lawns. **Red bishops** (39) parade in black and orange robes; even the **long-tailed widow** makes up for its funereal garb by a dramatically trailing tail. Of them all, the brightest must be the tiny **sunbirds** which dart through the flower beds like fiery jewels: the all-green **malachite**, the **orange-breasted** with its iridescent blue-green head, the **marico** with green head and back, black belly and purple and turquoise stripes across the chin, and the lesser **double-collared** (42) with green head, blue back, and scarlet chinstrap.

Scavengers Often treated with contempt, the carrion-eaters perform a valuable service, keeping the bush clean. To track a kill, look for the **Cape** (44), the **lappet-faced** and **white-backed vultures** (45) circling overhead. Often found at the same sites, or on a garbage dump, the huge marabou stork is one of the ugliest birds around, with a heavy hunched body, white front and black back, bald pink head and neck, pink fleshy pouch and huge yellowish bill.

ANTELOPE

Blesbok *Damaliscus dorcas phillipsi*; **Bontebok** *Damaliscus dorcas dorcas*; **Tsessebe** (49) *Damaliscus lunatus* Three closely related antelope: the blesbok (37 inches), found only in the north and east, has a rich brown coat with off-white underparts and blaze. The south western bontebok from the Cape (35 inches) has a purple-brown coat, white underbelly, rump, socks and blaze. The tsessebe (47 inches) has a dark red-brown coat, tan underbelly, and a hump. The long, ridged horns splay out and back.

Bushbuck (46) *Tragelaphus scriptus* Nocturnal browsers, bushbuck live alone in in well-watered woodland. The rump is higher than the shoulder (31 inches) giving them a hunched appearance. Males have thick, slightly twisted horns, up to 12 inches long. There are over 40 subspecies whose color varies from gray-brown to chestnut, always with white neck patches and white spots on the flanks.

Duiker The duiker (meaning "diver" in Afrikaans) is one of the smallest of the African antelope. Nervous, nocturnal browsers living alone or in pairs, they are widely distributed from rocky hills to grassland. There are three species in South Africa—the

common gray duiker, *Sylvicapra grimmia* (20 inches), the smaller, rarer red duiker, *Cephalophus natalensis* (17 inches) and the blue duiker, *Cephalophus monticola* (12 inches; actually grayish-brown). All have rounded backs and black marks on the face and top of the tail.

Eland (50) *Taurotragus oryx* The massive eland (7 feet tall; 1 ton in weight) has a light sandy body, faint white stripes across the back and strips of black hair along spine and belly. Both sexes have long, backward-lying horns with a tight spiral at the base. Timid diurnal browsers, they live in herds in scrubland and semidesert.

Gemsbok (51) *Oryx gazella* The beautiful gemsbok (4 foot) inhabit the semidesert scrub of the Kalahari, where they eat grass, leaves and tubers and need no additional water. They have a heavy body, a sandy coat with a black tail, black stripe along the flanks and upper thighs, white legs and black knee patches. The face has black and white patches and both sexes have very long, thin, straight horns.

Grysbok These small, nocturnal creatures (20 inches) have a hunched back and chestnut coat sprinkled with white hair. The Cape grysbok, *Raphicerus melanotis*, a grazer, lives only in the far south. Sharpe's grysbok (48), *Raphicerus sharpei*, is a browser and grazer found in the far north. It has a redder coat, a dark band along the muzzle and whitish belly and inside legs.

Impala (47) *Aepyceros melampus* Largest of the gazelles (3 foot), impala are charmingly pretty and easily seen, living in herds in open grassland. They have a russet back and nose, a white belly, white rings around the eyes, and black stripes on the tail and rump. Males have long, lyre-shaped horns. Both browsers and grazers, they can jump to a height of 10 feet and reach speeds of 60mph.

Klipspringer, *Oreotragus oreotragus* Little klipspringers (21 inches) browse and graze in small groups on rocky hillsides, bouncing on tiptoe from boulder to boulder on hooves the consistency of hard rubber. Their long, bristly, speckled coat varies from yellow-brown to charcoal gray. Males have short, straight horns.

Hard work
Most herd antelope split into male and female groups. The young males are driven out when nearing maturity to join a bachelor herd. The dominant male must remain tireless as he carves out and defends a territory, and guards and services a harem of anything up to 30 females and calves. To establish his own herd, a young male must either defeat him or cut out and kidnap a significant number of females.

Rare sightings
Other antelope seen infrequently in South Africa include the huge, magnificent black and white sable, *Hippotragus niger*; the heavy strawberry-gray roan, *Hippotragus equinus*, similar to the gemsbok with its black-and-white face; the small beige and white oribi, *Ourebia ourebi*; and the tiny red-gold suni, *Neotragus moschatus*.

50

51

SAFARI GUIDE

Kudu (56) *Tragelaphus strepsiceros* Found in the north and east, the powerful greater kudu (5 foot) has a sloping back, light grayish-brown coat with faint white stripes, a white crest along the spine, black beard, and white band between the eyes. Males have magnificent horns which curl backwards in an open corkscrew. They are browsers, living in small groups in scrubby woodland.

Nyala (55) *Tragelaphus angasii* Similar to the kudu, nyala (4ft.) are found in northern KwaZulu-Natal. They have a dark brown coat with faint white stripes across the back, white-spotted flanks, black mane and beard, white crest along the spine and a white patch on the nose. Males have long, twisting, backward-lying horns. Diurnal browsers, they live in small groups in dense thickets near water.

Red hartebeest (53) *Alcelaphus buselaphus caama* The hartebeest is large (5 feet) with a steeply sloping back, a rich red-tan coat with dark patches along the spine and thighs, and a long, gloomy face. Both sexes have thick, ridged, backward-twisting horns, shaped like a candelabrum. Diurnal grazers, they live in large herds in open grassland.

Reedbuck The Southern Reedbuck (54) *Redunca arundinum* (3 feet) inhabits marshland near water. Usually found in pairs, they are grazers with a dirty yellow to grayish-brown coat with a white throat patch. Smaller Mountain Reedbuck, *Redunca fulvorufula* (28 inches) live in small groups in rocky hills or steep river beds. They have a shaggy grayish coat with white underparts and a reddish-brown head and neck. Both males have short, forward-curving horns.

Grey rhebok *Pelea capreolus* Small, gray, furry antelope (29 inches) with powerful back legs and a hunched back, rhebok are browsers and grazers who live on rocky hills and slopes in groups of 2–20. They have large ears, white rings around the eyes, and a white rim to the tail. Males have thin, straight horns.

Steenbok (52) *Raphicerus campestris* Similar to the grysbok, the little steenbok (20 inches) often lurks in long grass or a disused burrow for safety. They have a chestnut coat and a white belly. The male has short, straight, very sharp horns. They browse and graze in open land, usually during the day, although they become nocturnal if under threat.

Waterbuck *Kobus ellipsiprymnus* Heavyset waterbuck (5½ feet) graze in small groups in reedbeds and river valleys. They have a shaggy gray-brown coat covered in a musky secretion that not only acts as waterproofing but smells evil and taints the flesh, guarding against most predators. They have a distinctive white circle on the rump. The males have long, ridged horns which curve out and forwards.

Wildebeest Technically an antelope, the wildebeest or gnu (5 feet) is said to have been made up of the pieces left over at the end of creation, with "the forequarters of an ox, the hindquarters of an antelope, and the tail of a horse." It also has the long face of a hartebeest, a thick black mane and the horns of a buffalo. They are gregarious, grazing open grassland in large herds. There are two species in South Africa, the common blue or brindled, *Connochaetes taurinus* (57), with a grayish-brown coat and faint black striping, and the rarer black, *Connochaetes gnou*, with a darker coat and white muzzle and tail.

National symbol
The springbok (6), *Antidorcas marsupialis*, has become South Africa's symbol and given its name to the country's national sports teams. Little could be more different from a rugby player than this dainty little gazelle. The only true gazelle south of the Zambezi, springbok (30 inches) are gregarious browsers and grazers who thrive in large herds in the dry open scrublands on the Kalahari fringe. They have a rich tan back, white underparts, rump and face, and black stripes along the flanks and tail and beneath the eyes. Males and females have ridged, lyre-shaped horns that curve out and back before hooking in at the top.

277

PLAINS ANIMALS

Buffalo (58) *Syncerus caffer* Deceptively cowlike but irritable and dangerous when roused, buffalo are huge (5–7 feet), with powerful bodies, dark-brown coats and short, massively heavy horns that clamp the brow like a Viking helmet. They browse and graze, in grassland and forest, live in herds, and wallow in mud for heat regulation.

Elephant (1) *Loxodonta africana* The largest land mammal, the African elephant (10 feet; 13,200 pounds; with tusks up to 11 feet) is a magnificent and surprisingly gentle giant, although swift to anger if alarmed. Sociable and intelligent, they live in matriarchal family groups with a complex social structure. Infants stay with their mother until the age of five, sexual maturity is reached at 15 and life expectancy is 60–70 years. They adapt to a range of habitats, from desert to montane forest, but are happiest in savannah woodland.

Giraffe (62) *Giraffa camelopardalis* Extraordinarily graceful and gentle, the giraffe (16/19 feet tall) has a hide resembling a tan and chestnut crazy quilt, a heavy, sloping body, camel-like face and small, fleshy horns topped with rounded knobs. There are only seven vertebrae in the immensely long neck and special valves regulate the blood flow to the brain when they bend. Giraffes live in large herds in open woodland and browse on the high leaves of acacia trees. Their only real defense is a powerful kick.

Hippopotamus (61) *Hippopotamus amphibius* Hippos (5 feet tall; 3,300 pounds) have massive barrel bodies, short legs, a tight, shiny gray skin and long, flattened face. They live in colonies of up to 15 and spend their days wallowing in shallow pools, surfacing to breath every five minutes, or lying with nostrils poking out of the water. At night, they walk up to 18 miles in search of good grazing. Totally vegetarian and placid when undisturbed, they kill more humans than almost all other wild animals combined, simply biting people, and even canoes, in half.

Rhinoceros The White Rhinoceros, *Ceratotherium simum* (6 feet 5,000 pounds), gains its name not from its color but from the Afrikaans word "*wydt*," meaning widemouthed. They are grazers, inhabiting grasslands and open scrub. The mouth is square and the front horn considerably longer than the back. The Black Rhinoceros (2), *Diceros bicornis* (5 feet; 1900 pounds), is a browser, living in thick bush. A darker charcoal-gray than the white, it has a pointy hooklip, the horns are more even in length, and it is smaller and more aggressive. Both species nearly died out through poaching, but a successful breeding and relocation program has increased the number of whites. The black is still very rare.

Warthog (60) *Phacochoerus aethopicus* Large, brown, hairy pigs (27 inches), with dark mane, small wide-set eyes, knobbly face and short, sideways curving tusks, these prodigious diggers live in underground burrows and eat tubers and grass. Usually seen as a family of male, female and two–three infants, they run in a line, tails straight up in the air. Their nocturnal relative, the bushpig, *Potamochoerus porcus* (25 inches), has a smoother face and squarer muzzle, has larger litters and keeps its tail down when running.

Zebra These sociable grazers live in large herds on open grassland. The irregular stripes act as camouflage and a system of identification as unique as fingerprints. The common Burchell's zebra (59), *Equus burchelli* (4¼ feet), has brown shadow stripes on the white sections. The rare Cape mountain zebra, *Equus zebra zebra* (4 feet), is slightly smaller, with longer pointed ears, narrower stripes with no shadow, and a plain white belly.

The Big Five

To see the "Big Five" is considered to be the goal of any successful safari. The definition of the five—lion, elephant, rhino, buffalo and leopard—came not from their rarity value or even their beauty, but from the early hunters. These were considered to be the most difficult and dangerous animals to shoot, and therefore the finest trophies. Lion, elephant and buffalo are relatively easy to find, while there are more rhinos in South Africa than anywhere else on the continent. Leopard are widespread but virtually impossible to see.

PREDATORS

Cheetah (63) *Acinonyx jubatus* Long (6½ feet), lithe and built for speed, cheetahs have gold coats with black spots and neat triangular heads. A few genetically aberrant so-called king cheetahs, with larger black splotches, are found in the far north. The fastest animals on earth, clocking up speeds of 70mph over short distances, cheetahs live in family groups and hunt in the early morning and evening.

Foxes The bat-eared fox, *Otocyon megalotis* (31 inches long), has a speckled gray-brown coat, darker bushy tail, small triangular face and huge round ears. It lives in semi-arid grass and scrub, in burrows. The unrelated Cape fox (64), *Vulpes chama* (35 inches), has a shiny golden-gray coat, dark tail and lives in semidesert scrub and mountain *fynbos*. Often shot as pests, both are harmless and even beneficial, eating mice, small reptiles and insects.

Hyena The common spotted hyena (67), *Crocuta crocuta* (33 inches), roams the open savannah and woodland in the north and east, while the smaller, rarer brown hyena (66), *Hyaena brunnea* (30 inches), inhabits the Kalahari region. Both have powerful shoulders, weak back legs and a sloping back. The spotted has a gold coat with black spots, a small, neat head and rounded ears; the brown has a dark brown coat, stripy legs and pointed ears. They are mainly nocturnal scavengers, but also prey on young, old and sick animals. They live alone or in pairs, gathering in groups during the mating season. The spotted has an eerie cry, ranging from a yap to piercing howls and manic laughter.

Jackal Regarded as scavengers, jackals (length 3¾ feet) are about the size and shape of a European fox and behave in a similar fashion. They do hang around kills, farmyards and garbage cans, but they are also efficient hunters of small animals, and even eat fruit and vegetables. There are two common

63

64

65

species in the region, the aggressive diurnal black-backed (68), *Canis mesomelas*, and the timid nocturnal, *Canis adustus*, with a white flank stripe.

Leopard (5) *Panthera pardus* Leopards (6½ feet long) prefer wooded hills, but accepting a wide range of terrain. They are solitary, nocturnal and virtually imposs ible to see. Their low-slung bodies have a red-gold coat with clusters of black spots. They hunt anything from mice to antelope, haul-ing carcasses into trees away from scavengers.

Lion *Panthera leo* The lion (35 inches tall; 8½ feet long) is the largest cat in the world. The young (69) have spots; but adults are a uniform gold; males have a mane which can range from light colored to almost black. They live in prides of up to 20 or 30 beasts. The females (smaller than males) do almost all the hunt-ing, usually at night or dawn. Not particularly speedy, they rely on stealth, breaking the victim's neck with a blow from a paw or clamping the throat and suffocating it.

Wild dog (65) *Lycaon pictus* Wild, or Cape hunting dogs have been feared and hunted by man and are now one of the rarest animals in Africa. About 26 inches tall, they have long, skinny legs, powerful jaws and huge ears. Their coat is brindled black, dark brown, yellow and white, the patterning on each dog unique. Strictly diurnal, they once lived and hunted in packs of up to 40 members.

Run rabbit run
There are several species of rabbit in South Africa, but those you see are most likely to be escaped European domestic rabbits. There are two common species of hare, the cape hare, *Lepus capensis*, and the scrub hare, *Lepus saxatilis*. The spring hare, *Pedetes capensis*, is not a hare, but a marsupial, with powerful back legs and tiny forelegs, like a small kangaroo.

PRIMATES

Bushbaby Small, tree-dwelling primates with huge eyes, bushy tails, and a piercing cry uncannily like the wail of a hungry baby, bushbabies are closely related to lemurs. They live in colonies, feeding at night on small birds, reptiles and insects, eggs, fruit and leaves. There are two species in South Africa, the thick-tailed, *Otolemur crassicaudatus* (19–23 inches long), and lesser, *Galago moholi* (14 inches long).

Chacma baboon (71) *Papio ursinus* Chacma baboons are large (4 feet long), with thick yellowy-gray coats, a long black muzzle and kinked tail. Highly organized socially, they live in troops of up to 50 in rocky, wooded hills. Omnivorous team players, they work together smoothly to hunt or defend, using formidable teeth as weapons. Their call is a sharp coughlike bark.

Monkeys South Africa's two species of monkey are both diurnal and gregarious, living in troops of up to 30, led by a dominant male. The vervet (70) *Cercopithecus pygerythrus* (3½ feet long), has a gray-brown back, pale stomach and black face ringed by a white ruff. The male has a bright blue scrotum. They prefer open savannah woodland, but range widely, are fearless and are highly curious. The elusive samango, *Cercopithecus albogularis* (4½ feet) is larger and darker with tufty side-whiskers and a dark brown face. They live in the upper reaches of dense montane forest.

SMALL MAMMALS

Anteaters Africa's vast army of termites supports several species of anteater, all solitary, nocturnal and rarely seen. The pangolin, *Manis temminckii* (31 inches long), has a heavy scaled, rounded body, flat tail, tiny legs, small triangular snout, formidable claws and a long, sticky tongue. It is covered with heavy, scaled armor and when threatened it curls up and exudes a foul smell. The aardvark or antbear, *Orycteropus afer* (23 inches), is low-slung, with a heavy body, short legs and pointy face. It has pale gold fur, a thin almost bald tail, long sharp ears and piglike snout. Great burrowers, they create vast underground networks of tunnels. The aardwolf, *Proteles cristatus* (35in. long), resembles a hyena, with a rounded back, long streaked black and tan fur, a black muzzle and pointed ears.

Cats There are four local species of small cat, all nocturnal and rarely seen, hunting small creatures, birds and reptiles. The caracal, *Felis caracal* (3½ feet long) has a red-gold coat, small head and large, pointed ears, tufted with black fur. The serval, *Felis serval* (3½ feet long), has a tan body, and black spots and stripes on neck and tail. The African wild cat, *Felis lybica* (35 inches long), looks like a domestic tabby, but with a sharper face and longer ears. Even more like a tabby, the small spotted cat, *Felis nigripes* (19–23 inches long), has a tan coat, black spots and stripes, and a rounded face.

Honey badger *Mellivora capensis* Also known as a ratel, the honey badger (37 inches) has a light gray back and a white stripe along the flank, while the head and underparts are a deep brown. They are nocturnal, largely carnivorous and regarded as pests because of their fondness for both chickens and eggs. Although small, they are aggressive.

Mongoose There are 11 species of mongoose in South Africa, of which six are common: the yellow, *Cynictis penicillata*; slender, *Galerella sanguinea*; white-tailed, *Ichneumia albicauda*; water (marsh), *Atilax paludinosus*; banded, *Mungos mungo*; and dwarf, *Helogale parvula*. All eat a varied diet of insects, small animals and eggs, and between the species they cover the full range of habitats. Closely related is the scrawny suricate or meerkat (72), *Suricata suricatta*, a highly gregarious desert dweller.

Porcupine (74) *Hystrix africaeaustralis* Solitary, nocturnal and vegetarian, this extraordinary rodent (29 inches long) has a dark face, white bristly mane and coat of hard, pointed black-and-white banded quills, which puff up to double their size and rattle when the animal is alarmed or angry.

False cats
Often described as cats because of their appearance, genets and civets are actually related to the mongoose family. With stretched bodies, short legs and black and tan stripes and spots, they are nocturnal omnivores, the genets nesting in trees or underground burrows while the largest of them, the civet, *Civettictis civetta* (4 feet long), is strictly terrestrial. The small-spotted genet, *Genetta genetta* (37 inches long), has a white-tipped tail, the large-spotted (73), *Genetta tigrina* (3 feet), a black tip.

REPTILES

Of all South Africa's reptiles, the Nile crocodile (75), *Crocodylus niloticus*, is king, a superbly designed killing machine already activated when the dinosaurs roamed planet Earth.

Smaller, but still dramatically big, is the largest of the lizards, the water leguaan or monitor, *Varanus niloticus* (up to 5 feet long). Many other lizards, skinks, and 10 species of agama thrive in hot sand and rocky crevices. Some, such as the blue-headed southern rock agama, *Agama atra*, or the red, green and blue common flat lizard, *Platysaurus intermedius*, are as brightly colored as a rainbow. Pale pinky-brown geckos lurk on bedroom ceilings and there are at least 20 species of slow-moving, rainbow-changing chameleon (4). Other reptiles include tortoises, terrapins and sea turtles; green, loggerhead (76), leatherback and hawksbill turtles all breed on the beaches of northern Natal.

Snakes have poor eyesight, but a keen sense of smell and excellent hearing; they prefer to stay out of the way. The great exception is the short, fat, black-and-tan patterned puff adder, *Bitis arietans*, which likes sunbathing on open ground, relies on camouflage, and is all too easily trodden on. Other poisonous snakes to watch out for are the bright-green, tree-dwelling boomslang, *Dispholidus typus* (77); the Cape cobra, *Naja nivea*; the rinkhals or spitting cobra (78), *Hemachatus haemachatus*; the black mamba, *Dendroaspis polylepis*; and green mamba, *Dendroaspis angusticeps*. The largest snake in South Africa is the common African python, *Python sebae* (10/16 feet long). It is not poisonous, killing by squeezing or constriction.

Snake drill

South African pharmacies sell snakebite serum kits: make sure you know how to use them before venturing into the bush. Don't clamber over rocks without checking where you put your hands; snakes will usually clear out of your way if you make enough noise. Should someone in your party be bitten, immobilize the limb and treat the patient for shock. Sucking out the poison is often harmful, and a tourniquet will only help occasionally. Never assume that the snake was harmless, get medical help as fast as possible, and give the doctor an accurate description of the snake.

Principal references are given in **bold**

A

accommodations 226–227, 258–263
Addo Elephant National Park 117
Adler Museum of the History of Medicine 157
Adler Museum of the History of Music 157
African Arts Centre 194
African National Congress (ANC) 22, 41, **42**, 43
Africana Museum 154–155
Afrikaans 87
Afrikaans Language Museum 87
airports and air services 238, **242–243**, 246
Albertinia 96
Alice 107
Amanzimtoti 200–201
Anne Bryant Art Gallery 106
Anreith, Anton **54**, 55, 57, 69, 115
Anton von Wouw Museum 164
apartheid 10, 14, 21, **40–41**
Ardmore Studio 209
Arend Dieperink Museum 179
Armored Train Memorial 202
Arniston 95
art 172–173
Ashton 77
Assagay Safari Park 201
Augrabies Falls National Park 134

B

Backsberg 92
Baden-Powell, Robert 144
Badplaas 176
Baker, Sir Herbert 58, 59, 67, 71, 115, 156, **166**, 185
Bakone Malapa Ethnic Museum 179
Bakoven 73
Ballito Beach 200
Balokwa Museum 129
Banana Express 201, **235**
banks 244
baobabs **176**, 180
Barberton 181
Barkly West 142
Bartolomeu Dias Museum Complex 97
Basotho Cultural Village 129
Bathurst 110
battlefield sites 130, **202–205**
Beaufort West 78
Beck House 77
Beira 224
Benguela 224
Bensusan Museum of Photography 155
Bergtheil Museum 201
Bernard Price Museum of Palaeontology 157
Bernberg Museum of Costume 148

Bertram House 54
Bethlehem 128
Bethulie 130
Betty's Bay 82
Bible Monument 108–109
Big Hole **138**, 139
Biko, Steve **43**, 104
bird life 268–273
Bisho 104, 105, **107**
Blockhouse Museum 207
Bloemfontein 12, **126–127**
Blood River 204
Blue Train 234
Blyde River Canyon **182**, 184
Bo-Kaap **54**, 64, 65, 115
Bo-Kaap Museum 54
Boers **32–33**, 34–35
Bonnievale 77
Bontebok National Park 83
Boschendal 92
Botanic Gardens and Orchid House 194
Botsalano Game Reserve 144
Botswana 216, 217, **222**
Bourke's Luck Potholes 184
Bredasdorp 94
Breë River Valley 76–77
Bruma Fleamarket 149
Buchan, John 179
Buffalo Valley Game Farm 101
Bulawayo 220
Bultfontein Mine 138
bungee jumping 96
Burgher Memorial 207
Butter Museum 85

C

C P Nel Museum 80–81
Calgary Museum 106
camping and caravanning 252–253
Camps Bay 73
Cango Caves 79
Cango Crocodile Ranch and Cheetahland 79
Cango Ostrich Farm 81
Cannon Island 136
Cape Agulhas 72, **94–95**
Cape architecture 114–115
Cape Flats 68
Cape of Good Hope 26–27, 28, 46, **71–73**
Cape Malays 16, 54, **64–65**
Cape Town 12, 46, **50–67**, 232, 233
Caprivi Strip 223
car rental 246
Castle of Good Hope 54–55
Castle Hill Historical Museum 116
Cederberg 84
Central Kalahari Game Reserve 222
Ceres 76
Cetshwayo 200, 212, 215
Chamonix 92
Chapman's Peak Drive 72–73
Charlotte Kritzinger Shell Museum 117
Cheetah Project 178–9
children 253
Chobe National Park 222
Churchill, Winston 169, 202
Cinderella's Castle 128

Ciskei 104, 105
Citrusdal 84
Clanwilliam **84**, 85
Clarens 128
Clifton 73
climate 244
coelacanth **106**, 109
Coert Steynberg Museum 164
Colenso 202
Colesberg 134
coloureds 16, **64**
Company's Garden 50, 55, **67**
conversion charts 255
Coon Carnival 65
Correctional Service Museum 165
Cradock 112
credit cards 245
cricket 198
crime 19, 148, **251**
crocodile farms 79, 87, 98, 179, 183, 200, 201, 214
Crossroads 68
cruise ships 243
Cullinan 170
currency 245
customs regulations 243
Cuyler Manor Cultural Museum 118

D

Dana Bay Nature Reserve 97
Daniëlskuil 142
Darling 85
De Beer Centenary Art Gallery 107
De Hoop Nature Reserve 95
de Klerk, F W 22, 41, 44
De Tuynhuys 67
Debengeni Falls 178
Dhlinza Forest 212
diamond cutting 151
diamonds 125, 138, 139, **140–141**, 170
Die Braak 90
Die Burgerhuis 90
Diepkloof Farm Museum 158
Dingane **212**, 213
disabilities, visitors with 254
District Six 55
Dorp Street 91
Dorpshuis 81
Double Drift Game Reserve 111
Drakensberg 208–209
drinking water 251
driving in South Africa 243, **246**
Drostdy Museum 83
drugs 243
Duggan-Cronin Gallery 138
Duiker Island 73
Dumazulu 213
Dundee 202
Dunn, John 213
Durban 190, 191, **192–197**, 232, 233
Dynamite Museum 158
Dzata 18

E

East London 105, **106**

Ciskei Eastern Cape 102–121
accommodations 260
restaurants 265
Eastern Highlands 128–131
Ebenezer Dam 178
Ecca Nature Reserve 111
Echo Caves 184
Education Museum 165
Elandsbaai 85
Elandskraal 202
electricity 255
Elim 94
embassies and consulates 250
emergencies 250–252
entertainment 232–233
Eshowe 212
Etosha National Park 223
Eureka City 181
Ezulwini Valley 219

F

Fairview 92
False Bay Park 214
Fanie Botha Dam 178
farming 20–21
Fernkloof Nature Reserve 83
Ficksburg 128
First National Bank Museum 154
First Raadsaal 126
Fish Hoek 71
Fish River Canyon 223
fishing 199
flora 74–75
food and drink 228–230
Forest Museum 185
Fort Beaufort 111
Fort Durnford 208
Fort Hare University 104, **107**
Fortuna Mine Trail 181
Foskor Museum 178
Fouriesburg 128
Franklin Game Reserve 127
Franschhoek 86
Free State, Northern Cape and North-west Province 122–145
accommodations 260–261
restaurants 265
Freshford House 127
fynbos 74–75

G

game lodges 226
game reserves 123–124, 215
Gamkaskloof 78
Gandhi, Mahatma 42, 190, **211**
Gansbaai 82
Garden Route 47–48, **96–101**, 105
Gariep Dam 130
Gariep Nature Reserve 130
Gately House Museum 106
Gauteng 146–173
accommodations 261
restaurants 265
Gemsbok National Park 222
General J J Fick Museum 128

INDEX

INDEX/ACKNOWLEDGMENTS

Author's Acknowledgments

Melissa Shales would like to thank the following people for their time, knowledge and hospitality: Paul Duncan, who helped write the history section; Mary Duncan for her assistance in compiling the hotel and restaurant listings, and Stephen Fowler, who gave up valuable holiday to drive around South Africa; Alison Whitfield and Liz Wright of African Ethos; South African Airways; Budget Rent-a-Car; Garth McFarlane and the staff of Kei Leisure; Dave Rattray of Safari Services; Elizabeth Taylor of Northern Cape Tourism; Dinizulu Tours, Timeless Africa; Small Exclusive Hotels of Southern Africa; Three Cities Hotels; Sun International; Southern Sun Hotels; Karos Hotels; and the tourist information officers throughout South Africa who keep the industry running smoothly.

Photographer's Acknowledgments

Clive Sawyer, photographer, would like to thank the following for thieir assistance: Hans van den Berg, Durban, Graham Stewart of Dumazulu fame; the Manager and staff of the Shamwari Game Reserve; Mr and Mrs Uys, Bloubergstrand, Cape Town; the Manager and staff at the Drosdty Hotel, Graaff-Reinet

Publishers' Acknowledgments

The Automobile Association wishes to thank the following photographers and libraries for their assistance in the preparation of this book. ALLSPORT UK LTD 199a (S. Botterill); DE BEERS 140a, 140c, 141a, 141b; BRUCE COLEMAN COLLECTION 131 (J. Burton); MARY EVANS PICTURE LIBRARY 23, 26b, 27b, 28b, 30, 31, 38, 144, 160b, 207; JOHN HOWARD 72; HULTON GETTY 40a (Keystone), 40b, 42c; HUMAN AND ROUSSEAU (PTY) LTD 228b, 228c; KATZ PICTURES (D. Stewart Smith) front cover; THE MANSELL COLLECTION 27a, 28a, 28b, 29a, 29b, 33b, 34b, 35a, 35b, 36/7, 36a, 37, 38/9, 39, 140b, 205b; NATURAL HISTORY MUSEUM 24a, 25; NATURE PHOTOGRAPHERS LTD B. Burbidge125, Baron Hugo Van Lawick 266 (2), 281 (65), (67), 283 (75); R. Daniel 266 (3), 267 (4), 269 (7), 270 (21), 272 (34) K. J. Carlson, 267 (5), H. Miles 269 (7), P. R. Sterry, 269 (11), (12), (15) (16), 271 (27), (32), 272 (34), 273(45), 274 (46), (48); R. Tidman, 269 (10); 270 (21), 272 (34), 272 (35), 280 (63); E. Jones, 269 (15), 283 (73);P. Craig-Cooper, 269 (13), (17), (18), 270 (25), 271 (26), (28), (29), (30), (31), (32), 272 (36), 273 (37), (38), (39), (41), (42), (43), (44), (45), 274 (48), (49), (52), (53), (54), 277 (55), (56), 279 (60), 280 (64), 281(66), (68), J. Karmali, 269 (19);J. Reynolds, 270 (21), 273 (40); M. Harris 272 (35); E. Jones, 277 (56), 283 (73); M. Gore, 283 (74); J. Sutherland, 284 (77), S. Bisserot, 284 (78), (79); PICTURES COLOUR LIBRARY LTD 141, 160a, 161a, 221, 222b; REX FEATURES LTD 16b (PH Nils Jorgensen), 22a (I. McIlgorm), 22b (J. Witt), 41a (M. Peters), 41b 42a 43a (J. Kuus), 42b (S. Bilco), 43b (M. Peters), 44a (Facelly); MELISSA SHALES 30/1, 198, 212, 239; SOUTH AFRICAN MUSEUM 132a; SPECTRUM COLOUR LIB-RARY 8, 74/5,100/1, 129, 136a, 136b, 161b, 209, 217, 219, 220, 222a, 223; ZEFA PICTURES LTD 224, 234a, 234b. The remaining photographs are held in the Association's own library (AA PHOTO LIBRARY) and were taken by CLIVE SAWYER with the exception of pages 15, 49, 153b, 156 which were taken by Malc Birkitt and the back cover (b) and pages 2, 4, 5a, 6, 11c, 16a, 32b, 45, 58, 59, 66, 68, 69, 71, 73, 75, 80a, 80b, 81, 84, 93, 95b, 98, 108, 113, 114b, 115a, 115b, 120/1, 120a, 128, 151, 189, 200, 206, 215, 218a, 218b, 225, 227a, 227b, 231a, 231b, 232, 233, 237a, 241, 242, 257, 270 (23), 274 (50), 279 (62), 284 (76) taken by Paul Kenward.

Contributors

Designer: Alan Gooch
Joint series editor: Josephine Perry   **Copy editor**: Audrey Horne
Verifier:Stella Isaac   **Indexer**: Marie Lorimer